M.
My Blessing In Disguise

By

B. R. Older

M.E. - My Blessing in Disguise

Table of Contents

Authors Note..4

Foreword...5

In The Beginning..7

The Onset of M.E.......................................21

The Effects Of M.E....................................24

I'm Off To Bart's..27

Songs..29

Dipping My Toe in the Water..................31

Time To Move On.....................................35

The Cause of ME?.....................................39

Buqi Lends A Helping Hand...................41

My Introduction to Spiritual Healing............50

A Proper Awakening................................64

I Join a Circle and Normality Returns............72

Spirit Speaks..87

Some More Happenings In 2003..........102

A Year of Travel......................................109

Inklings...122

M.E. - My Blessing in Disguise

Commuting Begins...133

More Acceptance..145

Big Moves..155

Rainbows...171

More Happenings In 2009...................................181

An Arrival and a Departure................................188

A Bit More Music...201

A Special Year...214

A Not So Good Friday...229

Kicks Up The Backside.......................................240

When The Pupil Is Ready...................................259

Thanks...264

Authors Note

The title of this book is not intended to cause upset or insult to those who suffer with the condition M.E./C.F.S. , or to their families, it simply reflects the changes that were brought in when I had the condition myself.

Many consequences came about during 7+ years in which I suffered with M.E./C.F.S., the blessing is the finding of my spiritual pathway during this time.

M.E. - My Blessing in Disguise

Foreword

As I sit here in front of a blazing log fire in an old stone house in Portugal, my mind is recalling memories, not the ones from childhood evenings spent peering into coal fires, in which I'd try to make out images amidst the flames, but those more recent, those that trace the journey that began on October 1st 1994. This house belongs to my friends Celia and Kelvin Stuart.

That was my original opening for the book and was written in February 2006, it has been changed as this book has taken so long to come to fruition. There was an eight year gap after the first twenty or so pages were written, it was very much on the back burner, in fact it was pushed into the back of a cupboard. It did cross my mind from time to time in the intervening years, but I only got started again after spirit gave me a kick or two up the backside in 2014, this was after all their idea in the first place.

Writing is not really my thing, it doesn't come easy to me, I've had to do lots of research and digging through my diaries, which began in 2000, a massive amount of notes involved, but without those diaries there would be no book, well it would be a lot slimmer.

This book is about my journey from the depths of ME to the finding of my spiritual pathway, on to complete recovery, and then forwards into my spiritual development.

I've tried to describe some of the many happenings that my spiritual awakening has brought into my life, but it's quite difficult to explain what is mostly intangible and often surreal. You may well find your credibility will be stretched to breaking point, and beyond, as I try to describe my experiences. You will see some words, such as beautiful, wonderful, amazing, wow, are used quite often, my own vocabulary is nothing out of the ordinary, and I didn't want to resort to the use of a Thesaurus, so apologies in advance for this.

M.E. - My Blessing in Disguise

My awakening and subsequent development have brought me many magical experiences. I do find it quite astonishing how Spirit can orchestrate and synchronise certain happenings in order to maximise their impact, when they feel it's necessary.

This book was written as Spirit wished me to make my experiences available for those who wish to share them.

M.E. - My Blessing in Disguise

In The Beginning

Hello I'm Brian, this is my story about how my having ME/CFS brought about a whole new way of looking at life and death, and also opened me up to recognise that I have some hidden, latent abilities.

In the summer of 1947 Eileen and Ron Older, my soon to be mum and dad, were living in a small flat in Milner Road in Brighton. The flat belonged to Mary, Eileen's mum, Mary lived there as well and also my soon to be brother and sister, Bob and Sylvia, so it must have been a little crowded. I popped out one day in July, apparently a day late, it was a long labour of love for mum Eileen. It seems that I was a little bit shy then, I still am.

Early in 1948 the family was allocated a new house at Carden Hill on a brand new estate up at Hollingbury, it's in the north of Brighton. Our three bedrooms were instantly full, and Mary came to join us as well.. The estate had shops, a school, a pub, and a factory estate was built close by.

My first memories are of tottering around the furniture, moving at a decent speed, but then crashing into the wall as I hadn't learned the art of stopping, I think that took a little while to master. I also remember Mary picking me up and putting me on a chair so that I could see out of the dining room window. She used to throw stale bread out of the window, and also place some on the window ledge, this would quickly bring in a flock of screeching Seagulls. I think Mary delighted in watching my face when they came right up close to the window, I'm sure I enjoyed the spectacle as we were just a foot or so away behind the glass.

I never saw Mary walk, I think that she had problems with the arches of her feet, she would go around the house on all fours, even up and down the stairs. I don't know if Mary left the house at all in those days, the family had a motorbike for getting around in, it would have been

M.E. - My Blessing in Disguise

impossible for her to travel in it. I hardly ever saw Mary smile, but I now understand that she had a difficult life. A few years later Dad graduated to cars, he would sometimes carry Mary up to the car when we were off on a family visit. Mum had two sisters, Elsie who lived at Ashford, Kent, with her husband George, and Margie who lived at Horsham, with her hubby Fred. Dad's mum Alice also lived close by, and Dad's aunt Amy did too, so Horsham was quite a frequent trip for us. In someone's house there was an old organ, a few sing-songs would happen after they'd had a stout or two, they also liked a game of cards. One thing I'll mention is that Fred, dad's uncle, was married to Margie, mum's sister, so he had an uncle and a brother-in-law in one.

Dad was an ambulance driver, sometimes he was able to borrow a wheelchair to take Mary out, mind you, he still had to get her up a lot of steps to the road, she was a large framed lady. Hollingbury was a good place for kids in those days, I was soon good friends with the Smiths next door, a very welcoming family with two boys of a similar age to me, Ken and Brian, there was also Muriel, who was probably about brother Bob's age. Bob is almost eight years older than me, Sylvia is two years older than me. We had the Clark's on the other side, the boys were a little older, so we didn't mix that much, but we all got on OK and other families moved in as time went on.

From the back of our house you could see across a lot of the downs, from Devil's Dyke to Ditchling Beacon, quite a view. Once we got to a certain age we were allowed to roam on foot or on our bikes, and if we went up through some twittens we could cross Hollingbury golf course and reach what we called the Roman Camp, a circular Bronze Age settlement, and onto the Devil's Foot, a deep, steep sided valley with a flat bottom, where football and cricket are played. We also went out and about across the downs, but times have changed and sadly a lot of children today don't get the freedom that we had.

We were a poor family, mum didn't work as Mary had her disability, and I had some eating intolerances. I was born a good weight, but became a sickly child when I was put onto solid food. It took a while to

M.E. - My Blessing in Disguise

find out the cause, green vegetables were the culprits; dad wouldn't have been impressed as he was a keen gardener, and a good one, and obviously growing your own veg helped out when money was tight. By the time I went to school I was physically way behind most of the kids in my school year, and remained so throughout my school life.
I was a poor scholar for the most part, and had untidy, spidery writing; my saving grace was that I was very good at mental arithmetic. Our dad was very keen on education, well he'd had to leave school at aged fourteen to go to work, I mention this because it was very rare for me to be off school. Every winter I would get a horrendous, barking cough. It must have driven my teachers and classmates mad, but no matter how bad it got, I was in school. The distasteful black medicine I was given didn't help at all, I remember my stomach and ribs used to ache like crazy, eventually my cough would just go of its own accord. I didn't help myself either, as I always wanted to run or play football, well that's what most boys do.

When I was aged ten I was knocked out at school. The PE teacher had split the boys into five or six groups to play cricket, the idea being that in small groups we'd all get a chance to bat and bowl. I remember I was running in to bowl, then someone was shouting 'lookout', no name was called so I carried on running in. The next thing that I knew was when I opened my eyes and I was looking up at a ring of faces. The teacher sent all the boys away to play their cricket, he sat me up and told me I was OK, then I had to go and sit at the edge of the playing field and wait for the home bell.

It must have been quite a shock for mum when I got home with a massive lump on my forehead. When dad came home he checked me over, he was trained in first aid because of his job, and also because he was a volunteer with the Red Cross. He decided that I was OK, no need to go to hospital, and bless him, I was back in school the next day. At morning assembly in school my class was on the stage, as the Headmaster came in, he made a beeline for me to see the state of my head, I think he made some jocular remark and carried on as normal, it was a different world back then.

M.E. - My Blessing in Disguise

I said how dad had moved onto cars, well on a Sunday we went to Ashford to see mum's sister Elsie, and George, Mary was with us. Our route took us through a town called Tenterden, as you approach the town there is a series of bends, on one of these bends a wheel came off the back of the car. The car turned over onto it's roof and spun around to face the way we had come. I remember my head hitting the roof and I saw stars, we were all basically OK, apart from shock, but Mary suffered a broken collar bone and had to go to hospital. What had happened was that the wheel had ripped off of the bolts that held it in place, it wasn't actually loose, now the next day was Monday, you've probably guessed that I was back in school. Mum's younger sister Margie had passed a few years back, a big shock to all the family. Mary herself passed a year or two after the car accident.

My one notable achievement at school was passing my 11+ exam, the result must have been good as I was placed in the top stream at Grammar school, perhaps that should read misplaced, as by the end of the school year I was in the bottom stream, floundering amongst Algebra, Geometry and French.

I left school at sixteen with one, scraped Maths 'O' level, leaving school couldn't come soon enough for me, it was such a relief to leave it all behind. It took me a while to find a job, when I did it was of the more physical type. T.T.S. employed me, they were based in Brighton. The company installed and serviced those roller towel machines, mostly phased out now, and I'm pleased to say that I worked with some good people, Christine, Barry, Brian, Frank, amongst others, it was good for my self confidence to feel appreciated. I've mentioned the part-physicality of the work, well I had quite a surprise several months later, I realised that I finally had a pair of shoulders, and had grown to a more average height, what a bonus.

T.T.S. opened a depot by Wandsworth Common the next year and a few of us were asked to move up to London, and I was shown some accommodation which had been recently refurbished. I was interested

M.E. - My Blessing in Disguise

and had a chat with mum and dad, they gave me their blessing, but years later dad told me that mum had cried all night.

It was either late '64 or early in '65 that this exciting change happened, I was 17, it wasn't all that common to leave home at that age then. We moved into a house that had been split into flats in Manville Road, Balham. I now know that Harry Edwards used to live locally before he took on The Sanctuary, though his name meant nothing to me back then. To begin with after the move, I traveled back to Brighton every weekend, but that of course would change.

The first weekend that I stayed in Balham I wandered down the High St. in the direction of Tooting, it was quite a culture shock and I couldn't help but notice that so many pairs of eyes seemed to follow me, not menacing I should add, curious was more like it. The reason was of course that white faces were scarce in this part of London Town, for my part I'd only ever seen the occasional black face. Brighton was a cosmopolitan town, but it had more of a European mix, Balham was so different to what I'd been used to. I soon made myself at home as I found a big stall selling records in Tooting's indoor market, I became a regular visitor there.

Sometime in the early sixties my sister Sylvie met her hubby to be Paul, he was in the RAF. They did duly get married in 1965 I think, Paul got sent to Singapore and Sylvie followed him out there a few months later, giving birth to Neil and Gaynor whilst they were out there.

After about six months or so we'd moved to Stoke Newington, the Stamford Hill end, our company had been bought out by a dry cleaning firm in Walthamstow, so a move north of the river was common sense for us. Our flat was in a house owned by a Welsh opera singer and his family, it wasn't that uncommon to be woken by his singing on a Sunday morning. Several new faces would come and go from our flat, Tony, Fred, Paul and later Bob, all good pals. I remember Fred had a smart Mk 2 Jaguar, Tony on the other hand had an old A40 which

M.E. - My Blessing in Disguise

required pushing on cold and wet winter mornings. A few of the guys were as much into music as me.

One of the good things about being in London was that there seemed to be loads of live music, mostly in pubs, one which had some good groups was the Bell in Walthamstow, it had a reputation for being a rough house, but I saw some good bands there. Strangely if I wanted to see acts from the charts, and I did, I would usually see them in Brighton. I saw The Beatles, Gerry and the Pacemakers and Roy Orbison all on the same bill at the Brighton Hippodrome. I saw all the main groups live in the sixties, including the Stax tour, and the likes of James Brown. One act I did see in London was at the Albert Hall, Bob Dylan in his crossover period, I enjoyed both his folk and rock styles, it wasn't a problem to me, though some people booed him loudly and walked out.

I guess music got into me at an early age, dad was always whistling and singing around the house, even if he was up at 5:30 for his early shift. The old wind-up gramophone had a fair bit of use, as time went on a Radiogram appeared, then brother Bob started buying Elvis, Buddy Holly and Fats Domino records, and a few other artists we wont mention. I lapped it up, but what a shock when Buddy Holly died, that took the wind out of me.

My own record buying began with the likes of the Shadows and Duane Eddy, but I soon had Elvis, Chuck Berry and Roy Orbison in my collection as well. I was lucky enough to be able to buy some records from Mike, son of Ernie and Nel, close family friends, he was getting married so I was able to get them cheap from him, one was the first Elvis album, still worth a listen. Dad and Ernie were close friends, they used to play accordions together, then they got harmonicas to take on holidays for sing-songs. When we were younger our family used to go to their house on Friday nights, the adults would pop down the pub, us kids would have Spam or cheese sandwiches. I would lay on the floor under the table watching TV, we didn't have one of our own, so it was a novelty, a lovely family, they were good to us.

M.E. - My Blessing in Disguise

Like most teenagers in those days I used to listen to Radio Luxembourg, and in 1962 I heard two records I really liked, one was 'He's a Rebel' by the Crystals, the other was 'Love Me Do' by the Beatles, their sounds were so different then, you know what happened next. My collection has built up over the years, I'm pleased to say that I still buy the occasional cd now, and I've managed to put quite a few songs onto my Ipod, but I'm no tech wizard. The big thing about music for me is that a song needs to have a decent melody. Since my life changed I've noticed that quite a lot of pop songs have spiritual leanings in their lyrics, whether consciously or not I don't know, or maybe my own interpretation of them has altered.

One more thing on the music front, I was in a flat off Clapham Common, and Bob G who had a guitar, spotted that someone was getting rid of a piano for next to nothing, you had to collect it though. It was across the other side of Clapham, I think four of us went to get it, we pushed it through the streets and traffic, and up a steep hill. We almost got it back in one piece, but somehow lost a wheel along the way. That flat in The Chase was always freezing, no matter how many people stayed over.

I had my first pint at aged 16, in a local in Brighton, the Wilmington, it cost about 1s 10d I think, there was no proper system for checking your age back in those days, I think I was with Kenny and Brian Smith, our other friends Kenny B and Sandy must have had their first drinks somewhere else . One of life's ironies caught up with me on my 18th birthday, I went with Fred to a Jeff Beck gig at a pub in Carshalton. Would you believe it! they refused to serve me, too young they said, I couldn't even cry in my beer as I couldn't get one.

I went out with Angie for sometime, a lovely redhead, but I was very quiet and had so little small talk, I expect she got fed up with me. There were one or two others that I should have made more effort with too, Chris was one and Joanne I think, but that's life.

M.E. - My Blessing in Disguise

My now ex-wife Sue and I started going out, one thing lead to another and we married in November 1969, our son Brian was 7 months old on our wedding day. We had to live apart for a while, but in the summer of 1970 we were given a council flat in Leyton, a stone's throw from the Orient football ground. I'd put myself through a computer course, they were apparently going to be the coming thing, and I got a job with a bank at Cannon St. Leaving my old job was no big deal apart from the fact that I left behind a few good people, Bob H, George and Bill, Alan B, and Tom.

We settled in at Church Rd and Alison was born there in 1972. It was a struggle getting in and out of our place as there were three flights of stairs to negotiate, fortunately I received a promotion in 1974, so our thoughts turned to finding a house with a garden. London prices were out of reach, and the bank had very strict rules about lending to staff back then, a local bank manager could even veto lesser staff from moving into his locality, archaic or what.

We moved to the Three Bridges area of Crawley, about a 5 minute walk from the station, and normally a good train service. It was a three bed semi with a reasonable sized garden in a road called The Birches, we were due to move in November. However, in October it became a bitter-sweet year when my mum had a heart attack, it came out of the blue. I was at work when I heard, I rushed down to see her at the hospital in Brighton. When I saw her she looked as bright as a button, apart from the attached tubes, she wanted to see the kids, but I hadn't brought them. I told mum that I'd bring them at the weekend for sure, but sadly mum had a massive heart seizure the next day and passed over, I carried that guilt with me for a long time. It would be years before I knew about life being eternal, now I know that mum will have kept an eye on Brian and Alison. I had my father's philosophy then, when you're dead you're dead. I remember the Smiths and I had some chats about 'what are we here for' and so on, of course we hadn't a clue.

M.E. - My Blessing in Disguise

I was getting on well at work, more promotions, and the kids were growing, so it was time to look for a bigger house. We moved to Somerville Drive in Pound Hill, Crawley in 1984, a stone's throw from a lovely, small lake that has trees on three sides, it was a 4 bed detached house, so a bit more space and a garage for the car. Back at The Birches we'd taken in a mostly black kitten, Ben, he was a cute and clever cat. He soon found out that he could open most of the doors in out house by jumping up and pulling down on the handles, so I think he used to end up in Alison's room overnight. Having moved, Ben decided the area wasn't to his liking, he found his way back to our old house, probably less than a half mile as the crow flies. The front door there had a very low door knocker, he surprised the new family by knocking on the door. Sadly they didn't want such a polite cat, he was lucky and was taken in by a lady who lived around the corner.

A few months later we had a new kitten, Fluffy, a tabby, and as time went on she had her own brood of kittens. We intended to rehome them all, but Alison fell in love with the smallest one and Babe became part of the family. A few years later I renamed him Porky, he'll feature a bit more as time goes on, he became a real comfort to me in the dark days to come.

I think it was in 1984 or 1985 that at work we lost our good friend Bazza, he passed with a cancerous condition. He was a good pal and a bit of a mentor for me when I was training on the mainframe computers. He backed me up a few times and we had a few beers. I remember he showed me the way to stop a computer running, just using the many switches on the front, not the stop button. It would set off an alarm bell and bring people running, by the time they got there the computer was running normally, I should add he only did it on what was called the testing system.

In 1985, a good friend at work, Murrey, talked me into going on his ski trip. I'd heard several people talking about skiing and how much fun it was, so I took the plunge and was off to Canazei in the Italian Dolomites. It was a real good fun trip, and although I wasn't much

M.E. - My Blessing in Disguise

good at skiing, I kind of got the bug and had many more trips over the coming years. I think I can safely say that I've fallen off every type of ski lift that I've been on. On one trip I took my video camera, now for the embarrassing bit, I was on a chairlift and went to get off but couldn't, the camera bag strap had got caught on the back of the chair, I was stuck. The lift attendant stopped the lift and I managed to unhook myself. He wouldn't let me ride back down the lift, he said I had to jump down. It was about a 10 ft drop, fortunately it was a soft landing in a pile of snow, what a plonker!

We had some good family holidays, including three trips to the USA. On one Florida trip we had coincided with a Space Shuttle launch, so we stood outside our rented villa and watched it rise up in the distance. We also hired a man with a Catamaran to take us out to an island in the Gulf of Mexico to search for shells. It was beautiful skimming across the sea, hardly a sound, but with appreciable speed. I saw a huge Ray surface just a few feet from the boat, it was a magical moment.

Working in the bank was a great experience, lots of friends were made, too many to mention here, they moved me around a lot so I really did get to know lots of people. I am still in touch with some of them I'm pleased to say. Until 1991 all my time in the bank had involved working shifts, suddenly I was told that I had a job on days which meant I had my own project to run,. I didn't enjoy working on days, it seemed all about politics rather than working for a common goal.

Sue and I went to Italy for a holiday in June 1992, we stayed at a lovely hotel which had been converted from an old monastery. It was situated in the hills about 30k outside of Florence, with a train station at the bottom of the hill, I didn't want to drive into Florence so the train was handy. That plan didn't quite work out as we had car trouble one day and I had to drive it into Florence to get it fixed.

 One evening we had walked down to a nearby village for our meal, the restaurant was quiet to start with, then the whole village seemed to come in and have a party. As we left the village it was very dark, then

M.E. - My Blessing in Disguise

we came around a corner and an astonishing and wonderful sight met our eyes, there were Fireflies everywhere, thousands of them, a beautiful spectacle, we'd never seen anything like it before. Several cars pulled up and the occupants got out to enjoy nature's beauty, it was just amazing.

A couple of evenings later we were having a drink outside in the hotel's grounds when I thought I saw a Hummingbird flitting around some of the huge flower urns, I didn't think they came that far north. After returning to the UK I found out that it was a Hummingbird Hawkmoth that we'd seen, it has become my occasional harbinger of change.

On my first day back at work after the holiday, I was just about to go into our building when a chap I knew came over and told me that my project had been dropped. This was a complete shock to me, it had come out of nowhere. Two or three months later I was on gardening leave, I finally left the bank at the end of the year.

Once over the shock I wasn't too upset about the job itself with all the political stuff, it wasn't me at all, but again, so many good friends would go out of my life, or at least be less available to see regularly. There are far too many people that I would miss to mention here, but I will briefly talk about Chris. I met him when I was moved to C shift in 1981, overall quite a young shift, I knew hardly anyone there, but they made me feel welcome from the off. Chris will appear in later chapters, he passed way too young with an unusual condition, he's been helpful and encouraging since my spiritual awakening.

I went to the reception of Trish and John in 1983, two good friends from work, many of the shift attended the wedding, some of us had to work that day, so I drove up to Woburn after work with Les and Al in my car. We were staying in a pub b&b just a few minutes walk from the reception. So we checked in and were soon off to join the happy throng. As we went out, someone mentioned that they lock their doors at midnight.

M.E. - My Blessing in Disguise

We had a very good evening, and it went on late of course, at one point I had to step back sharply as someone swung around from the bar with a tray of drinks. I'd had no option and no time to look and unfortunately I trod on a lady's foot. The next thing was that I had a very angry, man's face close to mine, and he was giving me a lot of verbal abuse. I tried to explain that it was an accident, then I recognised him as a now retired, former England bowler, well known for his fiery temperament. There were several ex-cricketers around, they were playing charity matches on the weekend, good for them. He did calm down I'm pleased to say, and we enjoyed the rest of the evening.

One sad note here is the fact that Trish ended up with MS and is now in spirit, I clicked with her from the off, she was among the closest friends I've ever had, I couldn't stop smiling whenever I saw her. Her hubby John is also a very likeable chap, I wonder what he's up to now?

Les, Al and myself made our way back down the street to our b&b, it was probably 2:30 or so, not surprisingly the doors were locked. We had a sing song after our knocks weren't answered, no one came down to complain about the noise darn it. Someone spotted a small window open, so Les was nominated to try and get in through it, he was the lightest and smallest. Al and I somehow hoisted him up and he made it through, so to our relief we got in and went to bed. The landlady looked a little surprised that we made it down for breakfast, but nothing was said. We went back up the road at lunchtime to see Trish, John and Trish's family, they are a lovely bunch, then it was off back home.

In the summer of 1992 whilst I was still at the bank and working days, my brother-in-law Paul roped me in to play cricket for Brighton RAFA, he'd played for them for a number of years, and they were a bit short of players. Incidentally Paul, who was a natural at most sports, went on to take 1000 wickets for the team, some achievement. My sister Sylvie was often involved with helping with the teas and scoring, and their son Neil also played for the team.

M.E. - My Blessing in Disguise

On leaving the bank I began to do more sport, golf, more cricket, some time on the exercise bike, and I took up Badminton. I really loved Badminton and did a short course to learn more about it at the local sports centre. I ended up playing two or three times a week with some people from the course. We went at it hammer and tongs, leaping and diving around, it was great fun. A result of all this exercise was that I felt so much fitter than I had been, probably the fittest since my teens, I'd also lost nearly two stone in weight. How ironic this was to become with M.E. awaiting me just around the corner.

On into my uncertain future then, I tried a few things, but I never really settled on anything. At some point I saw a news item about lots of the bigger companies going into, or expanding, their Financial Service Advice areas. This seemed to strike a chord with me, something to aim for, so now I had to find something to do until the recruitment stage began. I ended up being a minicab driver in East Grinstead, that started in June 1994.

Through being a minicab driver I met quite a few lovely people, but equally I also met some of the other kind, those who treat you like dirt, it meant that I had good days and not so good days. The best folks were often the ones who needed a little help, they were always appreciative, I don't mean through tips, it was their attitude.

The bad days were having an affect on me, more than I realised at the time, but stress can build up without you noticing it. Into mid-September and there was a mini flu epidemic going around, one of our drivers came in unwell and sat looking very pasty until someone could take him home. A few days later I started getting a funny head and I thought that I must be fighting off the flu. Also around this time, I spotted the advertisments for recruiting Trainee Financial Advisers, I sent off for an application form.

With my head a bit strange I asked to be left out of the next cricket match, alas they were short, so I was in. In our last match I'd not been myself, I'm not a wonderful cricketer at all, but tried to do my best,

M.E. - My Blessing in Disguise

such as throwing myself down to stop the ball, not necessarily with my hands, it shows willing. However in the last game I'd had trouble reacting, even off my own bowling, I couldn't seem to move myself to get down to stop the ball even when it was hit back in my direction.

My funny head continued , but nothing else seemed to be developing. The job application form arrived on Friday 30th of September, that day I got up and found that my head was clear, brilliant I thought, I've fought off the bug. I started filling in the form, but then I was off to work for the afternoon and evening, so I resolved to complete the form on Saturday.

I worked until around midnight and got back home still feeling normal, so I had a little relaxation and a nightcap, then it was off to bed. Until this point my life had been ordinary, but changes can come in when you least expect them to.

M.E. - My Blessing in Disguise

The Onset of M.E.

I was up once in the night for a normal loo break, the weird feeling in my head was back, perhaps a bit stronger than it had been. So October 1st 1994 dawned and I awoke around 7am. I felt really peculiar, I'd hoped to get up early and get that job application form finished. I soon found out that I could barely move a muscle, it took me about an hour and a half to roll over to get out of bed, I didn't feel any better once I'd managed it. My first thoughts were that I'd caught the flu, albeit a very peculiar flu. I spent the day on the sofa and went to bed early as aches and pains came in all over. After about ten days I went back to work, feeling a bit better, but not 100%.

A small digression here, November 1st was to be the 25th wedding anniversary of Sue and I, earlier I'd scouted around the local hotels with the idea of having a meal and a party in a place where people could stay the night if they wished. I was offered a good deal by one hotel, but I never went back to book it. In fact my ideas switched to a holiday and I booked us on a trip to the Canadian Rockies, one of those escorted tours, in some top hotels I should add.

We took our trip to the Canadian Rockies in the second half of October, the first stop was the massive French Chateau-styled hotel in the small town of Banff. Then we went out to Jasper, where our accommodation was in a log cabin, with Elk grazing outside the door, breakfast was brought by bicycle riding waiters who would keep forgetting things. The last stop was to the hotel that sits on the shore of Lake Louise. We were taken out on the coach in the daytime to see beautiful coloured lakes and wonderful mountain scenery.

After unpacking at Lake Louise we were out having a walk around the beautiful shore, just as we started heading back to the hotel it began snowing, a reward for our efforts in the fresh air as the whole scene took on a magical air. We had a meal in the bar that night, and some hot toddies too, I did sleep well that night.

M.E. - My Blessing in Disguise

My energy had drained as the week went on and we took to having breakfast in our room. I did still appreciate the beautiful scenery although I felt a growing tiredness. There was a Scotsman on our trip, he didn't seem to like wearing socks or shoes. One day we stopped to have a walk on a glacier, he got off the coach without them and put a foot on the ice, he swiftly returned to the coach for his footwear, so not as silly as he seemed.

Back in the UK I went back to work though feeling tired, it wasn't long before I had my first relapse. Had we gone ahead with the party as originally intended, I wouldn't have been able to attend, interesting!

I went to see my GP, after his examination he said everything was normal, but he believed I was ill, it made me feel very emotional. I was booked in for a series of blood tests. My GP thought that I'd had a virus, nothing was showing up so I was referred to the local hospital. After an initial chat with the consultant more tests were taken, then some more. It was quite a wait before I was given an appointment to see the consultant again. In the meantime a couple of people had mentioned M.E. to me as being a possible condition. It was getting a lot of news coverage at the time, labelled as 'Yuppie Flu' and the like, it was always spoken of in a disparaging way by the press. This was because there was no way to prove whether anyone had the condition, so it was thought of as a skiver's charter. What this widely held viewpoint failed to consider was the fact that lots of hard working people and high achievers were amongst the cases. Someone said to me that if it was M.E. then I'd better get used to it as there was no cure, you have it for life. I responded by saying that if that's what I have I'll see it off, I'm not putting up with this for the rest of my life, and I meant it.

I finally got to see the consultant again in April, she said that there was good news and bad news. The good news was that they've found antibodies of the Epstein-Barre virus in some tests, the bad news is that they had no cure for my condition. All she could suggest was that I go

M.E. - My Blessing in Disguise

sick and rest whenever the condition worsened - that I'd worked out for myself, so a disappointing day.

Back at my GP's surgery, he again offered to sign me off sick, he said that he had other patients with this condition, he called it Post Viral Fatigue Syndrome, he didn't like M.E. or its new name of Chronic Fatigue Syndrome.

Perhaps I'm stubborn, but I hated the idea of just giving in to this condition, so I decided to carry on working unless the tiredness built up too much. I wasn't getting a whole lot of other symptoms at this time. Somehow I was determined to get through this and rid myself of it, but I had no idea how.

It took me several years to realise that M.E. is not a condition that you can just fight off, you have to accept it, then try to find a way that slowly lessens its hold on you. There's no point in confronting M.E., it's not a fight that you can win that way. At this point I still seemed to have some control of my life, well intermittently, however that was soon to disappear.

May was a goodish month as I felt a little better, then I had a series of very early morning pickups, people who needed to get to the airport for their early flights. These people wanted picking up at 3:00 am, they often lived in the middle of nowhere, so I was leaving home very early to find them. I had a bad relapse in June 1995 and went to see my GP to be signed off work. This latest relapse hit me hard and work became a thing of the past as I began getting some peculiar symptoms and lots of pains. There was no doubt now that M.E. had taken total control of my life.

M.E. - My Blessing in Disguise

The Effects 0f M.E.

ME can hit you severely or at lesser levels, in my case it became severe, I cannot say if that was because I carried on working for several months, but it's quite possible. I should have spent most of the time in bed, but I soon developed horrendous back pains around the adrenal areas, and I also used to find that the back of my head would become very sore and uncomfortable when lying down. Consequently sleeping wasn't easy and became quite irregular, most days were spent sitting in an armchair or on the sofa, doing little or nothing.

I had no control over my life any more, it became very frustrating and made me feel fed up. It's a real life changer, no work and no play, life became very tedious. My brain was becoming increasingly fuzzy, short term memory virtually disappeared, I would walk the dozen or so steps from the lounge to the kitchen to make a cup of tea, by the time I'd got there I'd forgotten what I was doing.

It was almost impossible to have conversations on the phone, my brain wouldn't keep up with what was being said. Several friends called initially, but they got little sense out of me. Fortunately my close friend Sheila was very patient, as she realised that I needed much more time to absorb what she said. It was as if I was hearing everything a sentence or two behind. Sheila kept in touch throughout and did her best to keep me in touch with what was going on with our friends. It can give you such a boost when someone shows you that they care when you're struggling. I can safely say that Sheila was another that I clicked with immediately after we met, and we have remained very close friends.

Whilst my life had become so boring and monotonous, I just didn't have the energy to do anything most of the time, so it wasn't that important as days and weeks drifted past. Other symptoms came to the fore, aches and pains would come and go in almost every part of my body, usually there was no obvious reason, painkillers were no help at all. I had severe pains in the neck glands that are under my ears, but the

M.E. - My Blessing in Disguise

worst pains of all were in my shoulders, by that I mean right in the bones themselves. Imagine having toothache in an area that size, it's the only way I can try to explain it. I used to hold my shoulders to try and comfort myself, it was so awful. Those pains weren't there everyday thankfully, it could be the forearms, legs or anywhere, there was no rhyme or reason to it at all. The same could be said for some of the other symptoms, I had days where I would keep itching and the itches would move about the body, as if I had ants on me or something. My body temperature would go up and down at speed, that meant that I'd be either layering up or taking things off every few minutes. My brain as well as having the fuzzy, foggy feeling sometimes seemed to be being squashed from the sides, then from the front and back, like someone was making a pat of butter with it.

The only symptom that was predictable was the constant lack of energy, the others would be quite random, and at some point I also realised that my emotions were difficult to control. Before I had M.E. I only thought about how the effects of physical exertion can drain the body, now I knew that mental activity and emotional ups and downs could do as well, and perhaps they could do it more easily, it took me a while to realise that this was happening.

I joined an M.E. group, occasionally going to a meeting if it coincided with my energy being sufficient to cope, I wanted to find out more about M.E. and what was happening with regard to looking for a cure. It helped meeting others with the condition and I heard about how some had tried this or that therapy in their search for a return to normality. There were some who said that they'd had short term relief from such things as cranial massage, reflexology and acupuncture, but none had an overall answer, and peoples reactions varied quite widely with individual therapies.

One day, after two or three months of sitting around doing nothing, a miracle seemed to happen, I found myself feeling more or less normal, wow! It felt brilliant, my life was back, right then I'd better wash the

M.E. - My Blessing in Disguise

car and mow the lawn, and what about a good long walk, that would feel wonderful. Don't ask me what I started on first, but those were the thoughts that came into my head, and some would have been acted upon. The next day I was flat out again with my energy level at zero, what a come down. This happened several times over the years, it took a long time for me to get a grip of myself when the miracle happened, the temptation to just do things was overwhelming. The normality feeling could be there when I got up in the morning, or just arrive at any time of day. It was just a natural reaction to want to go out and do something after these periods of non-activity, something as simple as a good walk instead of a short trudge, I just couldn't help myself. It would be years before the penny dropped and I realised that stopping this reaction would be a crucial part of my recovery plan.

I've already mentioned how music has played a big part in my life, like many, I'll have it on in the car as well as at home, and the Ipod is very handy when travelling. I can still remember an old song that Dad used to have on a 78 record, 'Ain't it grand to be blooming well dead', yes it was a funny song, and I'm grateful for Dad's fondness of music, I know it's certainly enriched my life. So things took a not so funny turn when perhaps two or three years into M.E. I suddenly found that I was unable to listen to music, it seemed to hurt my ears. This went on for probably about 18 months, then it ended as quickly as it had started. I think my ears were very sensitive to most sounds through that period.

M.E. - My Blessing in Disguise

I'm Off To Bart's

I managed to attended a meeting in Hove of the Brighton ME group, there was a talk about ME being given by a Professor. He was working up at Bart's hospital in London on a project in which he was trying to find out the cause of ME. He had a theory about it, and a budget for a time, his study was intended to either prove or disprove his theory with regard to the cause of ME. At the end of the talk he mentioned that he was always looking for volunteers to help his study, any sufferer could come along, but they had to clear it with their GP.

It didn't take long for me to decide that I'd like to take part, so I had a chat with my own GP. A couple of weeks later I was given the go ahead, and so an appointment was made for me to visit the Prof at Bart's. This was in 1996, I still had my belief that I would somehow rid myself of this dreadful condition. I expected the journeys to be tiring, but I was looking upon this as an opportunity to either help prove the Professor's theory, or if it was disproved then it was one cause off of the long list of possibles, either way it was a positive move. Medical science was totally in the dark about this condition and it wasn't being taken seriously by a lot of the medical establishment, so why not help someone who did take it seriously.

I met the Professor and his Doctor assistant, and we had a long chat, he concluded that I was a classic case, although one or two of my symptoms were new to him. I think we finished with some blood tests that day, and another appointment was made for a couple of weeks time. As the appointments went on I also had CT and MRI scans.

One day at Bart's they had trouble getting the needle into a vein, reinforcements were called in, suddenly they struck oil, well OK - blood, it started spurting everywhere and caused quite a panic until it was under control. I looked upon this with some amusement, quite detached from it all, it was as if it was happening to someone else. For a week or two I was given a low dose of steroids, they did give me a

M.E. - My Blessing in Disguise

lift, so it was quite disappointing to be told that I couldn't carry on with them. One outcome from the scans showed that my adrenal glands were smaller than average, perhaps that accounts for those horrible back pains.

At some point as I attended Bart's, I had to go for a Department of Social Security assessment, and on the day in question I was feeling reasonable, but nowhere near normal. I made it totally clear to the examining doctor about the nature of the condition, as in I could easily relapse the next day, and my energy could not be relied upon in any way, well I thought that I had. I was listened to politely but to no avail it seemed.

A week or two later I received a letter telling me to go back to work, my benefits were stopped. This is an immensely distressing thing to happen when you're ill, it hit me very hard at the time. I showed my letter to the Professor on my next visit to Bart's. He said that he would be in touch with me, and when I received his letter I should appeal against the judgement. The appeal was duly won, I was extremely grateful for the Professor's support, I received no apology from the DSS.

I think it was in early 1997 that my trips to Bart's were stopped, the budget for this research was coming to an end , it was time for the Professor to draw up his report on the findings. Sadly his theory was not proven, but it was one possible cause removed, only 99 more to go then. I had no regrets about being part of his research, even though the journeys were often tiring, it had been a positive experience for me.

M.E. - My Blessing in Disguise

Songs

At some point in 1996 I woke in the night, nothing unusual in that, but I had this tune playing in my head, it kept playing, and soon after I had some lyrics for it. My fuzzy brain couldn't place who had sung it, it sounded a bit like Country, not my taste. I began to wonder if it was a new song, that would explain why I couldn't place it, if so, it must have been written in my sleep, such as it was. The song was called 'Every Cloud has a Silver Lining', and of course it's proved to be true for me.

I should say at this point that I had written some songs, none had ever been played or published, I wasn't a musician so I carried them in my head. I think I had a little panic as I thought about how bad my memory was, how would I ever remember it, come to that how would I remember my other songs, my panic grew.

In the morning I still had the words in my head, so they were written down, then I wrote down the words of my other songs, phew! what a relief. Somehow I'd also kept the melodies in my head, but this was a worry now. At some point I bought a Dictaphone to record them, just as well as more followed over the next two or three years.

I would go through spells where I was able to write songs or parts of songs about anything, news items, peoples conversations, anything that came to mind. I'm not going to say that any were fantastic, but some seemed OK to me, but music is very subjective. I even wrote a song about how boring my life had become with ME as my constant companion.

I now presume that there was a lot of spirit help coming in, perhaps they were trying to lift me, or maybe there were some writers who thought that they had unfinished business on the earth plane, there's certainly plenty of them up there. One strange thought is that whilst this was happening I was also simultaneously experiencing my period of not being able to listen to music, how weird is that.

M.E. - My Blessing in Disguise

My thoughts about writing songs started in the sixties when the Beatles were writing their own material, and the likes of Chuck Berry wrote and performed his own songs. It started my cogs whirring and somehow I figured out a couple of tunes. I'd best not forget the prolific Bob Dylan either, he seemed to be able to write songs about all kinds of things, from love songs to topical ones. There were several others , Roy Orbison for instance, who wrote some beautiful songs, but a lot of singers relied on songwriters for their material.

At some point I managed to get a few songs demo'd, but not to my satisfaction. I would send a tape away with a song or two on it, and try and describe how the song should sound, it isn't easy trying to explain what you want. One of the biggest problems is the fact that I have no idea what key my songs are in, crucial information for musicians. I also know that my voice lacked energy during some periods with ME, that's not to say that I have a wonderful voice normally, far from it. I've since been told that the only way to do it properly is to go into a studio myself and talk to the musicians and producer. Good advice I'm sure, but I've never plucked up the courage to do it yet.

I bought a keyboard and had a few lessons to try to get to grips with it, the problem was I still had ME, so it wasn't the best timing, and I had great difficulty in relating what I was hearing in my head to the notes on the keyboard, frustrating really. No matter, the songs have given me a lot of pleasure, even if I can't share them. They certainly helped to raise my spirits when the going was tough.

M.E. - My Blessing in Disguise

Dipping My Toe in the Water

This chapter may begin to stretch a reader's credibility, it certainly stretched mine at the time, you may think that I should have been sectioned, I guess it was my first intervention from spirit. I've since had countless happenings and intangible experiences, which to those who have not opened up to spirit may well seem like fantasies or the ravings of a madman. Come to that, there maybe those who are open to spirit who feel the same way, all I can say is that from here on in these are my perceptions of my experiences.

At the time of its happening , this was probably the strangest experience of my life, I'm sure it's been superseded many times since. One day I trudged down the local mini-supermarket at the end of our road for something or other, as I entered the shop I felt incredibly drawn towards the pile of freebie papers, which were stacked on the floor near the door. It was a struggle for me to get past them.

I must have bought what I wanted and then made my way towards the shop door. As I went to pass the stack of papers again, a voice began shouting loudly in my head, 'pick it up' pick it up'. It was shouted several times before I reluctantly managed to bend down to pick one up. It appeared that I was stuck there until I did as I was bid. Back home I put the paper on the coffee table shelf and left it there. I was still making trips to Bart's at this time, I'm sure I didn't mention it to them, or to anyone for a while.

It was most likely a week or so later, when for some reason I picked the paper up and wondered why I had brought it home in the first place. I began glancing through it, but then I was distracted by the telephone or the doorbell, so I just dropped the paper down. When I picked the paper up again, it opened at a page advertising Clairvoyants and Psychics. I think I briefly read through the ads, it must have started me thinking about them. I'd never had a reading before or even really thought about having one, but it began nagging in my mind.

M.E. - My Blessing in Disguise

It was probably during the week after that I decided to take the plunge, I'd been having a tough period and needed some sort of boost, perhaps this could help in some way. I was feeling a bit low and I didn't want to lose the hope that I had about recovering. These feelings would sometimes kick in after relapse or a prolonged period of low energy.

It was a strange feeling, making that call to arrange a reading, and then going to meet someone who was involved in something that I had no idea about, or any belief in it at that time. I'd phoned a number in Horley rather than Crawley, lest someone who knew me might spot me entering the medium's house.
Fortunately it was an easy house to find, and just a few minutes drive away. As I rang the doorbell I had no idea of what I was doing there or what to expect. A lady opened the door, as I stepped inside she said that she could see I was ill, she didn't need her psychic hat on to see that, her remarks were lost on me. She showed me into the room where the reading would take place, then before I could sit down the lady had collapsed to the floor, screaming and crying and hugging her shoulders.

She was in agony for perhaps a minute, I watched helplessly, I didn't know what to do and thought about leaving. The lady finally stood up and asked me if I had these horrendous pains that she'd just experienced in her shoulders, I told her I did, but I hadn't got them today. It was very dramatic, but didn't impact on me the way it would now with what I know. Spirit had made her suffer the worst pain that ME had inflicted on me, I'd be amazed now at a similar occurrence, as I'd know that it was incredible evidence to receive.

We sat down and I had to shuffle the Tarot cards, then they were dealt in what is known as a spread. We were looking at the recent past and it was so gloomy she said, everything had gone wrong, all that was missing was the death of a loved one, I told her that was correct. More cards were dealt and we moved onto the present. It was still the same scenario, the lady picked up on my trips to hospital, she said that on my next trip they would extend the interval between appointments, and

M.E. - My Blessing in Disguise

shortly after that, my trips would come to an end. This proved to be the case over the next few weeks.

Some cards were dealt for the future, she said that there was hope of improvement, but it was not imminent and progress would be slow, that has also proven to be true. I was given some evidence about things going on around me, and also some stuff about my car, that was correct.

At one point the lady gave me a most peculiar look, as if she couldn't believe what she was being told or what she'd seen. Whatever it was she must have thought it to be a most unlikely possibility, as I had gone there with absolutely no belief in the spiritual side, she never told me what it was.

The reading must have served its purpose as I went away feeling a little intrigued, my interest had been aroused, though it would be some time before I actually made any step forwards. I had no idea at that point how mediumship worked, if I had I would have been very impressed with the reading. Looking back, I felt sorry for the lady, she was put through agony just to get me interested, it does make you think.

I'm now convinced that this first reading was spirit putting a key in a door for me, a door that had been locked all my life up until that point, now all I had to do was turn the key and push the door wide open.

My next reading was about six months later with a lady medium in Horsham, she had a warm and sympathetic manner. I didn't dare go back to the lady in Horley in case she was made to suffer again. This time I was given lots of evidence that spirit was around me, and also evidence of survival, as my mum Eileen and her mum Mary came through, that was lovely for me. I was told to drink plenty of water and to stick with having sugar in my tea. For a few years I'd been taking sweeteners, but recently I kept forgetting to buy them, so a bit of confirmation and advice there.

M.E. - My Blessing in Disguise

I had a further reading with this lady about six months later, my health was talked about, Harry Edwards Sanctuary was mentioned as a place to go to for help. I was of course totally ignorant about healing at this point. I found the village on a map, but I wasn't sure about driving there. I played safe and was only driving on roads that I was familiar with in order to try and keep my stress levels down. I didn't have anyone close at hand who I'd confided in about my having had readings at this time, so sadly I didn't go. I carried on having readings about every six months.

M.E. - My Blessing in Disguise

Time To Move On

Throughout our married life I'd had very little illness, some time off with a back problem, but not much else of note. Sue wasn't used to having me around all day, but suddenly there I was, all day and everyday in the armchair or on the sofa, infringing on her space. I don't doubt that this had an effect on her, and overall there can be no doubt that my ongoing health situation contributed to the ending of our marriage. I'm also sure that we had drifted apart somewhat, we were married young and it seemed to me that we'd run our course. I felt tension building up between us, and whilst we mostly kept a lid on it, my stress levels were on the rise, doing me no good at all.

With all my sitting around, one of our cats, Porky, had taken to sleeping on me a lot. His favoured position was to have his front paws on my shoulders with the bridge of his nose wedged into the dimple of my chin. He had longish claws so I couldn't put up with this for long, so he'd just lay in my lap instead. He was a beautiful cat and his presence helped me no end, my spirits were always raised when he was in the house during those testing years. One sad aspect about Porky was that he became diabetic, this was due to his weight, which ballooned in a shortish time. The problem was down to the state of my short term memory, I would forget I'd fed him and basically I ended up feeding him on demand. I remember him as being so playful, even when an older cat, and as a source of loving in some tough times. He will feature in later chapters as he became a regular visitor after he passed over.

Son Brian bought a flat in Crawley around 1997, the next year our house went up for sale as Sue and I decided it was time to go our separate ways. It wasn't too long before we had a buyer lined up for our house, it took a little longer finding our new homes. Sue's idea was to move locally, Alison would be staying with her mum to begin with, and the cats would also be with them. It was a sad time, but for the best.

M.E. - My Blessing in Disguise

Eventually Sue found a house in Crawley, whilst I bought a flat down the coast at Shoreham-by-Sea, with the moves finally happening early in 1999. My flat was in a small block, just the one other flat below and a house at one end of the block, it was also just a stones throw from a large park. I did have a very small garden, mostly paved, so not much required to keep it in order. I'd decided that a flat was the best idea at this point, I was hoping that it would help to keep me out of mischief, by that I mean I was hoping for less relapses.

At normal walking pace I was less than a ten minute walk from the train station, with the small town centre leading on from there. Beyond that was a bridge across the river, then in another five minutes I could be on Shoreham beach. It was a good place to be, mostly on the flat side, so not too taxing for walking.

It took me a while to settle into my flat, eventually I realised why, it was painted in very pale pastel colours throughout. I needed to bring some colour in, I just hoped that the decorating wouldn't bring about any relapses. I took my time, and the lounge became red and a sunny yellow second bedroom/sitting room appeared. It helped no end, the rest of the flat was decorated over time, as and when my energy allowed.

I think I had one relapse around this time, an idea popped into my head about the way forwards, a way I hoped would point me towards improving my energy levels, and perhaps leading me to finish with this condition. It's very simple and no doubt totally obvious, but from being on the inside, it's not always easy to see things in a different perspective. I resolved to only do what was absolutely necessary every day, as I said simple. The problem with this approach would be in sticking to it, a very boring lifestyle, yes mine already was, but this would have to be rigid in order to have any chance of success.

I was required to have another DSS assessment at some point in 1999, surprise, they failed me and stopped my benefit. I had no professor to back me up this time, so I decided to let it go, rightly or wrongly it

M.E. - My Blessing in Disguise

seemed the least stressful option. The stress of going through an appeal meant that there was every chance I'd relapse, it was the last thing I wanted, so I decided to live off my savings for now.

My physical energy did slowly increase, so I made a little progress, then I had a reminder about how mental energy can drain the body. I started doing crosswords again and reading, I must have overdone it as I had several days when tiredness kicked in. It was a sharp reminder and thankfully I realised the cause and had to ration that as well. Any mental activity after about 5pm was inviting trouble, but I restricted myself much more than that, there was no choice.

The next challenge was when a 'miracle' day occurred, let's get up and go! It was a battle controlling myself, but one that I had to win, else these recent little steps forwards would've been wasted. The better my control, the longer the 'miracle' days would last, as in maybe two or three days, so it was crucial to behave myself.

At some point I saw a Homeopathist and she asked some very strange questions before I left with a remedy. I didn't feel any real benefit, but decided to look into it further. I did find the odd remedy that worked with helping pain relief, yes I was still getting some pains. I had some nasty spiky pains in the top of my head, I found that the Nat Sulph remedy kept these under control. I carried on taking them for sometime, slowly reducing the dosage, and eventually those pains were gone.

In the past few years my dad had been spending a lot of time visiting his cousin Renie in London, she was a lovely and lively lady with a good sense of humour. As kids they'd spent some summer holidays on their grandad's farm having a whale of a time. They got on very well, though Renie had health issues that prevented her from going too far from home. In the spring of '99 Renie had to go into hospital, a couple of weeks later or so she was gone. Dad never got over this, the fun had gone out of his life. A few months later he was going around telling people that he had cancer. His doctor examined him and could find nothing, but dad said he could feel something inside him, Later in the

M.E. - My Blessing in Disguise

year dad was proven right, he was diagnosed with cancer. His last few weeks were spent in hospital, he so wanted to go that in the end he refused his medication, apart from the pain killers, and he'd only eat ice cream. He passed away in the early hours of Jan 31st 2000, even though we knew he was going it was still such a shock.

The day after his funeral was a very windy and grey day, low clouds and low light. I took myself off over to Shoreham beach and let it all out. The waves were crashing on the shore, no one else had ventured out, I was alone with my grief. At this time I still only had an inkling about Spirit, I was convinced that life carried on after death, but my only involvement had been in having a few readings. However, the time was approaching when my eyes and mind would be well and truly opened.

My father had no belief in an afterlife, so what surprises must have been waiting for him. I'm very pleased to say that he's been through several times with messages for me, so it didn't take him too long to settle in and find out what's what.

M.E. - My Blessing in Disguise

The Cause of ME?

As far as I'm aware medical science is still no closer to discovering the cause of ME, and therefore no nearer to a cure. I've given a lot of thought to this myself, and although I have no medical training whatsoever, I do have the experience of having suffered with the condition and what's more of recovering from it, having been cured.

Several years ago I somehow formed my own theory on the cause of ME, certainly in my case anyway, I can't say if the cause is always the same for every sufferer. I believe that stress causes many of today's ills, I know that I was stressed at the time that I contracted ME. Although I was pretty fit back then, the stress brought on by my mini-cabbing job was most likely the cause of my downfall.

I believe that stress lowers the body's immune system and therefore makes us vulnerable to many conditions. Part of the body's immune system is the blood-brain-barrier, obviously there to help protect the brain. If the immune system is low then surely the blood-brain-barrier must also be proportionally weakened. In this scenario I suspect that it's possible that viruses can manage to penetrate through the barrier and enter into the brain itself, once there they can wreak havoc.

How correct I am I don't know, but it fits my personal scenario, and maybe that of many others, as viruses seem to be the common factor in those with this condition. To some this will seem a major assumption on my part, to me it's the only answer that makes sense.

To take this a little further I tried reading some medical books , I didn't get very far other than to find out that we all have neurotransmitters and neuro receivers in our brains. Our bodies rely on chemicals or hormones being produced as and when the body needs them. This is achieved by the neural network, it's responsible for the sending and receiving of messages to and from the brain in response to the body requesting more or less of a hormone. When the virus interferes with

M.E. - My Blessing in Disguise

the body's requests, hormone imbalances are likely to occur, as messages are sent and received to and from the wrong places. I believe that the consequences of this are the tiredness, lack of energy, and all the peculiar and unexplainable symptoms that ME brings.

This may sound a simple theory for a complex problem, but by addressing possible imbalances, and with other help, I managed to reclaim my brain and my life.

M.E. - My Blessing in Disguise

Buqi Lends A Helping Hand

As I've previously stated, the year 2000 had a sad start with Dad's passing on January 31st, just a few days before his 87th birthday. My life had to go on and it was still a struggle. I continued reining myself in, determined to try to not overdo things and bring on a relapse, especially on those days when I would suddenly feel normal again. This became very difficult after such a long illness, the urge was very strong, and probably grew stronger each time, but my discipline was mostly maintained somehow. The very thought that I could so easily slip back into the doldrums spurred me on to stay with my plan of this boring lifestyle, as a means to ending this condition's hold on me.

I went for an acupuncture session at a Chinese shop in Brighton hoping it would help. After the needles were inserted into my skin they were linked to an electric current, I hadn't expected that.
As soon as the current was turned on I felt some pain in my back, I told the ladies and a needle was removed and reinserted. On with the current again, I told them it was still hurting in one area, they told me it was impossible and promptly left the room. I stayed put lest I cause myself more pains.

At the end of the session they still didn't believe me and gave me a bag of small, brown pills. Somehow I lost the pills on the way home. It was not a happy experience, I now know through a friend of mine, Clare, a trained acupuncturist, that if a needle is in slightly the wrong place, not in its correct point on the body, it will hurt. She proved it to me, yes, ow!

One day I bought the local evening paper, it carried an advertising article about something called Buqi. It was described as being like acupuncture but without needles, as it worked on what are called the body's meridians. It is an ancient Chinese therapy, a type of vibrational healing, and I think it may have ties to Qui Xong . It sounded interesting to me, I was still looking for help of course to end my ME. I

M.E. - My Blessing in Disguise

went along to a talk and demonstration to a place called The Cornerstone in Hove, it's an old church that's been converted into rooms that are rented out to groups.

There were probably about forty people in the audience and a couple of people spoke to us about Buqi, there were three others with them I think. It interested me, but at the end of the talk several people were asking questions and comparing it to other alternative therapies. Reiki was the one that cropped up the most. At that time I knew very little about most therapies.

Now it was time for the demonstration, which a couple of dozen people stayed for. We were asked to stand in an unusual position and to try to hold our hands in a certain way, we also had to keep our eyes closed. There were four or five people working on us, and they started from the back of the room. After several minutes curiosity got the better of me, there was no noise so I had to find out if anything was happening. Out of the corner of my eye I saw a demonstrator waving their arms behind someone, so arms and hands were moving, but no one was being touched. I couldn't understand how this was likely to help anyone if there was no contact involved.

I quickly shut my eyes as I somehow sensed that someone was behind me, then quite inexplicably I felt a very strong, vigorous twitching behind my right ear, it was like a muscle jumping about. No one was touching me, it went on for perhaps five minutes, the demonstration was then soon over.

I was intrigued, most of the earlier talk had passed me by, so I decided to take a card of the lady who was setting up practice in Brighton. We had a brief chat, it was going to be expensive for me, and of course I'd given up my benefits and was living totally off my savings. The lady, Anita, made me a generous offer, due to my situation she would treat me for half price. A couple of days later I decided to give it a try and made a call to book an appointment.

M.E. - My Blessing in Disguise

I think I began seeing Anita fortnightly, after a couple of sessions, she asked me to try to stand in what she termed the Buqi position. Surprisingly this position didn't put any major strain on my body, but I did find that some of my symptoms were stirred up initially. Each session started with a chat with Anita about how I felt that things were going. I had begun to feel a lot of sensations in my head, tingles, itches and ripples, and one day it felt as if my brain had thrown itself at the top of my skull, this caused a flash of light.

I think it was during one of these talks that Anita suggested to me that I should start making notes about whatever was going on, or perhaps even keep a proper diary. I'm very grateful to Anita for her suggestion, else so much of what is in this book would have been forgotten. Anita was very interested in what was happening with me, I think a lot of this was new to her.

A few weeks in I had a strange feeling on top of my brain which made me feel as if I wanted to shiver. I then seemed to see inside my skull and I watched channels open in my brain, into which steam or smoke was somehow blown or sucked through, it all disappeared in a few seconds. I was left with the impression that my brain had been cleansed or fumigated.

It's difficult to say when Spirit began working with me, were these sensations in my brain to do with ME, a result of these Buqi sessions, or was it Spirit making their first moves, perhaps it was a combination as Buqi was opening me up.

Anita would sometimes adjust my body position, but once done there was no further physical contact, yet my body could feel as if it was rocking quite a bit, and my hands would sometimes bounce, with no one pulling my strings. Sometimes I would be sitting, and I had periods where I felt as if I was on a boat rocking. The sensations in my brain continued and I also began to feel pressure in my ears, once I felt as if a wave washed over me. Then I felt as if my body was being stretched and I was growing taller and my legs were lifted it seemed.

M.E. - My Blessing in Disguise

There were many pressures in my skull, the most common were in the front, just above the third eye, I could feel energy flowing in my face and some muscle moves in the body. My right knee cracked without any movement from me whatsoever, I also began getting tingles in different places, my feet, face and in the glands around my neck. I did feel pains in my wrists and thumbs for a while, but I think further energy flows around my body distracted me a bit from them. My spine also cracked of it's own accord, and I felt heat moving around my body.

These sensations kept happening whether I had to stand or sit in a session, rocking and swaying and the rest. I'd started carrying on these exercises at home after I'd mastered the position, the sensations were often present. It really is amazing that for most of the time Anita would be standing several feet away from me, just seemingly waving her arms about, yet triggering so many sensations in my body, some gentle, some quite intense.

At one session my stomach felt very tight, ripples began moving upwards, as if in a rotating drum, Anita seemed pleased, she thought that my 'Dan Tian' was rising. A couple of nights later just after getting into bed, I felt as if I was in an Earthquake. I was shaking all over for a while, I soon realised that it was only me and that there was nothing untoward happening.

These experiences continued, a few days later it felt as if a laser or some sort of gas was firing under pressure at the left side of my brain. The next day that side of my brain was very tingly, it seemed to me that the extremities of my brain had been reclaimed, with its circuits renewed and tested, it's the only way I can describe the sensations.

One day as I arrived for a session Anita said 'you've brought lots of friends with you today'. She then explained that she was seeing lots of little lights around me, all colours. At the time this meant nothing to me, but it sounded good. I had yet to experience the joys of seeing

M.E. - My Blessing in Disguise

Spirit lights, but it draws me to the conclusion that Anita is a medium and a healer, I can't say whether she knew it or not at the time.

The sensations I was getting continued at home, this prompted Anita to say that as well as practicing the exercises on my own, I should also spend some time sitting quietly. I had of course had to do a lot of this already since the ME began, but she put it in a different way. One day I felt energy flowing through me so strongly that it felt like I had water rushing through me, it made me feel weak for a couple of minutes.

I'd had a lot of soreness at the back of my head since almost the start of ME, one day I was shown a white ball being removed from the inside of the back of my head, it had been on a stalk. A few days later I had some strong energy flowing from the bridge of my nose, it felt wet, as if water was pouring out.

At our next session my right arm lifted of its own accord, this made Anita smile, she wasn't expecting this. It became a regular occurrence, and went on to happen with both arms. The night after our next session I was woken by a very strong trembling, which soon felt as if I was being physically shaken. The bed seemed to rock and roll around and an incredibly strong wind seemed to come out of my head, with my hair not surprisingly standing on end. I had to open my eyes to check that the ceiling was still in place. I think it lasted for about a minute, it just felt like a whirlwind was in the room, but it was almost instantly more enjoyable than frightening, thank goodness.

By now Anita had left the clinic where she'd rented a room and was working from home, so I got a train to Hove and walked from there. On my journey one morning, I felt something on my palm as I opened the carriage door, once seated I looked at my hand and it was all perfectly normal. A few minutes into our session Anita asked me what was wrong with my hand. I looked at it and saw an enormous bruise covering most of my palm, I was astounded and had no idea where that had come from. I told Anita what had happened on my journey with the train door, she thought it was some kind of hurt or sadness that the

M.E. - My Blessing in Disguise

treatments were helping to leave my body. The bruise grew fainter as the day went on, by the next morning it was gone, extraordinary.

With what I know now I would say that spirit were getting my attention in ways that I couldn't understand at the time. Perhaps they were wanting to reassure me that things were moving on, I was getting help. I continued my sitting at home, though no intention was set, but I guess spirit were taking advantage. My right arm began lifting up and I also started getting movement in my hand and fingers. I also am sure I felt my first touch from spirit, wow, and there seemed to be air flowing up through my throat. I'd had a feeling for a while of energy being stuck somehow in the centre of my forehead, around the third eye area, this blockage suddenly cleared. During a night in bed soon after, a yellow light passed through my head from left to right, I also seemed to lose feeling in my fingers and thumbs, it started at the tips and worked it's way down.

After my next treatment from Anita, I felt as light as a feather as I walked back to Hove station, I always felt good after a session, but this was on a whole new level. A few days later at home I was sitting reading on the sofa when I felt a light breeze, it was as if someone had walked swiftly past me. I was of course on my own with all the windows shut, and the curtains remained totally still.

A couple of mornings later I spent the morning trembling, I wasn't cold or anything. This recurred after a few days and was accompanied by a very strong airflow coming up through my throat, it kind of reminded me of a volcano. I say it was air simply because I have no idea of what else it could be. A week before Christmas I was having a treatment at Anita's, this day was the first time that I felt as if I was wearing a headband along my forehead, I then had pressure on my shoulders and spine, as if I was wearing a yoke, I've had these sensations many times since.

Over the next couple of days I felt strong energy flows in different parts of my body, I also felt tickles on my legs and it seemed as if my

M.E. - My Blessing in Disguise

socks had been rolled down to my ankles. Christmas was close now and I'd generally been feeling good with my energy levels pretty stable, so I was looking forward to the festivities. Then three days before it I got up feeling really rough with an ME head. All plans were pushed aside and I just sat resting on the sofa. Then a breeze brushed my face and it felt as if the inside of my head on the left was being dabbed, this eased some of the pressure there. Strangely I was also shown this happening, and it was followed by my seeing a tear in my brain, it was repaired as I watched. This was all very reassuring to me as I'd been thinking that I'd relapsed again.

On Christmas Eve I felt some cool touches, then something cool was wrapped around me, it seemed as if I was being gently hugged by two spirits, how lovely. I saw my family over Christmas, but kept it quiet and relaxing, thankfully that possible relapse did not materialise.

On and into the New Year I was feeling confident that I had ME on the run at last, there was obviously still some way to go, but I thought my energy level was probably at 65-70%, and was pretty stable, which was very encouraging. It is very difficult to quantify one's energy level unless it's at zero or 100%.
New sensations kept coming, I felt as if other hands were underneath mine, then I had a nasty taste in my mouth for no apparent reason. One day it seemed as if my forehead was being pulled about and squashed . Over the next few days I had many strong sensations and movements in my stomach, also lots of pains and energy flows. At the end of this period I received a very short, sharp pain on the back of my left hand, between my thumb and index finger, it was like an electric shock.

I've mentioned that I tried doing a little research about the brain's workings, the neurotransmitters and such, at some point I made a list of amino acids that I think occur in the brain. I was quite surprised to find most of them in H and B's, one was Phosphatidylserine, it was expensive, but fortunately it was in a half price sale, so I bought some. I was experimenting to see if by boosting the level of it in my body, that perhaps my brain and overall health would improve.

M.E. - My Blessing in Disguise

A week or so later I was laying down on the sofa, feeling energy flowing from my head to my feet. It appeared to be in every single cell of my body time, as if a complete diagnostic test was being run on me. It had begun in my brain where I was shown the whole neural network lit up in a beautiful blue, it was like an extraordinary mesh of electric blue wire. I felt as if something had been reconnected, and it felt really good. This encouraged me to try another amino acid from my list, I found L-Carnitine.

Just over a week later in early February, the glands in the left side of my neck began aching and vibrating for a while, vibrations also began in my left leg. In bed that night those glands in my neck ached and vibrated again, as this eased off I felt as if all of my cells were switched on for another diagnostic check. These happenings gave a positive feel for me and encouraged me to maintain the belief that I was getting better and better. As if to back this up, the next day I felt as if my body was bouncing when I sat quietly.

I have to say that if anyone chooses to take amino acids, I could not predict what reaction, if any, they would have, be it good or bad, it would be their own choice.

A couple of nights later I woke to find that I had wind in my face and hair again. Come the morning and my good feelings continued for a while, as I had very strong energy flows all over my body, but then whilst sitting I seemed to be thrown forwards. No harm, no pain, but what's that all about?

It may have been a warning for me that my bubble was about to burst, as the next time I saw Anita was to be the last. She said that from her perspective, she had done all she could, my channels were all clear. The disappointment hit me like a train, I had made a fair bit of progress with the help of this Buqi, but I knew that I hadn't finished off the ME yet. I was still being very careful not to overdo things mentally, crosswords, reading and the like, could easily tire me out. A sad goodbye to Anita,

M.E. - My Blessing in Disguise

but a lot of thanks for her, not just for my improved health, but also for the fact that Spirit were certainly intervening now, though I wasn't quite sure at the time.

I soon had a day which was full of prickly pains and I began feeling a little lost. I needed to find a way to help to keep me moving forwards so that I could finally banish this ME.

I bought some DHA tablets in the middle of March and had an almost immediate reaction as my cheeks felt red hot, but they showed no signs of flushing, the heat went on for about three hours. I then had a few minutes of tingling in the lower, central part of my brain, I seemed to be impressed with the idea that a lot of circuits had been reconnected, I slept like a baby that night. I should say that DHA is Docosahexaenoic Acid, it's a plant derived Omega 3 fatty acid I believe.

It was about time I had a reading, somehow I found a lovely lady who was a medium and also read palms, Maureen. I'd never had my palms read before, so I was looking forwards to meeting her in Hove. It was a positive reading, apparently from one palm the past is related, whilst the present and what might be to come is shown in the other. Afterwards we had a chat over a cuppa, I told Maureen that I needed to find a way forwards with ME. Maureen told me a little about Spiritual Healing and where I could go to receive it. The place was quite close by, in fact it was somewhere I knew already, The Cornerstone, where I'd had my introduction to Buqi, what a coincidence!

M.E. - My Blessing in Disguise

My Introduction to Spiritual Healing and More

Wednesday the 25th of April 2001 became a significant date for me, another stepping stone on my journey. I walked along to The Cornerstone not really knowing quite what to expect, but feeling positive about my first encounter with healing. I was met by a lovely smiling lady, Jenny, and we went and sat down for a longish chat which helped to make me feel comfortable.

I had to tell Jenny why I wanted to try healing and the background to my condition, Jenny told me how she worked, soon after her hands were on my shoulders as she tuned in to start the healing process. It wasn't long before I was seeing dark blue, not the normal dark blue, but a beautiful and comforting dark blue, that then seemed to wrap itself around me. As it did I felt as if I was being hugged, and a wonderful sensation came over me, to put it in a nutshell, I felt as if 'I'd come home' It's a feeling that I'll never forget in this lifetime, extraordinary. I think Jenny was pleased with my feedback afterwards, I felt fabulous as I walked back to the station, I was sure that I'd found the way forwards again. This group of healers were working on a donation basis for anyone who popped in, it was probably the best £5 I've spent in this life.

It was in the early hours of the morning after my first healing session that I woke, I was sweating profusely and my throat felt as if it was on fire, these symptoms lasted about 36 hours. I think it was related to the healing rather than a bug, the timing made my mind up on that. Whatever I'd decided to carry on having healing on a mostly fortnightly basis, how could I not, after that amazing feeling during the first session. Most of my sessions were with Jenny, more often than not I had feedback for her after, I also started telling her about the experiences that I was getting at home. As I've already stated, I am a

M.E. - My Blessing in Disguise

quiet chap, but Jenny was so easy to talk to, and as it turned out, she'd had some experiences herself.

One of the outcomes of our chats was that Jenny advised me to start reading some spiritual books, she recommended Betty Shine as a gentle opener. I soon found one and noticed that every time I was reading I was feeling sensations, such as my solar plexus would start turning, and the hairs on the back of my neck would stand on end. I had some nice correspondence with Betty Shine and I harboured hopes of meeting her, but it turned out that she was unwell, so it wasn't possible.

After I began reading that first book, I woke up in the night and saw a huge white oblong shape, a bit like a screen. Sensations kept coming as I sat at home, one day it felt as if something closed my eyes from inside my head, as if a blind had been pulled down, and I soon became very tired. In bed that night I started laughing and chuckling, I just felt so happy. Then there was a low buzzing in my left ear, it seemed to pass right through my head and went out of the right ear, more chuckling followed, I couldn't help myself. A couple of days later as I sat I saw white lights for the first time, there were four or five disc shapes that began moving and also grew in size, their centres became dark and then they all went off in different directions and disappeared.

I was getting so many different experiences now as Spirit seemed to be upping their game. A Sunflower appeared, then flower arrangements followed, but the colours weren't clear, then blue circles before I saw a white ball of light outside a window. They seemed to be working with me even when I wasn't sitting, but whatever, I was enjoying it all. At a healing session with Jenny in May, I felt my hip and thigh muscles moving, one of my legs was turned to the right, I also saw lots of white shapes and something seemed to waft through my brain.

I woke on the morning of the 25th of May and was shown a big bay window, across it's three sections were a row of numbers. I was a bit slow on the uptake here, but I think it was the first time I'd seen numbers, well certainly so many together. I suddenly realised that I was

M.E. - My Blessing in Disguise

probably looking at a phone number, with that thought the numbers vanished rapidly. The first number was '0', I think I picked out '464' in the middle window, but I was too slow to catch the rest, or perhaps I wasn't meant to. The significance of this would not become apparent for about a year, but in time this number would lead me further down my pathway, to awaken another ability.

Soon after this I began taking Glutamine, another amino acid, then Acetyl Cysteine, I felt more re-connections in my brain over the next week or two, I also had some spells of feeling happy. Lysine was another amino acid I took, these were only taken one at a time, not in combinations, and I finished one course before I moved onto a different one.

One morning in early June I was prevented from getting up, it was as if there were hands on my left hip and on my head, they were firm in a gentle way, so I had a lie in. I'd heard several phone rings in the night, most were certainly not my phone, then I was shown some images, now clear and with clear colours too. In mid June I was stopped from getting up again, this time it was as if a hand was resting on my brain. Shortly after I seemed to have a spiders web on my face, this feeling recurred for several days.

Things kept moving on as I was shown a wonderful iridescent light show, so difficult to do justice to it in words. Soon after I was feeling hungover and leaden, no booze had been taken, it was a real throwback, but fortunately it went. Two days later I was shown a face for the first time, quite a thrill even though I had no idea who it was. New experiences were coming thick and fast as I had a taste of fish from out of nowhere. I went out for a walk buoyed by these happenings, I may well have been walking a bit quicker than what had become my norm, suddenly I felt a hand pressing down on my head, the pressure was only eased when I slowed the pace of my walk, so it seemed that spirit were stopping me from overdoing it. My hair did seem to stand on end for a while, well that's how it felt. This was also the third day in a row that I'd had periods of tiredness and was feeling a little drained, it was the

M.E. - My Blessing in Disguise

21st of June, a day with a solar eclipse, perhaps my energy changes were linked to the eclipse.
It's a good feeling knowing that spirit are around and being helpful, I was soon to get another example of this. It was a hot, early summers day, there's a novelty, I was about to pick up a pan of boiling water when my hand became full of sharp prickles. I soon realised that I had nothing on my feet, not the best way to carry that pan of boiling water, so I covered my feet and the prickles stopped.

I began seeing more faces, a scene or two with people talking, some talking to me, but I couldn't hear what was said, I was also seeing more of those beautiful light shows, new sensations and happenings were becoming commonplace now. I felt strong pressure at the sides of my brain, as if bubbles were being blown upwards, a little later it seemed as if it was raining in my brain and it then went down the back of my neck, well I can be a bit of a drip sometimes.

The next morning in bed I was singing a couple of my own songs to myself, suddenly I had very strong energy flows all over me and my hair stood on end all over my body, it was an incredible feeling and I was also shown some musicians, who were all in white. That day I kept getting smells that reminded me of my childhood. A little later I heard my Dad say 'Hello Brian', that was delightful and so unexpected as Dad didn't believe in any afterlife, he'd been in Spirit less than six months, so he'd soon sorted that one out.

I have had some unpleasant sensations, here's one, I could feel something under the skin of my left cheek, it went upwards to the right side of my left eye and pushed under the eyeball, I fought to keep my eyes shut. There was no pain at all, but I don't enjoy having things done to my eyes, this process was repeated the next day. The enjoyment soon returned as strong energy began circulating around the back of my neck and shoulders, it kept swirling and it felt as if I was being given a lovely massage. Later that day there appeared to be fingers fiddling about in the sides of my brain. Soon after that I was impressed with the thought that my head had been sorted out, I'm sure

M.E. - My Blessing in Disguise

it's needed that for years. This was followed up by what I think were some hieroglyphics and a lot of white images.

However, spirit continued working inside my head, as I felt more re-connections inside my brain, then something seemed to be pushed between my skull and brain to separate them, this caused incredibly strong surges and ripples in my brain, which rushed down my arms and made my thumbs twitch.

One day I was sitting down with my hands resting on my legs, suddenly I felt this amazing energy which seemed to join my hands together, as if a bridge had been built between them. For a while I was getting spirit visitors walking around my flat making the floorboards creak, also my leather, swivel chair made noises as if someone had either sat in it or got up out of it. I got into bed one night and was shown a brilliant, white aurora, around it were even brighter white lights. I woke later in the night and it was there again.

Before July was out, spirit brought more discomfort to my eyes, with what seemed like a rod being pushed under my left eye. One day it felt as if a thread was pulled behind the left eye. I was also getting things pushed up my nose at this time, with a feeling of anaesthesia in my sinuses, this became a regular happening for sometime.

I was back at The Cornerstone for more healing in early August, Jenny was away so I received healing from Paul. My legs became so relaxed that they felt jellylike, after I got home, my whole body became very relaxed, almost weak and shivery. It's not uncommon for people to feel tired after receiving healing, I think this is spirit trying to help us make the most of what we've received, we're more likely to be co-operative when we relax.

My next healing was through Lucy, during this session I seemed to feel a cat walk up my right arm, across my shoulders, then down my left arm. I also felt as if I was being rocked for a while. Lucy told me that she felt some prickles come out of my left shoulder. The following day

M.E. - My Blessing in Disguise

my legs felt heavy and I had that feeling of going down in a lift, which ended with a bump at the bottom. I then had a strong buzzing around my head, which felt as if it was being held in place by a forcefield of some sort. Very strong energy flows all over my body followed, it felt as if the energy was the strongest I'd experienced up to that point. Later it seemed as if I had energy coming out of my ears, then with my eyes open, I saw a light show of incredible purples which rushed towards me and entered my head. A few days later I was shown a beautiful, brilliant, green light show, how lucky can you be.

I'll just reiterate about the strength of energies and sensations I feel, if there is any length of time between occurrences, then judging the strength really is impossible, as there is no way to quantify it.

Bobby H popped into my head one day, he was a boss of mine from back in the sixties, a really good guy, I remember he'd been a useful footballer in his day, it maybe that he's returned to spirit. I felt a lot of prickly sensations when I thought about him, it's strange how thinking of someone in spirit brings in different sensations.

Spirit seemed to back off a little in the second half of August, perhaps they needed a break, but one day I had a surge of energy that pushed up from my solar plexus into my chest, it made me have a good cough.

At the end of August our old cat Porky was around, I heard him walking down the hall, he'd passed over a few months before. He'd become overweight because of my bad short-term memory, I just kept putting food down for him. His weight ballooned and one result was that those claws that hang down at the back of cats legs would catch in the hall carpet when he walked down it. Now I was hearing that sound again, as his spirit walked down the hall in my flat, wonderful. He's been a regular visitor to me over the years I'm pleased to say.

Around this time I began to realise that I was getting fewer pains on a daily basis, though periods of prickles had become more common. One night in bed I had beautiful, white light pouring down on me, though I

M.E. - My Blessing in Disguise

couldn't see the source it made me feel peaceful and happy. A couple of night later in bed I was shown a lot of wonderful, geometric shapes that rippled and changed as they floated around, they looked so intricate.

The next day I was sitting on the sofa and I had another helping hand from spirit, my head suddenly became very tingly and somehow it made me get up, just as well as I had forgotten about the potatoes that were cooking on the hob, phew! Over the next couple of days I had what I can only describe as feelings of love being around me, I've no idea who was responsible, but it was so beautiful, I wish everyone could experience it.

I was reading Micheal Bentine's book 'The Door Marked Summer' when my right thumb began twitching for a while, it may have been Morse Code, sadly I've never learned it. I bought another book called 'Visions of Another World', I felt I had to as my brain had gone crazy after I picked it up, then I had prickles in my fingers as I carried it home.

One new experience was when I was shown a scene in which something happened that made a noise, at that exact moment I heard the expected noise outside. As I sat on the last day of August, I lost all feeling in my arms and hands from the elbows down, it gave me the impression that my hands were floating.

Into September and I was shown lots of letters, but for some reason I couldn't focus on them. In one sitting my chair felt as if it moved through 45 degrees and my hands curled up, I also couldn't feel my thumbs. I was seeing bubbles of colour, these have become quite common over time, and are none the less still beautiful to see. The following day lots of indescribably beautiful colours were washing over me as I sat, it felt so peaceful and comfortable just sitting there amongst it.
As I was walking along to The Cornerstone for my next healing session hopefully with Jenny, my enthusiasm waned and was replaced by a

M.E. - My Blessing in Disguise

feeling of anti-climax. I was hoping for a good chat as Jenny should be back from her holiday, but she wasn't there, still the healing was good. Whilst I was sitting outside awaiting my turn I was suddenly seeing everything in negative form, as in photography I mean.

Sitting on the sofa one day my head was gently eased backwards until it was resting on the cushion, it was only subtle pressure, then my shoulders were forcibly pushed down as far as they could go. Once they'd stopped going down I found that I was in a very relaxed position. Two days later I was treated to a wall full of complicated, geometric patterns which were illuminated by a moving, golden spotlight, there was also a man's head in the golden light. I then saw a map of England and Wales, it had pulsing, sky blue ice all over it and a large fish appeared off the Cornish coast. I think I saw the north island of New Zealand as well.

Later in the day I was out walking, then for a few steps someone took my full weight, by that I mean that my feet were still on the ground, but my legs felt free, wow! I was having trouble with my knees at this time, when the pains came I was hobbling around like a cripple. Then whilst walking in Brighton I got a lovely surprise, as I had a wonderful feeling of freedom , a total lack of restriction as I walked. It was a strange but very encouraging experience, although it didn't last.

The following day at home the words 'New Phase' came into my head, then for a few minutes my body went stiff and my jaw tightened. Later I had another treat as I saw a phosphorescent light show was shown to me, another wow! I felt so lucky and privileged to see it. The next day spirit turned a screen on, amongst the scenes shown were some beautiful images of space, something I can't get enough of. Porky was also with me as I felt his weight on my chest and stomach, and his paws on my shoulders, beautiful.

I sat in the morning before I went to my next healing session, there was a lot of high-pitched buzzing and energy around my head. Later I felt as if I was knocked on the head by something hollow, the object seemed

M.E. - My Blessing in Disguise

to explode and sent shock waves through my brain. I received healing from Jenny and a new girl, Debbie. I felt tremendous energy and I also seemed to get a relaxing massage. At some point in the session I had a golden arch over my eyes. In bed that night I saw lots of letters again, they seemed to form a message, but as before my eyes couldn't focus on them to read whatever was there.

Most days were full of experiences that September, one day I felt as if some force or energy came inside me, it went down my arms and legs and into my head. It made things feel tight between my bones and skin, it wasn't threatening or uncomfortable, it had me wondering if spirit had entered me.

I think it was Jenny who told me about the Spiritual Churches in Brighton, places to go where you could see public demonstrations of clairvoyance by mediums, up to this point I'd only had private readings. Jenny had told me that a couple of them were not easy to find, so I went into Brighton on a scouting mission to find the Brotherhood Gate Spiritual Church. Having found it I resolved to venture inside when a demonstration was taking place. My curiosity was aroused and on the afternoon of September 20th I went to see my first public demonstration not knowing what to expect, I went in rather nervously..

The medium on the platform was well known locally, and I can now describe her style as a no-nonsense, old-fashioned medium, that is complimentary. She began working her way along the front row, almost sequentially, if someone was missed out then she would go back to give them a message. Most of the messages were on the short side, but then one chap got a long message, and it seemed to be a bit on the personal side, I didn't like the idea of receiving a message like that so I resolved to leave.

I didn't want to seem rude so I decided to wait until this message was finished, then I would get up and go. I should say that I sat near the back, and there were three or four people between me and the chap getting the personal message, so I thought it was a good time to leave.

M.E. - My Blessing in Disguise

No sooner had I had that thought than the medium interrupted her message and pointed at me saying, "I'm coming to you next". Spirit had obviously rumbled me, picked up my thoughts and were having none of it, I was stuck. I wonder if I'd tried to get up and leave whether spirit would have stopped me, I suspect yes they would. I sat there in trepidation as I waited for my message to begin.

There followed a link with my dad, it was soon obvious as she told a story that he'd told me a few months before he passed, no one else knew about it. My recent situation with health and not working were mentioned, then a surprise, she said that I'd be starting work soon and was given the date of November 4th. It didn't make sense to me, my health was certainly improving, but going back to work was not on my agenda at that point. One other puzzle in the message was about a milk float, I couldn't relate to it, we'd had milk delivered of course, but other than that no connection, but mostly excellent evidence given.

I stayed and had a cuppa and had a chat with Betty, the medium, I said that there was no way that I could see myself back at work on the date given, she said that she wasn't given dates very often, they were always right when they came. The milk float puzzle would be resolved a few months ahead, after I joined a circle.

I was pondering on the message on my way back home, for some reason November 4th was ringing a bell, but I couldn't place why. On arriving home I checked the calender, November 2nd had Tenerife written on it, I was off for a week in the sun with an old friend, Mike, whose sister had timeshares there. Mike had generously asked me to go along on his trip, so how could I be starting work during that week, spirit must have got this one wrong.

There was no let up in the pace of happenings, I had high-pitched whistling and lots of buzzing in my ears, along with what I can only describe as someone fiddling about in my ears as well. I was shown some incredibly beautiful, kaleidoscope patterns, I hadn't seen those

M.E. - My Blessing in Disguise

since my kids were small, they're wonderful, I didn't want them to stop.

In bed I was shown a white staircase going upwards, at the bottom of it was a lit, white candle. I felt so humble, as if I was in the presence of some wonderful entity. At the same time I was feeling incredibly strong energy flowing throughout my entire body, all this together gave me a magical feeling. Many times I ask why me? What have I done to deserve this?

In the next few days I was shown a variety of beautiful patterns, composed of all sorts of things, such as Peacock's feathers, simple and intricate geometric designs, and the most amazing colours mingling together. My body became heavy and my head seemed to fill with light, and twice I had a white light just below my right eyelid.

At the end of September I had an interesting night. It began with what seemed like a short dream, in which I was somewhere where a telephone was ringing. I eventually found the phone and answered it, a voice said to me 'We think you're ready for the next stage of---', then there was a lot of noise around my head and I put the telephone down.

I now felt awake and I could feel a lot of energy at my back and whistling around my head. The energy seemed to hold my arms and virtually encompassed my whole body, but not my face. My body started rocking and bouncing around, I ended up on my back. Suddenly I was off the bed and was being whisked across the room to the chest of drawers, we passed that and went up to the ceiling, along it and down across the bed to the floor on the other side. Then we went back up to the bed and soon I was back to normal, it was over. I imagine that this was a kind of out-of-body experience, my first, it probably only lasted a few seconds, but wow! Most of the energy went very quickly, some stayed around my back and head for a while, my amazement stayed for a long time.

M.E. - My Blessing in Disguise

I was now seeing spirits out of the corners of my eyes, they'd disappear before I could look directly at them, it was the same with white shapes, which began appearing outside my windows. At night a smoke alarm kept going off, I could find no reason for it. I began to wonder how many more things could happen. Well I kept getting hot when I sat at my keyboard for a start, and my face sometimes felt distorted by fingers pressing into it, not mine of course. My midriff would feel as if it was sinking down, yet there was no pressure on it as such, but I felt sensations inside of me as it definitely sunk lower, how could this be?

One result of my visit to Brotherhood Gate was that I saw a poster for a healer named Michael Chapman, he travelled around giving healing through his guide Dr Lang. The strange thing is that his father George Chapman, who was also a healer, had his own guide called Dr Lang, this Dr Lang being the father of the other Dr Lang. So two fathers working together healing, then the two sons as well, what connections!

I made an appointment to see Michael Chapman for healing for my lower back, which had become troublesome. Just as he was about to start healing Michael said to me 'You should be doing this'. I had no idea why he said this, now I wished I'd asked him. At home a couple of days later I asked for absent healing for myself. I soon felt sensations at the sides of my head where Michael's hands had been. I then fell asleep for about half an hour, when I awoke the sensations were still there. My eyes were still closed as I saw a beautiful, naked lady, she was dancing on her own, she came over and gave me a hug, now that's worth a wow!

The next day someone kept coming into my vision on the extreme right, it was happening every few seconds for a while. I was also getting colours, mostly gold, that seemed to come out of my eyes, how do spirit come up with these things?

I was reading a Doris Collins book, every time I did I began hearing noises, knocking, phones ringing, chains rattling and others. Sitting one day my chair rocked noisily, then the chair was still but I was kept

M.E. - My Blessing in Disguise

rocking. I felt strong anaesthesia in my left cheek, then burning prickles in my left eyeball, I wasn't comfortable with that and said so, later there were cold prickles there. I know I'll have a lot of questions to ask when It's my time to return to spirit, I'm intrigued by many of these happenings, and what their purposes are.

Later I saw a smiling lady, she gave me a cuddle and asked me if it was OK, then someone was hugging me around my neck, as my chair gently rocked from side to side. The next day as I sat with my eyes closed, I felt a terrific wind around me, I opened my eyes and it became a gentle breeze. In bed that night I heard 'Hi Brian', later the doorbell was given two loud rings, it was as if the doorbell was in the bedroom rather than down the hall.

Another night I was shown some geometric patterns, mixed in with them were some white hands, this made these scenes all the more beautiful. I've noticed recently that when spirit are showing me things, some things try to push through what I'm seeing, it's as if there are more layers underneath.

In October 2001 I decided to belatedly go and see Harry Edwards Sanctuary, I felt well enough to drive there and see if I could get some healing. I never saw another soul there, so I just wandered around the lovely garden, I did get into a large room which was partitioned by some glass doors. Whilst there I felt a couple of small clicks near the base of my spine, where I'd been having some niggly pains, so perhaps my journey wasn't wasted after all. I should have realised that I would need an appointment.

Sitting at home the next day, I could hear ticking inside me, who wants to lock me up, ha-ha. It seemed to be coming from between my nostrils and lower throat area. In bed that night I had a nice rhythm playing in my right ear. The next day, before I went to the Cornerstone for healing, I saw an eye, it had two white lights in it. It has occurred to me that when I see things clairvoyantly I see clearly with both eyes, with normal vision my right eye is much weaker, it's very longsighted. As I

M.E. - My Blessing in Disguise

sat and waited for healing with Jenny and Debbie, a lot of strong energy seemed to flow out of my fingertips. Perhaps spirit were trying me out for sending healing, if they were I didn't know it at the time.

I'd seen some words recently, 'but Mcfadden', it meant nothing to me. In a scene I was shown there was a black lady, she was dressed in light blue, she said to me that I had come to see her at Hawarden, again this meant nothing, perhaps it was from another incarnation.

The end of October was fast approaching, bringing my sunshine trip to Tenerife ever closer. A few days before it was due, I felt incredibly strong energy racing through my body. It was sensational down my back and was in my hair and rippling under both eyes, as it ended in one area, it began in another, a truly astonishing and joyful experience. A little later my body felt heavy all over, something seemed to be pressing me down.

M.E. - My Blessing in Disguise

A Proper Awakening

Into November and an early start to get to Gatwick Airport for the Tenerife flight with Mike, so no sign of me starting work I thought, how could spirit get that so wrong. After the eats and drinks on the plane, I closed my eyes hoping for some sleep after the early start. It didn't happen, instead I found myself looking at a, huge, vivid, orange screen. I opened my eyes a few times, it was still there every time I closed my eyes. I tried to remember what it was normally like when I closed my eyes in the sunshine, it wasn't as bright as this for sure. I put it down to the fact that I was flying at nearly 40,000ft.

The next morning found me relaxing on the apartment balcony, I was treated to a range of extraordinary, brilliant colours that were so beautiful, there were also some faces who were wearing dark glasses. Every time I closed my eyes the colours were there, mingling and pulsing, they just kept changing. It was amazing just watching this, I had that feeling of being so lucky and privileged again.

Mike and I went out for a walk to have some breakfast, it was a ten minute plus walk down to the coast where there was a long line of eating places to choose from. As we were walking through the streets, I was suddenly surrounded by lots of little lights, they reminded me of little candle flames. It was an absolutely beautiful sight as they seemed to dance around, moving along with me. It soon became obvious to me that Mike wasn't seeing them, come to that, nor was anyone else. I was walking along with a beaming smile, why not, I had lots of wonderful, little companions with me, how could I not enjoy it. This was a brand new and incredible experience, one I'll never forget. It did happen three or four times during the week.

Every time I closed my eyes that day those vibrant colours were there, I then began to recognise some of those faces wearing dark glasses, John Lennon and Jim Morrison were amongst them. Later I heard a man's voice say 'Brian'.

M.E. - My Blessing in Disguise

The next day I was woken about 7am by the loud knocking of a metal door knocker in my right ear, which was on the pillow. A little later I was shown lots of clouds, something came out of the clouds and headed towards me. In big, bold, whitish letters was the word 'PAYOFF', it was November 4th, the date given to me at Betty Horne's demonstration.

As I went out onto the terrace lots of beautiful Spirit lights came with me. On closing my eyes, I immediately feasted on 'out of this world' colours. In amongst these colours was a dark centred eye, a fiery orange ring was around it, it was spectacular. I put my hands onto my eyelids and all the colours changed, wow! Some faces now appeared and I recognised Elvis, this was some start to the day. The colours became predominantly green and I felt as if I was walking through trees and shrubs. I soon saw a scene in which someone was on skis waving to me.

In the early evening I was sitting on the sofa in the apartment when something made me look up. Above me I saw a wooden cased clock on the wall, it had a pendulum moving to fro underneath, I couldn't recall seeing it before. I looked back down for a few seconds, when I looked back up again the clock had gone, how could that be? Later I had more colours, some in kaleidoscope type patterns, the beauty just kept coming. Then there was a strange sensation at the left side of my head, which seemed to jump to my left arm.

The next day brought me pastel colours, no less beautiful than the brighter ones, and they were back later, Roy Orbison and Jackie Kennedy also showed themselves. Out and about I had lots of little candle flames for company, my luck was holding. The following morning I was woken by the sound of radio pips in my head. On closing my eyes I saw the colours again, then some scenes appeared which seemed to be behind a curtain, it's difficult to describe exactly. I saw a beautiful, blue wall, it became a rich, deep purple, then the

65

M.E. - My Blessing in Disguise

mortar between the bricks turned red, fantastic! I then saw Buddy Holly very clearly, and Johnny Kidd too.

I was being shown many more faces, one lady became a caricature, there were also many eyes, most of which became animal eyes, then a curtain opened and the scenes I saw were much clearer. Later I had ripples running along the top of my vision every few seconds, also I had some touches on my palms. More eyes followed, faces too which didn't look earthly.

Wednesday morning brought in strong energy flows all over me whilst I was in bed. I saw Johnny Kidd again, then a tv screen was turned on in my head, it was so clear. On the screen appeared some white buildings and a view down over a village, somewhere amongst it were lilac coloured tiles. It became more surreal as the view changed, I seemed to recognise it but couldn't place it. The penny dropped and I realised that I was seeing the area in which we were staying, but I was seeing it from 30-40 ft up. When that realisation dawned I found myself back in bed with a start. It seemed as if I'd just had another out-of-body experience.

I had a lot of twitches in my right hand that day, they had started not long after I woke up. Relaxing after lunch I was seeing more scenes and colours, I heard my name called again, and felt some touches. Later it felt as if my left arm was being held just above the elbow, then my ankles were held. We had a meal/cabaret booked for the evening in the complex, it was to be held by the pool. Perhaps an hour and a half before the meal was scheduled, the heavens opened, quite a downpour ensued. The staff and a couple of guests moved a lot of stuff inside to a large, downstairs bar area.

Mike and I were amongst the last to arrive, we found a table with two spare places. The couple on our table were the guests who'd helped the staff earlier, friendly folk, and the staff made sure that our table was looked after throughout the evening. I got through most of a bottle of red wine and was hoping to get another glass to see me through, a new

M.E. - My Blessing in Disguise

bottle appeared. Yes I had more than one more glass, well I was really enjoying watching the Flamenco dancers, I'd never seen Flamenco live before.

Not surprisingly, I felt the worse for wear the next morning, it didn't stop spirit at all. At one point I was in the bathroom expecting to throw up, suddenly lots of very bright, candle flame lights were all around me, some very close to my head. I didn't know if spirit were laughing at me or comforting me, but these lights came so close it just made me feel wonderful amidst the hangover. It wasn't an instant cure though, perhaps spirit were showing me how non-judgemental they are. It was our last full day and we had planned to go for a decent walk, I settled myself down on the terrace instead. In no time it seemed as if my half-opened eyes were playing tricks, vague shapes began appearing on the tiles around me.

A little later I'd had enough sun and went back inside to sit on the sofa. I was looking at the blank wall in front of me when what looked like an 'O' appeared, it began alternating between being large and small . This strange happening was soon explained, as the 'O' turned sideways to reveal itself as a pouting fish, I had to chuckle. Soon after an enormous screen appeared on the wall in front of me, I began seeing scenes and faces, the faces being like a set of cards which I remember getting with packets of bubblegum when I was a kid. The picture switched to an outdoor cafe with lots of seats and a distant buzz of conversation. Soon in walked John Lennon, he sat at a table and was joined by his old buddy Harry Nillson, they began talking, but I couldn't hear what was being said. Lots more musicians turned up, Phil Lynott, Jimi Hendrix and Elvis amongst them, some were shown in close-up, so the faces were huge, as if on a cinema screen. I felt a little bit stunned with all this, but excited too, I also saw some writing and what I think were some autographs.

On the plane home I experienced lots of sensations in my brain and around the third eye area, there was also someone rubbing my left ankle. What a sensational week it had been, wow!

M.E. - My Blessing in Disguise

The day after I got back I was sitting again, I was shown a room with countless numbers of white candles, many lit, then into another room which was full of bottles and glasses, and no Tommy Cooper in sight. Later I either fell asleep or was taken off by spirit, I heard a voice telling me to 'wake up', it did the trick.

My next healing session was with Paul, I felt as if my chair was floating, and although my feet felt light, they were always on the floor. Sensations kept coming, I felt as if I was running upstairs, and as if my legs were lifting up. It also felt as if my hands were being held, my arms became heavy, but the overall feeling was gorgeous. Whilst walking one day my feet felt as if they were slipping sideways, I looked down to check, of course I was walking normally.

Sitting back home, I felt a strong surge from the middle of my brain which pushed out to the sides, it was as if someone had pushed through my brain with their fingers, it's the only description I can come up with. At the next days sitting things felt beautiful, my hands were held for a while, such a special feeling.

Before I went to the next healing session, I had the feeling that someone was gently pushing down on my chair, it seemed as if they wanted to spin it. Someone had a sense of fun as I was literally pulled down onto the sofa soon after. That day's healing was with Jenny, for most of the time I felt as if I was on a gently rocking boat. This was the first time I'd seen Jenny since my trip to Tenerife, so I had a lot to tell her. Jenny told me that I should try to find a development circle to sit in, she thought that spirit had given me a 'proper awakening'. She said that most Spiritual churches ran them, or would know of someone who did. I'd only ever been to the one, I wasn't sure that I was ready for another visit just yet.
At the end of November spirit treated me to a cartoon movie, it was shown to me on the lounge wall. Later I had strong energy flowing through my hands, so probably sending healing again. They followed this up with more healing the next day.

M.E. - My Blessing in Disguise

I'd better say here that I don't close down at all, therefore I'm available for spirit 24 - 7 as they say. I think I did the first few times I sat, but that practice soon stopped. Equally, I tried meditation when this first began, but spirit were soon coming in and working, so for me it's always sit to join with spirit, I have no need for meditation. I know many enjoy it, but it's not for me. I do not recommend that others sit alone or don't close down, you have to build trust with your guides, many are far too nervous for this, perhaps quite rightly, I'm not criticising. I had no real understanding of these things back in 2001, it's just the way that things developed, or perhaps that should read were meant to develop with me.

We're now into early December, the year has gone quickly, probably because the pace of my life is picking up as I am slowly doing more things, and therefore I have a much more positive feel about things. I had an interesting couple of nights, with the first one the ceiling took on an orange hue, then a creaking door opened in a corner of the bedroom, it wasn't the bedroom door. I felt strength in my thighs and strong pulsing energy working up through my leg muscles. It was refreshing somehow and continued for an hour or more. I did feel some pains in my left knee and shin, I sent my thoughts to spirit and the pains were gone immediately.

The next night I saw a lot of coloured lights, my eyes were open, I heard a voice say 'here comes happiness', then I heard a door clunk shut.

A couple of days later I was treated to some synchronicity whilst I was sitting, I was shown a gold ring on a table, it changed into a letter or symbol.. After the sitting I turned on the radio, the first song I heard was 'Band of Gold' by Freda Payne, I do enjoy things like that. Not so enjoyable was a sharp pain in my forehead, it was as if someone had drilled in there, when it stopped I had lots of happenings in my brain. I was shown some maps, a finger was pointing to a place, but I couldn't remember where.

M.E. - My Blessing in Disguise

Fluffy, our old family cat had passed earlier in the year, she was Porky's mum, she showed herself to me one day and gave me a miaow, lovely. That night in bed I saw a flash and heard a thunderclap, this was followed by what sounded like lots of heavy things falling. I could find no trace of any disturbances in the morning, inside or out.

Moving on, I felt a needle go into the back of my neck, it was soon pulled out. On another day I felt a pain in my right foot, I asked spirit for help, the pain seemed to roll itself up from the toe end and go into my ankle and just disappear. The pain was very intense as it rolled itself up.

Doing some Christmas shopping I felt a push in my back, there was no one behind me, someone must have wanted me to get on with it. In the run up to Christmas I decided to have a reading, it had been a while and I still hadn't found a circle. I went to see a medium called Annie, I didn't have to far to go as the appointment was in Shoreham. Annie quickly picked up about healing, but she was getting it from the angle that I was a healer, I put her right on that one, well I thought I had, but of course it was the second time that I'd been given that message. Annie picked up on lots that was going on around me, and we ended up with the healing message being reiterated.

We had a cuppa and a chat afterwards, Annie told me that she sat in a circle at The Healing Light in Shoreham, she said that she would talk to Celia, her circle leader, to see if it was possible for me to join, she gave me Celia's number. It was a week or more before I plucked up the courage to call Celia, I was told that I could come along in January.

On Christmas Eve in bed I had lots of energy around me, it brought back memories of my trip to Tenerife. Just before the years end I was getting lots of firm touches, this seemed to make me raise my hands, as my hands got near to my head there were loud cracks from the backs of my hands.

M.E. - My Blessing in Disguise

There's no doubt that things had moved on this year, I felt a lot better overall and all this spirit activity was very interesting and had me wondering where it was all going to lead.

M.E. - My Blessing in Disguise

I Join a Circle and Normality Returns

I was still receiving healing at the beginning of 2002, but a few weeks into the year Jenny said to me that I should stop going as so little healing was coming through. At that point I didn't think I was 100%, as that was my aim I went back a couple of weeks later. Apparently the healing energy stopped almost as soon as it started, Jenny said that nothing was happening. I thanked Jenny and said goodbye with very mixed feelings, I was so much better, no doubt about it, but I guess I wanted perfection. A little later I was reminded of something that Annie had said at my reading, basically the body takes time to readjust to feeling normal after having a long systemic illness, it appears that this was now the position that I was in.

This scenario was proven out as the year went on, I increased my activities by walking further and quicker, gardening and digging, and I also took in a skiing trip with my old friends. It was a case of building up my confidence in my own body, proving to myself that my ME was really behind me.

It's fair to say that before the year was out I knew that I had put that dreadful condition well and truly behind me and normality had returned.

Early in January I took up the invitation to audition for Celia Stuart's circle at the Healing Light in Shoreham, I put it that way as it was a trial period to see if it suited me, and also to ensure that I could fit in. There were a dozen or so circle members, most were developing clairvoyance, one or two were working at psychometry. Celia and Beverley had also both developed trance mediumship, I knew nothing about any of this at this time. The circle also had a working medium in it, Annie, with whom I'd had my reading. There were three or four men, the rest were ladies.

M.E. - My Blessing in Disguise

This was an opportunity for me to find out if all of these spiritual happenings could be used in some way, and also a chance to discuss things with others, over time it became obvious that my development was different to most of the circle. I had no idea of the time it can take to develop spiritual abilities, it does vary from person to person and time frames are not normally given to us by our guides.

To begin with, being part of a circle brought me a lot of frustration, as all the sitting I was doing at home meant that mostly there was lots going on for me. However, in circle it was mostly quiet for me, often very quiet, whilst others would be making links and bringing through messages. I know now reasons why it was as it was, that will come later, as it was revealed to me in a reading, but I didn't know that spirit had to harmonise energies and adjust to my sitting in a different situation.

I found it difficult, and at the end of my trial period Celia said that I was welcome to continue in circle, but she wasn't sure that I was happy. It wasn't so much that I was unhappy, it was the frustration of nothing going on for me. I did enjoy being able to talk to others about my experiences, and hearing theirs of course, the spiritual side is not something that you can just drop into an ordinary, everyday conversation, even with some close friends.

I did begin to feel energies around me, which I think helped me to decide that I should try and remain patient and carry on sitting in this circle a bit longer. In all honesty I didn't feel as if I had any alternative, I'd heard that most spiritual churches ran circles, but I'd only ever been to one once, so I didn't really know if I'd be able to join one.

Patience is something that all sitters need, I remember that we had some good evening sittings and it gave everyone a lift, only for it to be followed by a quiet evening, after which everyone would leave feeling disappointed. That's how it can be when you seek to develop, it's out of our hands, all you can do is make yourself available and let spirit know your intention.

M.E. - My Blessing in Disguise

I used to talk to my guides about how different it was between sitting at home and in circle, and I did mention that I couldn't see the point of me going to circle as I seemed to always be the one who had nothing to contribute. We did begin sitting in red light some of the time, this would eventually lead us on to sitting in complete darkness in time. Soon after my moan to spirit I did start seeing colours and a few images in circle, they didn't mean anything to anyone, but overall it made me feel happier and more settled.

In early March I was off for a weeks skiing with friends in Baqueira, Spain, my first trip for a few years. We had lots of sunshine and mostly empty slopes to ski on, this resort gets very crowded at the weekends when all the locals turn up, and boy do they go crazy. During the week it's just beautiful and generally peaceful with no queues, just those lovely empty slopes.

In bed the first night I seemed to be shown a warning that my body was going to take a hefty knock, I saw 'Sunday, Monday, Tuesday' and then this shock happened which wiped out Wednesday. Whilst skiing the next day, I thankfully had a lot of white lights for company, there were also lots of colours and bubbles about.

After skiing was over for the day we had a couple of drinks and decided to have a wander around the resort. In common with other newish resorts, many of the apartment blocks have shops and restaurants underneath them. We went into one such area beneath a block, I was slowly walking down some stairs when my legs seemed to be pushed or kicked out from under me. My feet came up to about head height and I appeared to go down in slow motion yet still hit the stairs hard. My back was painful as I gingerly stood up, apart from my back I had scratches on my arms too. The shock that I had been warned about had happened, and not in a way I was expecting, I was really shaken up for a while. It didn't make sense, if my feet had slipped or I'd stumbled I'd have just gone down the stairs in a heap, no way would my feet have shot up to head height. Perhaps the weirdest thing of all was that

M.E. - My Blessing in Disguise

there was no one near me at that time, the only conclusion I could draw was that spirit were responsible, why? I haven't a clue.

I didn't expect to be able to ski the next day, due to the pain in my back, but come the morning I felt fine, the pain was mostly gone. More white lights were with me as I skied, and when I closed my eyes on a lift I saw lots of images, including a wall or wooden panel with lots of writing on it. I received more images overnight and also heard a man's voice say 'Hello Brian'.

On Wednesday I was shown some beautiful colours with some extraordinary patterns in them, and lots of faces on a small screen. In bed that night, amongst the images I was shown was the word 'Friday', it had 'OFF' underneath it. On Thursday I had a brief lay down before skiing, I saw a newspaper headline about a riot at a political summit, I think the town's name was Stap or Skap, or something similar. I was still enjoying the skiing and felt no reaction to my 'fall' on the stairs.

We were late going out on Friday morning as the weather had closed right in, unfortunately this meant that our 'Piste Party' was called off. The Chalet staff were going to meet up with us at lunchtime, bringing with them food and drink, so that we could all sit around in the snow having lunch. We had done it before and it was great fun. What this did mean however, was that what spirit showed me on Wednesday night, was now proven to be correct, our party was off.

Somehow during Friday's skiing I got ahead of the rest, instead of waiting at the lift for them to catch up, I got on and headed back up the mountain to wait for them there. I soon went through some low cloud, as I came out of it I couldn't fail to notice a huge, glowing, white shape above the chair in front of me. It seemed to be a figure in a white robe and was traveling up at the same speed as me. I began to feel in awe of this figure, and yet also felt love and reassurance at the same time, as this Celestial continued to ride in front of me. After a minute or so my curiosity got the better of me, I wanted to get a good look at the face,

M.E. - My Blessing in Disguise

once I had that thought, the figure immediately began to disappear, leaving me with an amazing feeling of wow!

Did this happen because I'd become separated from my friends? Would I still have seen it if I'd had company on the lift? It was difficult thinking that this huge, white, Celestial figure was there just for my benefit, really?

Some of us only skied for half of the Saturday, the joy goes when the slopes become so crowded, and these Spanish skiers seem to take no care at all. The result of course was a number of collisions, enough was enough, it'd been a great week back in snowy mountains, so it was time to retire to a bar.

We were due to fly back on the Sunday, I was awake early and saw a bright, white light on the wall. A white Dove came along and was followed by six Weeble type characters, who were carrying their luggage as they wobbled along. I heard the name 'Stuart', then 'wrong', then a phone rang in my ear. In trying to make sense of this, I came to the conclusion that there was going to be fun and games with our luggage or skis. My circle leader's surname was Stuart, her husband Kelvin worked at Gatwick Airport as a baggage handler, so it was easy to figure that out, or so I thought. I also felt that as the Weeble characters had all looked happy, that spirit would ensure that we had a safe flight.

The flight was generally OK, a little bumpy as we got closer to Gatwick. The fun and games began as we closed in on the runway with the plane rocking about much more. We seemed to be about 50 feet from the ground when a fierce crosswind hit the aircraft, suddenly the engines were on full power as the pilot aborted the landing. We had to do another circuit or two before we came in again and landed safely, phew! The luggage and skis were collected by us all without any hiccups.

M.E. - My Blessing in Disguise

Looking back afterwards, it had been a wonderful trip for me, so good to be back skiing and to see the mountains covered in snow, and lots of sunshine too. I also had some amazing spiritual experiences, the figure on the lift, astonishing really, though I'm still puzzled by the shock on the stairs. Those experiences will stay with me there's no doubt, it's also obvious that my precognition was working, even if I haven't quite got the hang of its interpretation yet. I was glad that Sheila was on the trip, it meant that I had someone to talk to about these happenings. Sheila had a strong interest in the spiritual side then, although no involvement, nowadays she is healing and developing in circle.

One last note on this trip, the political riot I was shown took place in Spain on the Friday and Saturday after we arrived back home.

My first circle back after skiing was very quiet for me, I went home quite deflated, talk about highs and lows, what a contrast. Things picked up though, and in an early April circle my arms and hands were raised up in the air, what's more they stayed up for ages. There was no way that I could keep my arms up for that amount of time, so it had to be spirit doing it. I was expecting to feel lots of aches and pains in my arms either after circle or the next day, but there was no reaction whatsoever.

The top of my body was moved around a lot, jerking and rolling, still my hands were being kept up around head height. I enjoyed it, I'd had control at home before, but this was taking it on further. I felt as if I'd made a little progress in circle for the first time.

Shortly after this, some of the ladies were talking about going to a séance, they asked me if I would like to join them, I had to say yes. Someone tried to explain a bit about what happens at one, there was nothing to put me off, so I thought let's give it a try. Apart from our weekly circle, all I'd experienced up to that point was an evening of trance with Celia and Beverley from our circle, when spirit came and spoke to us, so a visit to a full blown séance seemed a logical next step.

M.E. - My Blessing in Disguise

In circle things were still happening for me, various sensations were ongoing, also control, and I was now getting spells of feeling very woozy, I was comfortable with all of this. In bed after circle, I was shown a mass of tiny honeycomb type hexagons, my fingers were sticking up through them, as if they were coming within my grasp. Later I woke up to find that I had a lot of wind in my hair and I was then rolled onto my side, it felt good and exciting.

The first Saturday of May arrived and I made my way to a house in Haywards Heath, a log cabin had been built in the back garden, someone told me that Colin Fry had owned the house and it had been built for him when he was involved with physical mediumship. We all went in and were told where to sit for the séance, I think there must have been thirty to forty people in the cabin, it did get quite hot after a while, David Thompson was the medium.

Being someone who was new to this, I was one of those picked to help tie the medium to his chair, this is normal practice for mediums who sit in the dark, the idea is to ensure that they can't move around and create phenomena by trickery once the lights are out. In these situations it's really dark, totally black, you cannot see anything unless it has a light source, such as the luminous tags that are placed on the séance trumpets.

We were soon under way and singing heartily to help raise the energy. I was soon seeing colours, then little lights were moving around, that meant that the trumpets were up in the air, they touched me a few times. I should mention that I had a large, white light glowing above my head for the first couple of minutes of darkness.

Spirit voices came out of the dark, some footsteps too could be heard as a spirit doctor moved around the circle. He came to give a lady some healing, when the opportunity arose I asked for some for my troublesome knee, I soon felt his hands there. It was becoming hot and sweaty, but the energy around me felt amazing.

M.E. - My Blessing in Disguise

The evening was about to get better as a spirit spoke to us asking who knew the name of Downs, no one spoke up. The spirit asked again and said that they knew someone present knew of someone with that name. Suddenly the penny dropped for me, my sister Sylvie and husband Paul had recently taken in a lodger, Downs was his surname. I'd actually been thinking that we'd had neighbours called Downer when I was a kid, and thought that was close, time to speak up then.

The spirit spoke to me and said that he was an uncle of my mothers, he gave me some evidence about her and one of her sisters. He said that I could ask him questions, I didn't expect that to happen, and I found it difficult to think of much to ask. He soon said that he had to go, but that there was someone else who wished to come and speak with me.

It wasn't long before a husky voice came through, he had what sounded to me like an Indian accent. He introduced himself as Rashid, he told me he was to be a guide who would work with me in the future. Rashid said that he knew that I wouldn't be able to believe now what he was going to tell me, he would be using me to bring Spiritual Philosophy through to many people. I asked for some guidance, the response was to be patient and to remain committed to developing my abilities, he was gone soon after.

I now know that this was a real 'wow' moment, I believe it's quite unusual for guides to come through like that at seances, it's much more likely to be loved ones who speak to us. Initially however, I was not that impressed, I knew nothing of spiritual philosophy, I'd only ever seen a couple of men speaking about philosophy on the tv, and to follow the conversation I would've needed to constantly consult a dictionary, I couldn't see the point in being involved with that sort of thing, surely a very small audience.
When the lights went on I had to check the medium to ensure that all the ties were still in place, then I could ponder on what had been an amazing evening. I loved the phenomena, the spirits speaking, and the whole atmosphere, but I wasn't too sure about the message I'd received. The ladies from our circle thought that I was lucky, they said

M.E. - My Blessing in Disguise

once it started that it would all be done for me, I only had to turn up and let spirit get on with it. Whereas with clairvoyance demonstrations it meant that the medium had to work, it would be easy for me, I didn't quite know what they were getting at then. As I went to leave an Asian chap came over to me, he was thrilled, he wanted to hear Rashid speak again, he shook my hand warmly and wished me well. I paid for a cassette of the evening as it had been recorded, yes I've played it a few times over the years.

I'm writing this over thirteen years later in 2015, it's only recently that Rashid has finally come through and spoken briefly through me. I believe the wait has been all on my side, changes had to happen with me and in my thinking, and in my overall being, it's taken a long time. Since that séance I've read books by White Eagle, Ramadahn, Silver Birch and Red Cloud, so I now know a bit of what spiritual philosophy is about, and beautiful it is too, if anyone who may read this hasn't read any, please do.

A week after the séance I attended a demonstration at the Healing Light, my first since I received my message through Betty, which of course had been the only one I'd been to. I again got a message with some good evidence, though some of it was difficult to take, but on reflection it was pretty accurate.

Back home I was woken about 4am by what sounded like dripping noises near the bedroom door. The dripping started moving towards the wardrobes, then back to the door. It soon went along to the wardrobes and carried onto the radiator. Enough, I got out of bed to see what was going on, as I turned on the light the noise stopped, I looked around and found nothing untoward. Back into bed and off with the light, yes it started up again, the dripping sound, I thought that it had to be spirit playing about and ignored it.

In late May I went to Crawley for a reading with a medium, I found her to be an unusual personality and didn't take to her at all. Strangely

M.E. - My Blessing in Disguise

though, the reading was mostly accurate, the fact that I could be healing also cropped up again.

After demonstrations at the Healing Light, the audience are invited to stay for tea and biscuits and a chat if they want to, many spiritual centres do the same. I went to one at the Healing Light, afterwards no one stayed for a cuppa, very unusual, so three or four of us went into our circle room to have ours. I began reading the notices that were on the noticeboard and spotted a new poster, it was for a lady named Celeste, who does readings in astrology, numerology as well as being psychic. The phone number on the poster seemed familiar somehow, so I made a note of it.

The next day found me looking through my diaries because of Celeste's phone number. I realised that spirit had been giving me her number, drip-feeding it to me over the past year. How strange, but there must be a reason for it, but I'd had a reading very recently, so I wasn't looking for another yet. I decided to double check the number when I went to circle, if it was right well then what? This was the number that I'd woken up to about a year ago and I'd only remembered part of it, I'd recently been seeing the last two characters very plainly, I couldn't miss them. On circle night I checked the poster, there was no mistaking it, the numbers matched.

Around this time Celia wanted to start up a group for people who wanted to learn how to become healers. I was half interested , as I thought of the good it had done me, but I was put off by the fact that I know I received some counselling as part of it, I couldn't picture myself doing that, so I didn't put my name forward. I had of course been told three times now that I could, maybe should be healing. First Michael Chapman, had told me, then Annie when I had a reading, and most recently at the reading I had in Crawley. Celia said her group would be starting in June, I reluctantly said that I may be interested, but left it open.

M.E. - My Blessing in Disguise

The business with Celeste's phone number was puzzling me so much that I called her and arranged to go for a reading, although it was only two or three weeks since my last one. Celeste did a three part reading, I'm not sure of the order, but Astrology, Numerology and Tarot were used. I was given things about spiritual development and working, the main thing that kept coming up was healing, so It looks as if this was all about spirit making a final push, and what timing, with Celia's healing course starting the next week. Perhaps I wasn't meant to remember Celeste's phone number when I first saw it, yes I would have been interested, but I wouldn't have known whose it was. Had I found out then I would most likely have had a reading, but as it happened the timing again made a big impact on me.

The next week I was on my way to Steyning to a healing group for beginners, I was the only man amongst six or seven ladies, some of whom I'm now good friends with. The idea of course was to try to attune ourselves to the healing vibration, learn about the etiquette involved, and hopefully at some point be able to help others by giving them healing.

The day after the healing group met I went to London, I sat and relaxed on returning home and suddenly I had lots of strong sensations in my left hand. Then someone began holding it, wow! Spirit is holding my hand, absolutely beautiful, there's no other way to describe it.

As the healing group continued I was feeling more and stronger sensations, I was giving Celia healing and one of my hands was on her forehead, it was suddenly pushed away, not by Celia. After as we chatted I was told that some healers are controlled by their guides, I wasn't aware of this, so much to learn it seems. Each week Celia would talk about a different aspect of the course, then a general chat which was followed by us pairing to give each other healing. At some point Celia introduced a couch, we all took turns to receive on the couch as the rest all gave healing to the lucky one.

M.E. - My Blessing in Disguise

One evening after about five months of the course, I was giving healing to Jeannie. By this time I'd worked out the way that I wanted to work, it was mostly down the spine, so much comes off of it or runs through it that for me it was the place to be centred on. I was making my way down Jeannie's spine when suddenly my right hand shot up to her right shoulder. What's going on I thought, and I promptly moved my hand back to her spine. It was probably 20-30 seconds later that my right hand again was moved to Jeannie's shoulder, this time I couldn't move it back, I had to wait until spirit had finished giving healing there, then I could carry on with my normal routine.

Afterwards Jeannie told me that she'd been in a car accident at some point, since then she would get intermittent pains in that shoulder, she was very pleased that spirit took control as it had been hurting her that day. I had no prior knowledge of her injury, so it brought it home to me of how much in control spirit can be when they feel the need, and also that perhaps I shouldn't be quite so rigid in my thinking.

Most days I was still sitting three times a day on my own, so it wasn't surprising that so much was happening at home. It was a routine that I'd fallen into, willingly for sure. I was going off into trance quite often, but I didn't know of course if anything happened whilst I was away, but sitting with spirit felt so comfortable and natural, why stop?

Somehow I'd heard that there was going to be a demonstration by a trance medium at Henfield, so I went along to see for myself. The medium was bringing forth spiritual philosophy, sadly the words of wisdom seemed to come across in a very dull and boring manner, not inspirational at all. I wasn't the only one who thought so, lots of the audience became fidgety very quickly. I sent my thoughts to spirit, if you want to use me in this way in future, it must be more interesting and hopefully valid to the audience, else what's the point.

Spirit made sure that my evening wasn't wasted, they took control of my eyes and had them zooming in and out like crazy. It was as if I was a camera, sometimes the centre was clear and the outside of my vision

M.E. - My Blessing in Disguise

blurred, I've never known anything like it. This had started early on when it felt as if a hand was placed on my head, I couldn't move my head or eyes, in fact I couldn't even close my eyes or blink. I felt sorry for the medium, who apparently had a good reputation, but it was down to whoever was coming through her. I couldn't complain, spirit had kept me entertained and made it memorable for me, and I'd had the opportunity to give them my thoughts about how we might work together in the future, would they listen, only time will tell.

One Sunday morning in October I went to the Healing Light service, I was attending more events now. That Sunday I received a message from the platform, in amongst some good evidence was an intriguing, mysterious line, 'there maybe a little detour in your development'. It meant nothing to me at the time, but it may have been the first hint about my future time in Portugal.

Things were moving on in circle and we were spending more time sitting in the dark. Most weeks I would spend some time with my arms flapping like a bird, spirit had also been putting my hands into the prayer position. I began experiencing spells of extreme cold, this is down to spirit energy, you cannot get warm if it comes, no amount of layers or blankets can make any difference, it gets under everything. Spirit had also started moving my mouth and making noises, most of which seemed to come from my throat.

We had a couple of evenings when the circle was used for rescues, that is to help souls who have become lost between the worlds. The idea is to talk to them and get them to look for a light, then if they can move towards it there will be those who can take them through to spirit. I've no idea why this should happen to any soul, I think only a small percentage are affected in this way. In our circle it was usually Beverley or Sarah who would get these links.

I did try automatic writing for a while, but my interest soon waned. However, I did get some lines of numbers a couple of times, one line

M.E. - My Blessing in Disguise

had the numbers back to front and upside down, it was written much neater than I could ever write them.

There were a few different circles running at the Healing Light and one evening I went to a different one, as they had a guest psychic artist come in. I'd never seen psychic art so an opportunity had been presented. Jan drew a man's face for me, it was similar to an old photo of my dad, Jan also gave me some good evidence with the drawing. Overall I enjoyed the evening and it made me realise that not all circles are run the same. I also met Debi for the first time that evening, we have done quite a lot of sitting and working together since. I count Debi and Jan as good friends now.

Just before Christmas Annie had a link with my dad in circle, he was excited and saw me battening down the hatches at the start of a trip. He said that something was drawing to a close and he wanted me to be confident about what lies ahead. He then said that I would be going somewhere warm for a while, but I would come back. It's turned out to be the case, quite prophetic, but at that point it wasn't even a twinkle in my eye. It was also mentioned that I would have lots of travelling to do, that's turned out to be equally true.

I also had a cat climbing on me at circle that night, I think it was old Porky, who'd passed a year or so earlier. He was visiting me a lot at home, I often heard his loud purring, an occasional miaow, and also his collar bell that would tinkle as he cleaned himself. It's a beautiful thing to know that he still wants to be around me.

Spirit were trying different ways of building control with me, sometimes it felt as if I was playing guitar or piano, if only. I also started feeling weight on my hands, and occasionally felt as if I'd caught something in my hands. The control was also growing when I was at Celia's healing group.

I continued to feel many sensations in my body and one evening I had some pain around my right ribs, this happened after I'd felt something

M.E. - My Blessing in Disguise

moving around inside me there and also a little further forwards. The significance of this pain would come to the fore in the future.

I went through a spell of getting unexpected tastes in my mouth, rum, blue cheese, cough medicine, there were also some smells which came out of the blue, bleach, cigarettes, cigars and others, I had no idea what the purpose of this might be.

I've had many wonderful sensations when sitting for spirit, I've been kissed on the lips, I've felt that I was holding a baby, I've felt that I was surrounded by peace, love and beauty, and have also had my hands held by spirit, and I've had cuddles and hugs from spirit. In one sitting spirit had me laughing in different ways, by that I mean like Tommy Cooper and Popeye, good fun of course.

Spirit lights come and go around me, one day there was a cluster of them moving around in the kitchen for a while. Noises in my flat were becoming more common, I heard footsteps in my kitchen and sounds around the dining table.

All in all 2002 was an amazing year for me, that my health came back to normal was wonderful in itself, but then learning and experiencing much more about the spiritual side is a tremendous thing. Knowing my development is moving forwards is very encouraging, although spirit have used that frightening word 'patience' to me on a few occasions. An exciting year ends and I look forwards with anticipation of what might be to come.

M.E. - My Blessing in Disguise

Spirit Speaks

Initially it was a quiet start to the year, though after a few days spirit were up to their old tricks of waking me up when they felt like it, other noises were happening as if someone was walking around my flat, oh well I guess it's company of a sort.

At the Healing group at Steyning I used to talk about my experiences when the opportunity occurred, this was not always with Celia's approval. However, it must have created some interest as in late January Celia started a development group there on alternate weeks to the healing Group.

One day at home I felt my brain physically wobble, a very weird thing and to what purpose. I was shown a scene in which a girl was throwing snowballs, one hit a window, making a soft thud, at exactly that moment I heard a soft thud on my window. A bit later that day I was playing some music, before long spirit were playing with my stereo, making the sound alternate between the speakers, it went on for several minutes. Then suddenly I had what felt like a heavy weight in the middle of my chest inside me, but no pain. It stayed for about fifteen minutes and then slowly lessened.

When I sat the next day I thought I could feel heavy water rippling on my feet for a while. Then my head went forwards, when it came back up lovely heat spilled out of my neck and down my back, beautiful. At that night's healing group I felt like a cork bobbing about in all directions as I received healing from Celia.

I was still sitting at home three times on most days, one day I somehow realised that in my morning sit with spirit I was being used to send healing. It may have been happening for a while, but I was still newish to this, and with so much else going on not everything was immediately obvious. Light trance with control kept developing, as the year went on I was going off totally for periods into deeper trance. The deeper trance

M.E. - My Blessing in Disguise

happened almost exclusively at home at this point, in circle I was still aware of what was happening, even though there were times when I was unable to speak.

In both circles I spoke about my experiences when I could, Celia didn't think it was appropriate, but it was an outlet for me. Shortly after ,Celia spoke to me and questioned whether it was safe for me to sit alone, I think she was mostly concerned that others may try it, and perhaps they wouldn't have been suited to developing that way.

On the day following our conversation, I decided to ask Spirit if I should be sitting on my own, and when I did, was I protected. I was sitting on the sofa when I spoke to spirit, suddenly something made me look up, there on the ceiling was something large, white and feathered going backwards and forwards across the ceiling, it looked like part of a bird, a huge one at that. I took this to be a positive answer to my questions, I'd never seen anything like it before, and it felt good. I told Celia what had happened when I next saw her, she agreed with me, that I should carry on sitting at home.

I was still scouring shops for spiritual books, and still occasionally get strong signs that made me feel that I should read that particular book. It was probably during this year that I bought my first White Eagle book, Rashid had aroused my curiosity about spiritual philosophy, it was time to learn about it.

Some days concentrating on writing this book is easy, sometimes not so, by that I mean it'll be easy for me to be distracted. One family who own neighbouring land keep some chickens, these can be very annoying as they are allowed to wander wherever they like. All well and good for them, but they've taken a liking to coming onto my land and getting in amongst my plants. Once there they do what chickens do, have a good scratch about and sometimes dig quite deep holes to sit in. This has caused several of my plants to die, the neighbours do not seemed bothered as when I complain, albeit in English, I am met by a shrug of the shoulders.

M.E. - My Blessing in Disguise

I'm pleased to say that spirit have intervened here, they find ways to get my attention, tingles on my hands, lights around me, touches. When it happens I go and look out of the window, more often that not the chickens are encroaching, so I go out and shoo them away, then get back to writing this book. It saves me being on a constant lookout and helps me concentrate on what I'm doing. I should say the reason the chickens come is because there is shade under my trees, the neighbours have chopped down all their shade giving trees to grow a few more crops. It's good to have some cooperation, and after all I'm writing this book because spirit want it out there.

I'd begun getting lots of tickles and sensations in my throat, some made me gasp, and spirit would take control of my mouth, as in opening and closing it, and putting it into odd shapes. Sometimes noises would come out of my mouth, as if someone was trying to speak. Around this time I also began getting what I call 'tuning fork' noises in my ears, they literally sounded like a tuning fork, sometimes high, some low, long or short, soft or loud, quite a variety overall. I still get them today, there's no way of telling how often they happen, there can be a lot in a short time or longer intervals between them.

It was at a Wednesday circle in Mid-April that spirit made their breakthrough, 'Yes' was spoken through me several times. It was a strange feeling at the time, but I think that I was relieved overall. Lots of unusual noises came out of my mouth that night, they all seemed to happen on my out breath. My breathing seemed elongated and my stomach was pushed out a long way. They pulled back my head and a lot of noises started when my face was pointing at the ceiling, my throat felt strange and stayed that way all evening. By the time circle closed I felt happy, Spirit had spoken through me. It was in part confirmation of what Rashid had told me, only one word, but all journeys are started with a first step.

When I got home I talked to spirit and asked why my head had to be pushed right back, as this was a very uncomfortable position. I was impressed that things will change as the techniques are refined and improved.

The speech continued for a while as single words with the vocabulary slowly broadening, 'you, who, shoe, hello, I see, easy' and so on. Shortly after the speech started through me, Celia had a spirit with her at one circle who was interested in what was happening with me. His name was Boddington, he'd been involved with investigating psychic phenomena when he was last here. I have since read a book written by him.

Spirit moved the speech on, managing 'hi, good evening', and after a struggle 'Hugh'. A few days later 'Dave' got through, and there was also a deep, growling voice trying to speak. It did seem that several wanted to try their luck, 'Gordon' was the next name given.

Sitting at home I had some noises that sounded like a Bullfrog gargling, then a surprise, 'you were a voice in spirit', as the fluency was slowly improving. Gordon seemed to be speaking the most and he did encourage me to ask questions, unfortunately I have no record of what I asked or the replies given.

By the middle of May, Gordon could speak for a while, he was interrupted one evening at the healing group. A high-pitched voice began coming through, not without difficulty to begin with, one night the alphabet was recited, followed by it's phonetic sounds, later the name of 'Eve' was given. I've no idea why so many spirits would want to speak through me, or why some find it very easy and others struggle.

The next change was with Gordon, as he spoke one evening my arms and hands began moving about in the way that some people do when they gesticulate as they talk. Another spirit named 'Ishtoo' or similar became a regular visitor for a while.

One night at circle the speech was poor, but I had the company of a spirit who I'd come to call 'laughing boy'. When he was with me my belly felt larger, I also seemed to have a cigarette in one hand and a

M.E. - My Blessing in Disguise

glass in the other. After that it began to settle down with three or four regular visitors who could speak fluently.

One evening a foreign voice came through, so spirit were still trying things out. I did sometimes feel a little confused with all of this, I thought the idea was for Rashid to speak, but there had been no sign of him at all. I had no idea of how long it would be for him to come through, and equally no idea of the reasons why.

During a circle in early June I experienced some involuntary deep breathing, strong energy built up in my chest. Then a strong, powerful, serious voice came through speaking in another language, as he spoke some members in the circle began picking up things to do with Native American Indians. He came and went a few times, the last few things he said seemed to me to be in a totally different tone. Jeremy, who was trying to develop voice, was making noises, he later told us that he felt whoever was trying to speak through him, understood what had been said through me.

The following morning at home Gordon came through and confirmed that it was a Native American Indian who had spoken last night, he said that it was a serious message about understanding what development is really for and how it should be used. Our Native American came through later in a milder tone, but still with the power. A couple of days later an Oriental type of voice came through to join the throng.

I shall now begin referring to the Native American Indian as 'Our Friend', it's much shorter. Our Friend became the main communicator for a while, but one night at circle someone else came through and joined in a link. Apparently it was female and I didn't hear any of it, I was only told about it after the circle was closed. Certainly an interesting development.

At home the following day, Our Friend came through and brought another friend with him, he spoke in English some of the time, my head

M.E. - My Blessing in Disguise

seemed to swivel as he spoke. A high-pitched voice also came through in that sitting.

A strange occurrence around this time was that I kept getting helicopter noises coming through my stereo systems speakers, usually through just one speaker, and sometimes through the tv. I can make a tenuous link between helicopters and Native Americans, as there was a tribe called Chinook, and of course there is a helicopter called after them, and they do fly over Shoreham sometimes. Could it be that Our Friend is from that tribe, it's only speculation on my part.

The second Native American was speaking regularly, usually starting in his own language and then switching into English. One day one of Our Friends began chanting through me, my lips hardly seemed to move at all, it's possible it was a newcomer.

A bit later I had a good walk in the June sunshine and I ended up having a pint at The Bridge, a pub that has a good sized seating area overlooking the river. I bought my drink and went outside, it was fairly crowded but I found a table and settled down to relax. I was looking at a patch of sky with cloud around it. The cloud was in a shape that seemed to be a combination of a ray, Concorde and a big bird, the sky colour was deeper at the head of the bird.

I carried on supping and enjoying the river view, when suddenly I could feel energy building up in my chest, I had company, Our Friend was here. The energy had grown very strong, Our Friend wanted to talk, somehow I managed to keep him quiet, I can only guess at what the reaction might have been had his voice boomed out. I've since learned that he loves to be near water.

At home that evening our Second Friend came through, then the high-pitched voice as well. I became so incredibly hot that I closed the session early. Our Second Friend came through at the next Steyning circle, the last thing he said was 'all in good time'.

M.E. - My Blessing in Disguise

The Healing Light had moved to a new centre at East Steet, Shoreham, we now had a converted basement to sit in, a lovely room and of course dark. One of the circle leaders called Dave had done most of the work. So we all were hoping for a special evening as we sat there for the first time. Our two Friends came through quickly and my hands were soon moving as if playing a drum, our Second Friend said 'we welcome you'.

At the following weeks healing group Our Friend had a lot to say, I felt as if I was wearing something heavy on the top half of my body. We had cold coming and going, there were also plenty of creaks, some of which came from the empty chair that was next to me.

Back in Shoreham for the next circle Our Friend was through immediately, after he spoke there was singing and chanting, this came and went a few times during the evening, he seemed happy. Sitting at home the following day Our Friend was talking almost non- stop, and also singing, he was very happy and excited, exuberant you could say.

A couple of days later I took a walk along Shoreham beach, it was almost empty, which is often the case as there are no facilities there. The energy built up in my chest, so I let Our Friend boom out for a while, he always wanted me to face the sea when he spoke. At this point I wasn't sure how much I could control the voices, or whether I should even try to, I didn't want to interfere with my development and I was enjoying hearing spirit speak through me.

I went to the Sunday Service and received a message through the medium, Pam. The link was with my dad, he said that there were some around me who weren't happy with what was happening with me, and that they would put me down, I shouldn't worry, just carry on. There was something about my pathway and a door to be opened when the time is right, it will also bring in extra protection. All in all it was a lovely, positive message, and I had a chat with Pam afterwards.
Our Friend continued to speak regularly, singing and laughing some days as well. Some others did come through, but Our Friend seemed to

M.E. - My Blessing in Disguise

be the main player. I was getting the feeling that some at the Wednesday circle were getting fed up with Our Friend, as he only spoke in his native tongue. I voiced this at home and spirit told me that they understood the situation, they said that changes would happen soon.

Celia started a Friday circle at the Healing Light, Annie had a link for me that talked about a book I was reading called 'Reach For The Stars', I had asked spirit if Valentine, who the book was about, could come to our circle, so that was a lovely touch. After the link spirit began whistling through me, it was the 'Hovis' tune for the tv advert. Annie then had a link for Celia, apparently the spirit linking used to whistle a lot. At home I found out that the tune I'd been whistling was from Dvorak's New World Symphony. I had the tune on a compilation cd, the booklet with it had a write up and a picture for each tune, the picture for the New World Symphony was of a Native American Teepee, wow, some synchronicity there.

When spirit spoke through me at our next circle I felt pressure around my head, it was as if I was wearing something on my head, maybe a headdress or similar. A few days later at home I saw the eye of an Owl, then lots of rapidly changing faces, some of them were American Indians wearing headdresses.

Our Wednesday circle came around and Our Friend had a lot to say, and a little sing. He was patient , always waiting for silence before he spoke, it seemed to me that he was offering encouragement to those who were getting links or trying to allow spirit to speak through them.

At home the following evening, Our Friend did his talking, chanting, singing thing, then I went off. After I came back I went to close, but I was dragged back down a tunnel it seemed for a few minutes. There was a very strange new sensation which rippled around my face and left me feeling incredibly woozy and exhausted for a while. In the next few days sittings at home I kept feeling woozy at the end, and I also had lots of muscle moves around my face and mouth.

M.E. - My Blessing in Disguise

Our Friend was speaking so much at the Healing group that I reluctantly had to suppress him, after all we were there to be learning about healing.

A new spirit came through at circle with a few words, 'Cook', and 'Dick', that was about it. It was very uncomfortable in my throat, I coughed a lot and had a burning sensation in my chest. The next day at home I felt a sensation on the out side of my throat, then it felt as if a hand was placed on the right side of my face, with the fingers between the eye and the temple. A voice came through as the 'Communicator', he answered my thoughts and usually gave more, he told me to look forwards to working for spirit. He came back in the evening and was followed by another voice, who I took to be Bertha, because of the speech and its phrasing. Bertha had been through several times in our Wednesday circle through Celia. The Communicator spoke at a few more sittings, always in the evening.

One day I sat privately with Celia, she wanted to find out more about what was going on with spirit and me, several voices spoke to her. Spirit told her that they wanted me to sit in red light at home and to also be regularly sending healing. It was also mentioned that there is a band of Native American guides around me, I presume that this is to do with protection. After this I sat a few times alone in our circle room in red light, it's not much over a ten minute walk for me. In those sittings I felt control and cold, but there wasn't much speaking from spirit.

One Wednesday circle was very interesting, lots of voices were around, one gave the name of 'Jig', both Celia and Annie knew of Jig. Sarah had a link with Houdini, she was wondering if he'd been telepathic, as she said that I was shown a bright, aqua tick, confirmation there. A little later I began to feel really fat, Sarah was given 'The Blue Ridge Mountains of Virginia', whilst Annie felt a tap on her head. It all seemed to tie in with a Laurel and Hardy film. Celia had the voice of Walter Stimson come through, he said that we should have a physical

M.E. - My Blessing in Disguise

circle. At one point my right hand was up in the air, then it felt heavy, as if some one was trying to push it back down, but it didn't fall.

At home the following day I sat in red light, but it wasn't dark as I had no blackout materials. Spirit came through, then I went all shivery as a different voice came through. His voice was weak and my stomach went tight, he said that's how he had been when he passed. There was a following deep vibration when he spoke, as if a speaker was distorting, it seemed to come from the lower part of my throat.

Sitting at home one evening I was shown some clear liquid or jelly which had layers of twine or rope through it, a bit like diamond shaped webs which were linked together. The weak spirit voice came through and told me that this is the protection around me, and there would be more to come. Our friends had stopped coming through recently, the Communicator and the Weak voice were the main speakers at the time.

On the first Wednesday morning in September I was sending distant healing, Weak voice came through to say that 'spirit are looking forwards to an interesting evening', wow, I'd never had a message like that before, can't wait.

As we met for circle I decided to keep the message to myself for now. Soon a voice was trying to come through me and my neck seemed to have grown, there was a feeling of something at the outside of my throat. I couldn't understand what spirit were saying, but Debbie picked up Churchill. He was in my body, first my neck, then my chest, legs and arms. The voice became clear and he said a few things about the war, his attitude towards it and about those who delayed taking action. He said that allying to Russia was the lesser of the two evils at the time. Others in circle picked up on sadness, Eleanor and similar war links. Another voice came through briefly and spoke about being so hot, Annie said that she saw a red glow over me. I was impressed with air raids, so perhaps he was an ARP or a fireman. Annie saw a white dove at the end of all this, So spirit had been right with their message in the morning, it had been a very interesting evening.

M.E. - My Blessing in Disguise

That circle was on September 3rd, it was the 64th anniversary of the start of WW2, obviously Churchill's part in it is well documented. Something made me look up Winnie's age when the war began, he was 64, now that's some synchronicity.

Winnie came through at home the following day and said that he hoped to be able to come through at our circle again. One day I was reading the paper at home when Weak voice came through and said 'we're ready', so before I knew it we were sitting. There were some new voices, when they started speaking I got a ball of heat in the middle of my chest, this remained there for sometime after the sitting finished. Incidentally, Winnie came into my body on a regular basis for a while.

I was playing some music at home one day when Our Friend came through to interrupt the song 'Fools Like You' by Blue Rodeo. The song is about how the American Indians were cheated out of their lands, not surprisingly Our Friend had strong feelings about this. The morning after I was receiving healing when spirit again came through to say that they hoped for an interesting evening. At circle there wasn't a huge amount spoken, but some things I received tied in with a link that someone else had, I also gave off the names of two dogs that were known to others, so interesting for me as this is unusual.

I was also given a little more evidence at the Steyning circle, Spirit came through talking about a watch, this tied in with a message that Barbara had received at a demonstration a week before. At our next Wednesday circle spirit joined in a link that Sarah had for Cherry, a couple of items were given. Both Sarah and Cherry thought that the voice was much closer to them, as if it had moved from where I was sitting, to me it seemed much quieter, as if it was further away from me, now that could be interesting.

At our next Steyning circle I felt as if I had something on my head for a while. A spirit voice struggled through and said that he was the Duke of York. He talked about how he had suddenly had to take on more

M.E. - My Blessing in Disguise

responsibility, which had initially made his speech problem worse. He then mentioned abdication and that he became known as George V1. This was a welcome surprise for me, I had to check it up as I hadn't realised that Bertie had been the Duke of York before he became the King.

In fact the following day I went to the local library, as I picked up a book titled 'Battle Royal', I had an incredible tingle around my right elbow. The book is about Bertie and Edward and the abdication, yes I borrowed it. That evening I sat at home and seemed to be communicating with several spirits by thought, it was all very clear and obvious. Just before I was finishing it all went totally black, yet the red light remained on, something was somehow shielding the light.

At home a few days later, Prince George came through for a chat, he'd been the Duke of Kent in the 1930's. I had some constriction in my chest which seemed to cause some distortion, but some of his speech was clear. I continued to read Battle Royal and received lots of sensation as I did, sometimes very strong, especially those in my brain.

At the Wednesday circle I had a lot of sensations in my chest, when spirit spoke it seemed to me as if the voices were speaking through my chest. Our Friend came through and spoke a little in English, he said that he was helping to protect me. The following day at home I was impressed that the sensations in my chest were to enable spirit to bring through more than one voice at a time. Spirit went on to say that this was experimental and would need some refining.

A week or so after that message I had two spirits come through and they were almost talking together, no pauses, it was amazing. Then the following day it sounded as if three or four voices were having a conversation, I didn't know the language, but it was incredible to listen to. This was followed up the next day with several voices mingling together, and my hands felt as if they were being held for a while, wonderful. A couple of days later I taped a sitting as the voices chatted

M.E. - My Blessing in Disguise

together and also Our Friend came through, I can't find the tape now, but there are others with speech on them.

That evening at circle spirit spoke and said 'Grey', a short delay and then 'Owl', it was spoken quietly. A couple of times the next day I was shown white arrowheads, one of them was very bright. I ought to mention Hector, a visitor who spoke from time to time. One evening after spirit had spoken, a spirit had a bit of a sing-song through me, it takes all types.

An evening sitting in early November brought lots of voices through, some speaking, some singing their words and others in different languages, one kept singing 'Going to Sunshine' to me, I don't know if it's a song or just something that they made up. A day or two later I had my hands held as the spirit voices mingled, but I was getting the odd day when spirit were quiet. Wednesday circle came and spirit spoke ' stick or twist', it was repeated, then ' You always win if you twist in your development, you must strive' was said.

One evening we had a new sitter in circle, spirit spoke to him very quietly 'You took your time'. Later another spirit spoke and asked 'Where was Joe', at the time I had a burning sensation in the centre of my chest and pain to the left. I began wondering about it and I briefly saw the crosshairs of a gunsight, so perhaps Joe had been shot, but no one had any idea about who Joe might be.

Jan, our psychic artist friend, occasionally joined us at Steyning circle, she said that I should record my sittings in case spirit wanted to try for direct voice. I did take this advice and did so for a couple of years, the bugbear is the time it takes to listen to the playbacks. Earlier that day I'd sat at home and something had been pushed into my throat, no explanation of course.

At Wednesday circle spirit spoke through me 'there's a surprise'. Later spirit spoke through Celia, they talked about changes to come in our circle. That night the light changed a lot from pitch black to seemingly

M.E. - My Blessing in Disguise

quite light, I wasn't the only one to notice this. I felt incredible energy around me and then saw a huge, head-sized, yellowish-white light to the right side of my head, it reminded me of an aliens head, if I knew what one of those was. I became very groggy and the energy stayed with me after the circle was closed.

At a Wednesday circle in early December I did a lot of coughing, I hadn't coughed at all before circle, a couple of people picked up that Helen Duncan had joined us, several got the smell of stale smoke and tobacco. In the run up to Christmas at circle, I felt a heavy weight on my chest and I had difficulty breathing and talking. It came and went a few times, then a voice said 'he was crushed', and 'get it off'. I couldn't get any more information about him, he soon left us. For about the last the minutes or so of the circle my head was pulled back, I felt incredible energy in my hair, it seemed as if the energy was flowing through my hair like water.
Some spirits were trying to speak through me for a week or so, they finally made it through on Christmas Eve, the main voice had a slight distortion to it, I think it was one who had been through a while back. I was treated to a couple of songs from spirit on Boxing Day morning, but otherwise it was quiet for the rest of the year.

Quite a bit earlier in the year I'd decided that I should look for work, soon after I had lunch with my brother Bob and a friend of his, who told me of a particular office to go and check out. It was tucked away some where in Brighton, so the next time I was in Brighton I went and found it. I was on a tight schedule that day so resolved to go back in the near future.

It may have been the next week when I set out to see what jobs might be available. I got a little way down Buckingham Road on my way to the station when one of my knees exploded in pain, it was really bad, the only thing to do was to slowly limp back home. It took a few days to improve, then I gave it a few more to get trusting it again.

M.E. - My Blessing in Disguise

Then there was only one thing to do, go to Brighton to look at those vacancies., This time I didn't even make it across the Old Shoreham Road, my knee did the same thing and had me in agony, so I was off home again. Whilst my knee was getting better I seemed to get the impression that I wasn't meant to go to that office, I didn't think the problem with my knee was psychosomatic, after all my funds were getting low, but it was looking to me as if someone was putting me off. Somehow I came to the conclusion that I'd have to wait a little while longer before I tried again.

I think It was this year that I somehow found my way to a séance in East Brighton, it was held up in the attic of a house, I think a dozen or so of us were there. It was partly in the dark and got a bit lively at times, water was thrown over a few sitters, I can't remember the medium's name. What stuck in my mind was the behaviour of a small table, the lights had a strobe effect I'm sure at that point. Whatever, the table lifted up and began moving around the circle above the sitters' laps, it went faster and faster, rotating as it built up speed. It didn't touch anyone, if it had it would have hurt, as its circuits were rapid before it finished.

M.E. - My Blessing in Disguise

Some More Happenings In 2003

I've said that I was going to more demonstrations and Sunday services, I usually ended up being on the door collecting the money, or else checking tickets. As time went on I began to get a pain in my right side at the demonstrations, I think it initially started about ten minutes from the end, but it soon began earlier and earlier. I did go to my GP to get it checked out, but he said that there was nothing there. I often ended up leaning to the left to try to ease the pain, it didn't help much. One Saturday in September it started at home, about an hour before I was due to leave for the demonstration, I was on the door so I couldn't pull out. The pain stayed with me all the way through the demonstration, it was a good one too, Val was the medium. I still had the pain the next day, I made up my mind to stop going to demonstrations, well perhaps my mind had been made up for me. I do remember feeling that spirit had put something into my right side, if it was something that could do this, why, what's the point? All I'm doing is taking an interest and supporting the group. The outcome of this is that I kept away from all demonstrations, the next one I would go to would be in 2011 or 2012.

I'd had another ski trip back to Baqueira in Spain this year with the usual group of friends. There were lots of little things happening, like my chair being kicked at breakfast several mornings, of course there was no one doing it. I saw lots of colours and lights when I was on the slopes, one day I saw a beautiful orange formation, it reminded me of the cloud shapes that you see on Jupiter. I had some noises in my room, this included the sound of a fluttering bird, twice. One morning I woke up to find my forehead being stroked, that was very nice. So nothing of major proportions, but confirmation that spirit were with me.

One day at home I felt some sensations in my fingers, I picked up a pen and paper and seemingly without any effort or knowledge of what I was doing, I drew what looked like 3DG. I soon made a connection with this as Celia and Kelvin lived at 3 Dacre Gardens. This scenario was repeated a week later.

M.E. - My Blessing in Disguise

Here's a good one, I was alone at home when I felt some itching on my right arm, before I could scratch it someone else had, how's that for service. It would be good if they could do that for those ones that you can get in the middle of your back, now that would be something.

I got home one evening and it was dark, the outside light was out, I was fumbling to find the keyhole when a small blue light shone on it, that is very helpful. Yes it was just like one of those led's that you can get on keyrings now.

Sitting one evening I felt some unusual sensations in my body, it was as if something had been wrapped around my vertebrae. Then it was like someone holding and squeezing them, all of this was inside my body, I felt no pressure on my skin whatsoever.

Another days sitting brought in lots of noises, it seemed as if several people were jumping into my bedroom, no one was there of course. Soon there were noises in the loft, then more in the bedroom again. There was a chair type noise near the door, although no chairs had moved. These noises were repeated about ten days later.

Spirit have also played with my ears, they push things into them, sometimes pulling them out, one day things went into both ears, seemed to go through my head and come out of the opposite ears to which they went in, my thumbs both gave me a thumbs up sign when they were done.
Quite intriguing are the sensations when hands, fingers or feet feel as if they are joined together, I've looked more than once when this has happened, sometimes they are inches apart or more. I expect I've mentioned the feelings where I think that my hands are inside gloves, or someone else's hands are inside mine, it may be the same feeling, I can't tell, but I can't describe these happenings any other way.

One evening I drifted off, as I came back I heard myself seemingly reading a book aloud, as if someone was there with me. As I questioned

M.E. - My Blessing in Disguise

this with spirit in my mind it stopped, then I snorted for some reason and someone copied it. Spirit stayed close to me, later someone wrapped their arms around me, how lovely is that. I've said that I'll stretch your credibility, well try to.

One evening at circle spirit were so close to me and my body was alternating between feeling light and heavy, then someone was inside me, I asked spirit who it was , immediately I was given Michael.

A night in October I'd just got into bed when there was some energy next to the bed, it was moving and making a wind like noise. The bed appeared to spin in a clockwise direction, I felt light, perhaps weightless, but the bedclothes ll stayed in place. It made me feel slightly euphoric and there was a cold breeze or breath on my forehead.

About three weeks later I awoke in the night and my hands were being held and I felt tiny. Then we began to move and there was wind in my face, it feels exciting as we are flying around the bedroom. I get a little concerned as we fly towards the chest of drawers, so large now, trust fills my mind. I relax as we start to change course, but at the last second we fly straight into the chest and through it. We then fly at and through the wardrobes and all the contents. Suddenly it's all over and I'm back in bed feeling totally exhilarated, we seemed to have flown so fast with the wind in my face, and yet so slowly, perhaps because I felt so tiny, it was a truly wonderful and thrilling experience.

As in previous years I've been shown lots of beautiful images, the one that stood out for me this year was when I woke one night to see the most beautiful, glowing, white elephant. There were some words with it and other images floating around, sadly the words have been forgotten.

Earlier in the year I saw a brilliant, creamy-white light which grew in size and brightness, it kept changing shape and grew more until it burst open into lots of tiny lights, some of which bunched together. It was like looking at stars of many colours, so wonderful and some groups made patterns. A few days later whist sitting in the afternoon I had a

M.E. - My Blessing in Disguise

beautiful experience as my body suddenly felt very light, as if about to lift off. My right arm raised very smoothly from the elbow, then it went down with the palm up. I could feel something soft touching both of my hands, then the right hand came up to my heart, and the left hand came up across my right arm. I then had a magical feeling as it felt that I was holding something very precious, wow! Two or three minutes later my arms were lowered.

Another beautiful experience happened to me in early July, I woke up in bed to find an amazing, glowing white light was shining down on me, it was phosphorescent. Then colours began drifting through it, purple, blue, pink, it all covered me and felt wonderful. A little later that night I heard someone speak inside my head 'She rocks the water, but we don't know how', I have no idea of its meaning.
One summer's evening I heard spirit walking around my flat, then there was the sound of someone noisily rolling or folding paper or posters. The following night I was woken from my sleep as someone shook me! Spirit were on a roll it seemed and as I sat the next evening spirit voices came through, then a lot of my muscles got tightened up, especially the stomach ones(the six pack didn't stay though ha-ha). Then spirit gave me a rhyme of sorts:-

My name as you know is Georgie,
And I used to be such a naughty boy,
Till along came a man with a cane,
Who made me stand out in the rain,
Without a single toy --------- to kick.

From summer to winter, on the evening of December 8th we were sitting in the Steyning circle, I was soon impressed with John Lennon and he began giving me his thoughts on the anniversary of his passing. He said that the shooting was so quick that he didn't see it coming. He was pleased that he'd used his ability as well as he had and also pleased that the songs had lasted, he was in the right place at the right time. Everyone should keep working at their abilities as they may suddenly have the opportunity to use them in a wider context. He realised that it

M.E. - My Blessing in Disguise

was not easy for everyone to reach their potential, sometimes circumstances or their character would stop them, so always be open to opportunity. I asked him if he had any advice for modern day celebrities, his response was to say that they should remember where they came from and always show respect to others, status does not make one person better than another. Later at home I became groggy and confused, then for a while it felt as if I was holding a guitar in my lap.

I was fortunate enough to receive some messages from the platform during the year, one was through Laurence. That evening I had strong energy around me and spirit kept closing my eyes and showing me white neon tubes. Laurence gave me some good evidence and described my lounge very accurately, and its contents, no, he'd never been there. He finished with a reference to my dad's attitude towards material things, he said that I should bear this in mind as I have a decision to make in the next six months. I think that was a reference to my moving house at some point.

Annie had linked with my dad before in circle, she brought him through again. Dad said that he wanted me to talk to him as he was now very interested in all of this. He'd been a total non-believer, but now he was as keen as mustard and wanted to help if he could. Towards the end of the message he gave the name of Egremont Place in Brighton. I'd heard the name, but I didn't have a clue whereabouts it was located, it had no meaning to me at the time, but all would become clear in 2014, so the explanation will come later.

Friend Barbara, whose house in Steyning we used for circle and the healing group, had a reading with a medium named Anne and she sang her praises. It made me realise that I hadn't had a reading for a while, so I made a note of her number. I didn't make a call though, but a week or so later spirit spoke to me at home and said that it would be a good idea to do so. Spirit had never said anything like that to me before, so in due course I called Anne and went for a reading.

M.E. - My Blessing in Disguise

As the day arrived I kept thinking about my pathway, and how it seemed so different to the others that I sat with, so I went for my reading hoping for some insight into this. From the start we were getting messages about my pathway and what was going on. Spiritual philosophy came up and it was said that it will be used daily once it starts, which I was hoping wouldn't be too long now.

Anne said that I was trying to find away to cross a bridge, but it was not straight forward to reach it, I had to cross some stepping stones first. My guides were trying to help enlighten me and to raise my consciousness, this was in order to prepare me for the future work.

The reason I was frustrated at circle was because I'd used several abilities in past lives, I needed to use new abilities in this life. It was like I was climbing a ladder, each rung I climbed equated to one ability. As I climbed a rung an ability awakened but there was no time to use it. I had to climb this 'Ladder of Remembrance' in order to reach the level where the new abilities began.

At this point spirit closed the link, we were both disappointed as the reading had only lasted about twenty minutes, so we had a cuppa and a chat. Anne was pleased to talk to someone with whom things were slightly different, she told me of some of her own spiritual experiences, saying that she could never do this with those who sat in her circles, as most wouldn't understand. Since then I've had similar experiences with other mediums, the links get cut and we end up having a good chat, perhaps I'm meant to be a listening ear for other mediums.

After our tea Anne got another link for me and she picked up on moving overseas in the future, and that writing would become important. I was well pleased that spirit had listened to my thoughts beforehand and had given me an explanation about my development so far.

One thing we didn't get any explanation from spirit about was why so many voices are coming through, I'm pleased that my development has

M.E. - My Blessing in Disguise

moved on this year, it took some time, but since the breakthrough spirit have made a lot of use of me, but to what purpose? There are those who say that it's all nonsense and spirit don't waste their energy without good reason, that spirit only come through with specific messages or philosophy, they don't come through to pass the time and talk about the weather. I can see their argument, but our pathways are individual, and none of us know what is behind spirit's thinking. The only theory I've come up is with the benefit of hindsight, it's taken a long time for me to have made whatever changes were required before Rashid would speak through me, so once spirit have got my voice going, why not use it. Who are the voices and why those ones? Could it be that they are spirits who will one day speak through other mediums, if so then why not have some practice while you can? It's all I can come up with, whatever, I don't lose sleep over it.

Quite a year for me with the communications from spirit really coming to life.

M.E. - My Blessing in Disguise

A Year of Travel

New Year's Day 2004 brought with it a wonderful feeling of peace and stillness, then waves of colour and spirit lights entered. When sitting, cold spells became common and were sometimes intense, those tuning-fork noises were quite regular happenings in my ears.

Spirit voices kept coming through, not always in English, and several were likely to come through in the same sitting. I continued to get lots of touches from spirit, and one day as I walked down Buckingham Road , heading towards the centre of Shoreham, Spirit hugged me around the shoulders, wow! I wasn't expecting that, but what a delight, there's no mistaking the amazing feeling.

When I sat there were often noises around my flat, and those unexplained smells were still happening, tastes too. I was starting to get regular spells at circle of going off into trance, previously I think it'd only happened once, and my guides did begin to join in conversations in circle, and answering occasional questions. So my development was continuing to move on, and it was also time for me to move on as I sold my flat.

During one sitting before I moved, I was impressed with a Greyhound, some of my new neighbours would have two rescued Greyhounds, perhaps a sign that I was moving to the right place.

My house move was made near the end of January, it was a rented house in Upper Beeding, a small village four or five miles inland to the North, with the river Adur still close by. I moved for two reasons, one was my financial position, the second was that now I had my health restored I'd begun to find the flat quite restricting. The flat had been great whilst ME had its hold on me, but last summer I hated the idea of going in and closing the door, it was a complete cut-off. The little garden was downstairs and round the corner, not one that you could

M.E. - My Blessing in Disguise

just step out into, so the only answer to that feeling of being trapped inside was to move out.

Spirit wasted no time in settling into Downland Road, I think they settled before I did. On my third day there I was startled by some loud noises from the spare bedroom at the back of the house. I had been washing up at the time, but I immediately raced up the stairs to see what was going on, who had been stamping or jumping on my ceiling. I should have known better of course, there was no sign of anyone. This episode was repeated a day or two later, I was again washing up when the noises happened, I don't enjoy washing up so I'm easily distracted from it.

On the night of those first thumps on the ceiling, my bedroom door opened in the night and I saw a white light out of the corner of my eye, I closed my eyes and saw a series of glowing, white footsteps. I was of course soon sitting at my new home and spirit were very soon taking me off for long spells, sometimes I only had to sit for relaxing and I was gone.

I still traveled down to the Healing Light for circle, one night there I was shown a beautiful golden cross, as with the Egremont Place message from my father before Christmas, the significance of this would only become apparent in 2014, as I researched my diaries to find material for this book.

Another night in bed had spirit showing me lots of pieces of paper moving around, there were many names on the papers, such as 'A.Live', someone's joke, but I didn't need any convincing by now. One night in the middle of February, still less than three weeks since my move, it was pitch black as the street lights were turned off after midnight or maybe one o'clock, I began hearing noises as if someone was going around the house. Suddenly the bedroom door flew open and I could hear the sound of something dragging on the carpet and coming towards me. I jumped out of bed and turned on the light, nothing there of course, had there been, then I would have bumped into it as I went to

M.E. - My Blessing in Disguise

the light switch by the door. Darn it, I wanted to kick myself afterwards, I think the sound would have been made by one of those old heavy gowns worn in times gone by, or a very long coat, either way I wished I'd stayed put and then I might have found out. What a twit I felt, I had a strong trust in spirit by this time, but human instinct kicked in I guess.

The next night I slept well, but the bedroom door was open in the morning. The following night the door opened again, I heard some odd noises and purring, perhaps Porky was around, I was also shown a lighted doorway with someone standing in it.

Upper Beeding joins onto another small village called Bramber. St Mary's cottage is in Bramber and it was frequented by Sir Arthur Conan Doyle, Arthur had visited us on a few occasions at our Healing Light Wednesday circle. I was still sitting in the Steyning circle, it was now almost on my doorstep, at one circle it felt as if my hands were joined together with my fingers interlocked, I opened my eyes to check and they were a few inches apart.

I was now taping my daily sittings at home in case something of interest came through from spirit, as Jan had suggested to me. One evening towards the end of February, there was something on the playback that I couldn't remember happening. Normally if I went into trance there would be nothing on the tape, so this was a first. A couple of evenings later there was a spirit voice on tape talking about a list. Sometimes the voices were nigh on impossible to understand what was said, some of course were in foreign languages.

In March I went off on another ski trip to Bacqueira in Spain. I had lots of spirits around me that week with lights and touches, but no major happenings. I did give my friend Sheila some healing on a chairlift, it was through one hand, well ski poles were being held in the other hand. It was to calm her as we'd had a very rocky start, someone put the brakes on very hard and bounced us about.

M.E. - My Blessing in Disguise

One night after returning I was watching a tv programme about A.C. Doyle and the fairy photos, suddenly everything blurred except the tv, as very strong energy came in and around me. My eyes were wide open and I couldn't close them, all the influence disappeared as the programme ended.

Towards the end of March spirit were speaking a lot when I was taping, sometimes the words on the tape seemed to me to be different to what I heard at the time, also some unusual robotic/electronic voices were coming through. One evening I was gone for a long time and there was quite a lot on the tape. I wished I'd made notes, but it would have meant a lot of writing. I do still have some tapes, but again it's finding the time to listen and if necessary create a transcript of any points of interest.

On April 1st the joke was on me, I fell asleep on the sofa near bedtime, I was woken by loud white noise, as you used to get when the tv programs had ended for the night. I opened my eyes expecting to see a blank tv screen, but programs were still being shown, yes the noise stopped when I opened my eyes.

Two evenings later I saw a white bird shape for the first time, I now know that is my main guide/guardian, he shows himself to me in this way whether my eyes are open or closed, I'm very thankful he does. It's an image that I have probably now seen more than any other.

Shortly after this I was shown a scene/dream in which a lovely, smiling, young lady was coming towards me, she was wearing a blue Fedora, when she took her hat off I recognised her as Lisa, who used to sit in circle with us at the Healing Light.

A month or so later, I was about to go down to the Healing Light to tend the garden at the back of the shop, I should say that it was a Health Food shop run by Celia. I was delayed by the phone ringing and I think I then forgot something, so I ended up a few minutes late on my schedule. When I was parking my car I should have already been in the

M.E. - My Blessing in Disguise

shop's garden working. As I got out of the car, Lisa called out to me, a nice surprise, so we had a brief chat and arranged a meet. Lisa told me that she had to move out and needed somewhere to stay for a while, as I had a three bed house I asked her to come and take a look. She liked the back bedroom and in due course moved in.

Things were OK for a while, but after about three to four months we had an almighty row one morning. Lisa really blew her top and was shouting very loudly at me, just inches from my face. After initially responding and probably making things worse, I found myself going quiet. Energy began to build in my solar plexus, Lisa kept shouting as the energy grew, it began filling my body as it moved upwards. It felt so beautiful, that despite the cacophony going on, I found I couldn't stop myself from smiling as my whole self had filled with love amidst all the anger. Lisa suddenly noticed what had happened with me, it stopped her in her tracks and she turned around and walked out. A few days later she had moved out. On reflection I have to take some of the blame as I didn't lay down any ground rules, so blame on both sides. I'm pleased to say that I have seen her since and all is good between us.

I'll just mention that some time around here I had another burst of song writing, I don't know what or who inspired it, but I'm not complaining.

I was now in the habit of sending healing on a daily basis as I now knew that I could, control had developed and my hands were often moved around as we sent. In April 2004 it seemed that a major change had come in, I began to feel as if my hands were touching someone, I could also feel my hands on people's auras whilst sending.

As the year went on this developed more, sessions became longer, and most days it seemed as if two people were being helped. Most were ladies and many had breast cancers, and yes somehow it felt as if my hands were on their breasts. I found this a little unnerving to begin with, although I have seen pictures of Harry Edwards with his hands on a lady's breasts as he gave her healing at the Albert Hall.

M.E. - My Blessing in Disguise

Spirit seemed to impress upon me that at least some of these ladies we were helping, were involved in spiritual work themselves and had asked for help. Some days I could feel their emotions, some sadness and almost despair in some, but it changed to joy when they could feel the healing coming to them. I know I've cried with them, the sad tears, and then the joyful ones as their emotions came through.

The most beautiful times for me with this was when my hands could sometimes feel them breathing, amazing, and also the days when their hands would press into the backs of mine, as if to check that it was really happening to them, quite sensational. Don't ask me why, but I have felt the full weight of some breasts, and my hands raised them up a little, perhaps to assure the recipient that they weren't dreaming. One thing I believe about healing is it's important for the channel to remain detached from it all, that may seem like a contradiction as I've just talked about emotions, but they belonged to the ladies, they weren't mine, though they would've been after we finished.

Hips, legs, stomachs and backs have all been worked on in this way, I've come to call it distant hands on healing. This type of healing went on for some time, how and why it was through me, I can't say, as long as it helps then fine. Some days the sessions were long, once we started I never set a time limit, it just went on as long as it was needed.

This healing aspect is also something that may stretch a reader's credibility or incline them to think I've got a screw loose, as before I can only give my interpretations of how it feels. I don't feel delusional at all, but I understand it maybe hard to accept, even for some who work for spirit.

Six months had passed since my last reading and as it was a good one for me, I decided to return to Anne. This time my main guide gave Anne his name, she was told to tell it to me and that I had to keep it to myself. Anne was also shown what happened back on February 4th 2003, when I raised the question of my protection with spirit, Anne described to me what she was shown and it matched what I saw that

M.E. - My Blessing in Disguise

day, you can't get much better than that. Anne also described his booming voice. The reading went on with more general evidence, some of it was about a possible future location for me. This time the tape recorder wouldn't restart when we turned the tape over, so it was time for a cuppa and a chat, but I was very happy with what I'd been given.

I was still talking about my experiences at circles, some of this was about to do with how the distant healing was working now. Beverley at Wednesday circle, who I now know is also a trance healer, became interested, and she asked if we could get together to give healing to each other. We did this perhaps three or four times, then Beverley brought in Debi from another circle, I had met her before.

Debi has been into Reiki for some time, healing too, and she had some regular clients. |It was decided that we would work together as a group, all of us working on the same client. We arranged to rent a room above Celia's shop, where we would work on a donation basis. It was only one morning a fortnight to see how we went, and of course it had to fit in with peoples schedules, Celia's shop was also quite central for us. A couple of months later we were joined by Barbara, it was her house at Steyning that we used for the healing group and a circle. A little further on and Debi was inspired with a name for our group, it was The Pyramid of Light, we all liked that. We had a few regular clients and over time spirit began speaking through me, usually at the start and also sometimes at the end. There was often encouragement with thanks at the end, sometimes other little messages were given, so it was also an outlet for spirit too. The group carried on for several years, and once the shop changed hands it was moved to the back of Debi's house in Southwick. I know we had a lovely atmosphere when we worked together, some more experiences with the group will appear later.

In late May Mike asked me to go to Tenerife with him, well after that last trip there with my proper awakening happening, I could hardly say no. The first couple of days brought me lights and lots of colours. Then I was on the terrace having a cuppa when strong healing began coming through, it was the 'hands on' type for one of the ladies, it went on for a

M.E. - My Blessing in Disguise

while. Later that day someone was holding my leg for a while, as I sat on a bar stool, well I wasn't rushing to go anywhere. In bed that night I saw 'GUINNESS' on an enormous glass, yes, in my dreams and all that.

The colours and faces kept coming, also what I'll describe as large, white plankton shapes too. More 'hands on' healing came through, no problem to me, and I had a lot of muscle moves in my lower right leg. One day I took a walk and got to a rocky outcrop by the sea, 'Our Friend' wasted no time in coming through to speak, he seemed to be using my upper stomach this time.

I was laying on a sunbed when strong vibrations came up through it, then there was energy in my left leg as someone seemed to push into my left side, they obviously wanted to share the sunbed with me as I seemed to be pushed over a bit. Later on the sun terrace, yes these relaxing holidays are hard work, I was shown some words when my eyes were open, 'Giselle', 'Fun Brian' amongst them. In bed that night I felt very strong vibrations coming up through the floor.

So no repeat of the last trip, but plenty of spirit company and beautiful colours. The healing just switching on was a surprise, but I wasn't doing anything, so why not.

In September I had a short trip to Ireland for the wedding of my son Brian to Noelle, a lassie from Limerick, it was a lovely time and we received typical Irish hospitality, and they made a happy couple. I travelled with Sylvie and Paul and a couple of days after the wedding we dragged ourselves away from Dirty Nellies and found ourselves at the cliffs of Moher, on Ireland's west coast. It was incredibly windy there and I witnessed an astonishing sight. I was in the car park when a car towing a caravan was passing by on the road, a gust of wind caught the caravan and tipped it over, in a matter of seconds the caravan disappeared into a million little pieces, it just instantly disintegrated. There were a few larger pieces which landed in a field, a herd of cows charged over to check it out, hoping for some titbits I guess. As I

M.E. - My Blessing in Disguise

walked around the cliffs in that wind I could feel very strong hands around my ankles, holding my feet to the ground, thankfully someone didn't want me to be blown away.

We had an afternoon and evening in Tipperary, I remember being somehow led around a few streets by spirit, but it never came to anything. The trip was over way too soon, so it was back to reality.

It could only have been a couple of weeks later that I was driving down to Wells and Glastonbury with my friend Barbara. We made it up to the top of the Tor, having got our breath back we held hands and closed our eyes to see if we could pick anything up. An eye kept coming and going, then a series of beautiful, blue/aqua, sparkling lights appeared, they formed a 'T' which then became some sort of symbol. It looked wonderful, so beautiful, then spirit came through and said 'we are home'. This symbol, which I couldn't make out at the time, appeared in Wells Cathedral, and also when I was driving us about, it was always beautiful and sparkling. I now know what I think the symbol was, this will come up much later in the book, I did show the symbol to several people, but no one could figure it out.

During this time I was still getting knocks and other noises at home, sometimes when sitting, sometimes in bed, or wherever. One morning I was sending distant healing when I heard wings fluttering, I went to the kitchen door where the noise seemed to come from, but there was nothing there. The 'hands on' distant healing was still happening most days.

Early November arrived and I was off on another trip, this time I went across the pond to the USA. Thanks to a contact I was upgraded from Gatwick, and had a relaxing time as we crossed the Atlantic, unfortunately I had to change planes in the States and the internal flight felt a bit like a cattle truck. I'd flown into Las Vegas, but I was only there for a couple of days, for me it was enough.

M.E. - My Blessing in Disguise

After a night or two I was shown a white card in bed, as I looked at it again it became a white bird and it flew, good to know that my protector is here. I drove to Flagstaff and got quite a shock as I had to climb over about three feet of snow to reach my room. The next day I went out and found a thick sweatshirt I don't know why I hadn't expected it to be that cold, it was November after all.

I visited the Grand Canyon and found a quiet point, 'Our Friend' came through, it's certainly a spectacular place to see. That night in bed I was woken when my brain appeared to be pressed down twice. Experiences kept coming, as I was eating dinner in a restaurant one night, I was surrounded by freezing energy. In bed another night someone spoke to me, 'Have you had a decent offer on the desk Brian', this still doesn't mean anything to me, unless it's a hint at all the writing I've had to do..

Most of the trip was spent in Arizona and Utah, I walked to the top of Volcano Lennox, I had to stop and take some really deep breaths at the top. Whilst I was up there, spirit came with some lovely energy, but it was also freezing around my hands. I closed my eyes and held a nearby tree, those beautiful blue/aqua sparkling lights came in and made what to me looked like a Scorpion shape, it made it a lovely experience.

I went to an old abandoned Native American village, 'Wupathi', 'Our Friend' was with me and came through, especially at a blowhole, the blowhole reacts to air pressure. I went inside an old Pueblo and 'Our Friend' became very excited as he talked, there were also white lights and flame coloured lights around me. One day I was driving and I had the face of a good looking brunette in the windscreen of the car, she was on the passenger side.

In my room that night I had a bright, golden light over me for a while, there were also some noises near the door. I was questioning in my mind what I was doing there, the golden light came back again and it felt lovely and comforting.

M.E. - My Blessing in Disguise

I stayed a few days in Sedona and had a good look around. I had my aura photographed, and the lady gave me her interpretation, this included 'whilst I have friends that I can talk to on spiritual matters, most cannot understand the depth that I was into'. She also said 'I have lots of regular travelling to do', how true that's become. 'The spiritual side has taken me over'. I should say that the photo was predominately blue.

I booked on a trip to see a Medicine Wheel and to experience a ceremony, Nancy was my driver. Sadly there are apparently very few Medicine Wheels left, most have been deliberately destroyed by people for whatever reason, so we had to make do with a makeshift one. Nancy started the ceremony, but she got a surprise as 'Our Friend' came through and joined in, he then took over. Was this the reason I felt I had to come to Sedona I wondered, if so it was for Our friend's benefit or mine? Perhaps both. I certainly found it interesting and enjoyed Nancy's company. I wanted to stay and have a chat with her, but by the time I got back to town I was absolutely freezing, so I had to get back to my hotel and layer up for warmth.

In bed one night I was shown a large, purple crystal, then some wonderful golden light sparkled and shone from it, just beautiful.

One day I found myself at another old Native American site, it was more or less situated in an almost circular cliff that the Indians had lived in. I wandered out at its floor level and found a small secluded stream, as turned a corner there was a lady giving a Tarot reading, sadly she wasn't looking for another client. It was certainly a beautiful setting for one, or for any kind of reading or healing come to that.

After I left Sedona I headed up into Utah, driving across the old movie set of 'Monument Valley', I wanted to see some of the national parks, Arches and the Petrified Wood, all the while 'Our friend took his opportunities to come through. Overall I really enjoyed the trip, it would have been better with company to share it with no doubt.

M.E. - My Blessing in Disguise

I had allowed enough time to get back from Utah to my last night's stop, I took the turn off I needed, but soon came across a sign which read that snow chains or snow tyres should be carried or fitted to any vehicle that wished to go further, it was a police sign. I hadn't realised that this short cut took me over some mountains, and obviously in November there was the possibility of snow. To change my route would add at least two to three hours to my journey, so I sent my thoughts up to spirit and decided to go for the mountain road. The road was clear of snow, lots piled up at the sides, but I made it over and thankfully never saw any of those Cherry Tops. On the flight back spirit gave me a lovely brain massage, I expect that they wanted to make sure that it was still there.

A few days after I returned home I was at Barbara's, helping out with some gardening, I suddenly felt someone put something in my pocket, Barbara was in her house at the time, I still haven't found out what it was.

At our next Wednesday circle I was shown a 1928 halfpenny landing on a pavement, no one could take it. Soon after the Wednesday circle split into two, we had received messages about a change coming, so there it was. Spirit spoke an intriguing message through me 'Is this the calm before the storm, or the calm after the storm, when the driftwood and the flotsam and jetsam are washed up on the beach, and the curious feeders come to eat'. I'd also received warning of this through my reading with Anne in May.

At our now smaller circle Annie had a link with my Uncle Fred, just a short message,' Uncle Fred does exist and is for real', I have no doubt about it. Several time I was given the name of Thomas, but it was spelt 'TOMAS', he said he was a psychic and medium from a long time ago.

I had a strange sensation whilst sitting at home, I felt strong pressure in my chest and it seemed as if my heart had grown larger. Then I heard a heartbeat that seemed to move about me, it lasted a while and eventually went between my ears.

M.E. - My Blessing in Disguise

Another day at home I felt I needed to light a candle, it's not something that I do too often, so I lit one, and something that resembling a spider's web covered in dew suddenly flew off of it, wow that was beautiful.

At the healing group it seemed as if the couch dropped down and moved, no one else noticed that. When I received healing that day, once I got on the couch I couldn't move at all until it was finished.

I gave Barbara some healing and felt what was now becoming a regular sensation of her body moving away from me. When I received from her I felt as if my body shrank leaving my spirit consciousness in the air. Whilst sending healing one day, I felt as if a cloak was draped across my shoulders, it was then fastened at the throat.

At home one evening, spirit spoke in a new and strange language, also in a high voice, this was repeated a few days later.
We get to the end of a busy year, spirit making their share of noises in the house, including the sound of an ice cream van. It was good to see my white bird in flight on a regular basis, it brings me peace of mind.

This is a drawing of the image I was shown at the top of Glastonbury Tor.

Inklings

The year of 2005 turned out to be a year with a lot less travelling than the previous one, probably not a bad thing as travelling can take its toll on you. I speak from experience as I've had to do far too much in the last few years.

My spiritual commitments carried on as before, then Barbara started a trance group at her house, so I joined that. Celia's temporary Friday circle evolved into an Earth Healing Group, and soon had quite a few attendees. The Pyramid of Light was now well established of course and I remained in the Wednesday circle. At home I was sitting regularly and sending healing, which usually included the distant hands on healing, so plenty of spiritual connections, but that's the way I like it.

I was still living in Upper Beeding, and in bed one night I felt a whirlwind around me and I could feel my hair blowing about, the bed seemed to rise up for a while, and the wind became stronger before subsiding. It was one of those amazing experiences, very similar to those that I'd had in my flat at Shoreham.

Another night I was woken by the sound of loud footsteps on the carpeted landing's floor. Then I heard very loud footsteps in the small bedroom, which was also carpeted. There followed the sound of a sash window being opened in the small bedroom, then there was a thud on the garden path below, as if someone had jumped down. I then heard the sound of hobnail boots running down the road, I did get up and have a look, but it was pitch black outside. The house has no sash windows at all, but the sound is well known to me, and of course there were no windows open. Nothing had been disturbed, well except my sleep, and no clues were left for me to try to figure out who my visitor might have been. Later in the night I woke and my body was rigid, I couldn't move a muscle. These experiences are often exciting and beautiful in their own way.

M.E. - My Blessing in Disguise

Quite often now I was taping my sittings, as before a lot of the voices were not in English, some were in languages that no one could fathom. Some voices had quite strong distortions that I could feel in my throat as spirit spoke, there were also a few robotic type voices.

On my American trip in 2004, I'd picked up some magazines, I was reading one when I came across a lady called Almine. She did a lot of channelling, some of it was in unusual languages. I managed to get some of my voice recordings onto a cassette, I sent it off with a covering letter. A few weeks later, out of the blue, Almine called me from Oregon. She said that the voices on the tapes were guardians who travel the universe, their messages are about Earth changes, she thinks that I'll come to understand them in time. Soon after our conversation the voices stopped coming through, still I'm grateful to Almine for taking the time to contact me directly.

One of the taped sittings produced a message which didn't mean much to me at the time, but it's meaning is now clear. It was a message about changes to come, 'In some I have no choice, it's out of my hands', that's proved to be prophetic. Another message was ' One way forward, no diversions, you cannot miss the path now, it is impossible to take a wrong turn'. Before those two messages, spirit came through with a message as I was sending healing, 'You have crossed the line, there is no going back, this is your destiny'. Shortly afterwards Annie gave me a message about how I was now crossing the Rubicon. I knew the meaning of that word as I'd recently heard it or seen it, and I looked it up. So it seemed that spirit had put a few things together, some confirming others, and from different sources. All very clever, all that was missing of course was an overall explanation of how it would affect me in the future.

Later in the year some more messages were put on tape for me, one talked about 'The opportune time for changes was approaching', 'The moment to stop the changes has gone, it cannot be stopped, just look forwards in a positive way', 'Voyages of discovery take knowledge to others, that's what they do, it's about returning home afterwards so everyone can know, spreading knowledge is generally the idea'.

A few days after that message came another, ' You begin some new work, there is a heavy workload, some time of course for rest, but you will be worked hard, much of the schedule you will be able to control, manipulate even, but certain things may happen at short notice and require immediate attention, so you will have to put up with that, we shall watch with interest'.

As I was taking notes from my diary in preparation for writing this book. I had to give immediate attention to a couple of small roof leaks, some synchronicity there.

Before we leave the subject of tapes there was a sentence one day that began in English, but finished in what I took to be German. Another tape that I played back a couple of weeks after the sitting, had a lady's voice on it. I'm sure that it wasn't there when I originally played back the tape. Lastly one tape had some unusual words on it, such as perpendicular. At the next circle someone was given perpendicular by spirit and gave it off. I think that spirit were proving to me that the speakers are genuine. I have questioned where all their conversations come from, as in is it my mind or elsewhere?

When sitting I was quite often taken into trance for a while, some of the sittings were two hours or longer. In one I sensed light and felt heat on me, as if I was sitting in sunshine. A little later I felt tremors in my feet, as if in an earthquake, the tremors spread throughout my body. I was briefly shown a Portuguese flag. I think that I was getting an inkling of what I was in store for me with regard to Portugal at that point. There had been a massive earthquake in Portugal that destroyed half of Lisbon a few hundred years ago. During another sitting the house was shaken, no earthquakes were reported, only I felt it it seems.

I drove to Avebury stone circle one day, my first visit, I've wanted to go back, but things keep getting in the way. Whilst walking around the

M.E. - My Blessing in Disguise

stones I put my hands on some, it seemed to me that some stones gave me energy whilst others took it from me.

I spotted three crop circles as I walked around I've loved their designs ever since I heard about them, there's something magical about even the simple ones, and of course some are so intricate and beautiful. I entered into one, it wasn't new and had obviously had lots of visitors. Whilst in the circle Spirit came through, I had a tingly, shivery feeling in my brain.

I think any who visit these circles must take care not to damage the crops, I've heard that some farmers trash them straight away, so as to stop people ruining their crops, we should surely be able to compromise on this, but people need to play their part. As I was driving around the area my car radio-cassette kept cutting out, there was nothing wrong with it.

The night before my birthday in July I went to bed and was shown a Good Luck message, it was signed by Elvis and other well known folk, how good of them. Then the fun started as I had someone blowing wet raspberries in my ear, ha-ha, yes of course it was the ear that was on the pillow. I had more raspberries the following night on my birthday, good job that they're amongst my favourite fruit. Incidentally I saw a Raspberry tart in the local Lidl today, a nice piece of synchronicity, I must buy one before they go.

Spirit were still walking around the house, I should have sold them tickets. Talking of which, on one of my tapes three clear, loud footsteps could be heard, the room I sat in was fully carpeted. At the house in Beeding there was decking outside the back garden's patio door, I decided to make up some pots with herbs and flowers, to brighten it up. On August 22nd I was about to go out into the back garden when I saw a Hummingbird Hawkmoth flying around my pots. I watched it for a while and couldn't but help remember when I last saw one in Italy in 1992, what a harbinger of change that one turned out to be, yes this one would prove to be the same. Until I saw it around my pots it I hadn't realised that we had them in the UK.

Within a week I received a letter from my landlords, they needed to move their family back in, so I had to begin searching for pastures new once more.

At circle one evening Annie gave me the name of ESNE or ESME, neither meant anything to me at all. That night in bed I was shown a ram's head on a man's body. It sounded Egyptian, but I had no real idea. Looking into the names that Annie gave me I found that ESNE is a town in Southern Egypt, it has a temple dedicated to the God of Life and Fertility. The name of the god is KHNUM and amazingly this is depicted as a Ram's head on a man's body, how about that, wow! Spirit certainly know how to keep me interested.

A couple of days later I looked up ESME on the net, I found an ESME in California, she is a sculptor and she contracted ME/CFS. She was almost in despair when a blue light appeared before her and began communicating with her, she was told to 'heal herself'. She subsequently achieved this and is now a healer herself, wow, that is a beautiful story.

One day whilst sitting I sensed someone in front of me, I could hear their energy. Hands were rested on my shoulders, and then ran down my arms and picked up my hands, it was so beautiful and their hands were warm, just such a wonderful feeling, I could wow a long time. My mouth was dry, but it suddenly became wet with something or other, our friend then backed away, these moments are so precious.

We had a mix of stuff at circle on September 21st, Annie was given Hermes, later Celia got a man with a goat's head, apparently this is Pan. It turns out that Pan is the son of Hermes. Pan will turn up in Portugal on a Fig tree. I and others were picking up things to do with the Battle of Britain, I felt as if I was wearing a jacket, Celia had it given that it was a flying jacket. There was of course HMS Hermes, it

M.E. - My Blessing in Disguise

was the world's first purpose built aircraft carrier, and was launched in September 1919.

October came around and I was soon moving to my next port of call, Manor Close in Henfield, a bungalow in a very nice village. Spirit of course moved with me and I soon had the regular happenings. I was soon finding doors open in the morning, doors that I know I'd closed the night before, luckily they left the front and back doors alone.

After I'd been there a couple of weeks or so I was woken by a loud thud in the spare bedroom, here we go again I thought. It sounded as if someone had jumped into the room, before I could get up I was flooded with spiritual energy, it was so beautiful and reassuring. I was soon raised off of my pillow and hugged, wow! I was then lifted by my legs and shoulders, lifted right off the bed so that I could be rocked like a baby. I don't know how to describe the feelings I was having, other than thinking that I'd been blessed again! What a night. On another night I woke up and felt I received real kisses and cuddles, am I crazy, no, I know it's no fantasy.

A week or two later I was woken by wooden knocks, as I opened my eyes I could see faces on the wardrobes, George Harrison was amongst them. Being in Henfield, I was thinking about the Trance evening that I went to a couple of years ago, where spirit played with my eyes. The next thing I knew was that they were doing it again, this time they moved my eyes independently, then came the zooming in and out, they know how to have fun.

One day at the Pyramid of Light we were giving our own Debi some healing, for some reason I felt that I needed to ask spirit to show me where Debi needed healing. I felt pressure on my right side and up by my chest, so I aimed to concentrate the healing there. Afterwards Debi told us that a cyclist had crashed into her and the pains were in the areas that spirit had impressed me with. Two days later in a taped sitting at home spirit said ' Never doubt your feelings, the impression from spirit will be correct'. Perhaps I should work that way more often,

M.E. - My Blessing in Disguise

although I trust spirit to send the healing to the area where it's needed the most.

When we began the Pyramid of Light I was mostly healing hands on, now it had changed to mostly hands off. Debi and Beverley thought that a Chinese guide was working with me, I think one of our clients saw him as well. I often get some strange sensations when healing with our group, such as feeling I was on a roundabout that was moving anti-clockwise, and I felt the floor tilt sideways for a long time. Another day I felt as if something had been attached to my shoulder blades, I asked spirit about this and was shown Angels wings, yea right! Another time I seemed to be holding an energy ball, then my hands felt as if they were joined together, I looked and found that my hands were at least 8 ins apart, the energy ball was raised and placed on my head.

One day whilst healing our Barbara, I was nearly taken off in trance, I couldn't hear the music or the birds singing outside, I seemed to drift up into a small corner of my mind. We had a young lady who came for help as she said that she was under psychic attack, this was new to me, I don't understand how anyone could be allowed to do this. As we gave her healing I saw a small black shape leave her body, then a white shape, like an upside down 'T' appeared near her head. I then experienced shaking from head to toe, it left through my feet. When I sat down I felt incredible aches in my legs for a while. This was my first experience of this type of healing, I can't fear these things, we channel healing to help others and are protected when we do so.

Roland came to us for help and I know his forearm was moved up and down, my hands were on him but it was spirit doing the manipulating. The next time he came his forearm received more manipulation, there was no effort from me at all, I know my healing guide showed himself to Roland. I do find myself put into different positions by spirit when healing, being crouched over was common for a while, also being very upright, I presume this reflects the guide's own posture.

M.E. - My Blessing in Disguise

At most of our sessions spirit would speak through me to open at the beginning of the healing group, it also became common for spirit to close through me. These words often had the ladies reaching for the tissues, I don't remember what was said.

Now for some other experiences whilst healing outside of the group. One day I had some incredibly strong energy through my hands and it seemed that there was a presence inside of me, it just felt wonderful. Another time I experienced heat through one hand and cold through the other. Whilst sending from home one day, I felt I went inside someone's body, then someone else's hands were joined to mine in there. Whilst sending hands on healing one time, my hands seemed to hold someone else's.

I was giving healing to Charlie at her mum's, as I got up from having my hands on her ankles, I was forcibly pushed back into my seat. A couple of times whilst giving healing I've heard the sound of wind and then something dragging across the carpet.

Here's a few more experiences whilst sending distant healing:

Feet as cold as ice. Palms cool yet fingers full of heat. I was impressed that I was holding a baby, it felt so beautiful and loving. I had a ticking noise in my throat for a while.

Near to closing one day, cold came up and filled my body, this was repeated the next day. Spirit said that the cold is both inside and outside of me, a new guide was working with me. This has become an occasional experience since then.

Another day I saw a ball of blue energy, next to it appeared a white wing, then another on the ball's other side, this made the image look like an amazingly, beautiful bird.

Our circle leader Celia, along with her husband Kelvin, had made a few trips to Spain, as they looked for a house, not finding what they wanted,

M.E. - My Blessing in Disguise

they had turned their attention to Portugal. After a chat it was decided that I would accompany them on their next trip in November 2005.

I guess I was curious, as in several past readings the subject of me living and working abroad had been given. I had no idea what was meant by this, it was usually Spain mentioned, but Portugal was next door. I also didn't know what exactly the mediums had seen, you could get very similar images for Spain, Portugal or Italy for instance.

In the run up to this trip I saw a white arrow pointing south- westish, so in the direction of Spain and Portugal, spirit also showed me ' STOOK' twice. I had to look it up, it's an old Scottish word meaning shock, mmm, that made me ponder a bit.

We arrived in Portugal on a sunny day and headed north towards Central Portugal. It was about 20c as we turned off the main road and made our way down a long track to find the cottage that we had rented. As we pulled up I was already thinking of getting changed into shorts and a t-shirt.

Having met the owner, we were shown inside the cottage, ow! What a shock, or should that be stook, it was freezing inside the cottage, 9-10c at most, and very unexpected. We were pleased to find that there was a wood burner in the lounge, that was going full tilt in the evenings and did a good job of warming the lounge. In bed that first night mum Eileen and gran Mary showed themselves to me, that was encouraging I thought. Incidentally I got into the habit of laying on my bed for about 10 minutes before getting into bed, that way the bed had warmed through a bit.

We were out most days, Celia and Kelvin had arranged meetings with agents, so they would drive us all around showing us whatever properties they had to offer. It didn't seem to matter what you wanted, although they did ask at the start, or what area you might think that you want to buy in, we were just zoomed about all over seeing a variety of properties, they showed you as many as possible in the time available, it's a tiring and quite confusing process.

M.E. - My Blessing in Disguise

We had one free day, I fancied a lie in, I expect the others did too. The sun was up, but I was snug in bed, then there was a tapping sound coming from outside the bedroom window. I reluctantly sat up and peered behind the curtain, half expecting to see Kelvin outside having a ciggy, he likes a joke. I saw nothing and so snuggled back under the sheets. It wasn't too long before that tapping sound was back, this time I caught sight of a Robin as it flew from one side of the window to the other, what a rascal. The Robin started making a fuss as if it wanted me out of bed and outside in the sun, oh dear, au revoir bedclothes.

One night whilst there I was shown a sword, it was beautiful like Excaliber. It was floating in the air, no one was holding it, yet it seemed perfectly balanced and was glowing bluish-white.

On the last day of our trip Celia and Kelvin settled on buying a small house that nestled into a hillside that was part of a bowl. It wasn't too far from the town of Lousa, and whilst not perfect, their need was pressing as they suddenly had a buyer for their house in the UK, so it was a base to start with.

In bed that night I saw a stunning crystal cross inside a crystal heart. As we drove to the airport a beautiful red sun was rising in the east, and a gorgeous full moon was descending in the west. On the plane I was shown a lovely hand which was palm up, it was either white or silver.

I'd been getting a lot of those tuning-fork noises during the year, and had been shown lots of pyramids, sometimes with a ball inside them. One night I was shown some pairs of hands linked together, they all had gloves on.

A couple of times after I returned to the bungalow from circle I heard voices as if from upstairs, there was no one there, it's not surprising as there was no upstairs. On one of those occasions the voices were foreign.

M.E. - My Blessing in Disguise

In December rainbows kept cropping up, and spirit spoke through me in circle to say that 'Rainbows are consensus for opposing elements', an interesting thought. A couple of nights later in bed I saw a huge Alien floating, there was also a rainbow in sections on the ground. That rainbow idea will crop up again later in the book. Following that, at our next Wednesday circle both Celia and Annie were shown rainbows, I hadn't said a word.

At our last circle before Christmas spirit spoke through me about change, and how we sometimes needed to work with all sorts of people to achieve it, even those we would normally avoid. Spirit used the image of the rainbow to illustrate beautifully what can be done if diverse elements co-operate. On Christmas Eve night I saw series of rainbows in parallel. On Christmas Night itself, I saw myself inside a house in Portugal, it wasn't a house I knew, I seemed to be deciding what I could do with it.

Another year passed by, some interesting aspects and some beautiful spiritual experiences for me. Hindsight tells me that subtle pressures were building up behind the scenes, all I knew was through the odd inkling.

M.E. - My Blessing in Disguise

Commuting Begins

Until 2006 began any flights I'd taken were for the purposes of holidays, well apart form the recent one with Celia and Kelvin, which I thought was about satisfying my curiosity. That was all about to change as I became a sort of commuter between the UK and Portugal.

New Year's Day was a Sunday, and I began it by sending healing, the energy was beautiful. Soon after finishing, a large, white light appeared and moved around the base of the Christmas tree, what a wonderful way to start the year.

At the first healing group of the year I was giving healing to Debi, I saw white light come out of my little fingers, my left elbow was also held, as if to guide my hand. Interesting happenings continued as a few days later whilst sitting, I was shown a large, white hand and wrist, it seemed to be a part of me. Spirit came through to tell me that it was time to begin new projects.

The next day I was driving when someone grabbed my left arm and held it for a while, there was no problem in controlling the car. I continued sitting at home, and managed to fit one in as I packed my things for a trip to Portugal the next day. This time the spirit voices that spoke were whispering to say ' Sit back and accept what is going to happen, don't be nervous, trust your guides, you will always be connected and protected ', so what does that all mean I wondered.

It was 19th of January and I was leaving the British winter behind for what I hoped would be a week of Portuguese sunshine. Celia and Kelvin had flown out to Portugal a couple of weeks earlier, complete with three black cats, who unfortunately had to travel in the hold, a nervous and fearful experience for all five of them. Kelvin was having to return to his work, so I was going out to offer support for the week, I would then travel back with Celia, as she still had the Healing Light shop to run in Shoreham.

M.E. - My Blessing in Disguise

Celia met me at Lisbon airport, she'd just seen Kelvin off on his return flight. We took a taxi across Lisbon to the Orient train station, then it was a train to Coimbra and finally another taxi to their house as there was no direct bus route from Coimbra.

The small stone house was cold with a damp feel, despite the fact that a fire was burning every night and a heater was on. It was basic and would take time to get it up to scratch, but it was a starting point. It was never going to be the height of luxury living, but Celia had been impressed that she needed to be in Portugal, albeit on a tight budget.

They had no transport at this point, so most mornings we had a very cold and frosty walk to the train station at Serpins, then the train to Lousa, so that Celia could buy some more things for the house.

After those cold and frosty starts, there were some hot and sunny afternoons, probably 20-22c, so it was shorts and t-shirts on the terrace, once the weeds had been cleared. Sitting on the terrace facing away from the road it was beautiful with tree covered hills curving round in an arc shape. We did have a couple of days with quite torrential rain, an idea of coming back was forming in my mind, but not until late May or June, when the cold and rain should be long gone. Despite those sunny afternoons the house remained cold until the fire got going in the evening, even then it didn't really warm through the rest of the house, as it was tucked away in the far corner of the kitchen, which was at one end of the house.

Celia hated the idea of getting on a plane and leaving her cats behind, fortunately she had found a couple who lived nearby who had said that they would feed them whilst she was away. Also on Celia's mind was the fact that the house would be very cold and damp by the time she came back again. This was the scenario for the rest of the winter and spring as Celia had worked out the idea of a roughly two week turnaround between being in UK and Portugal. These old stone houses in Portugal have very thick walls, say approx three feet thick, the idea

M.E. - My Blessing in Disguise

is to keep out the summer heat, not to let in winter sunshine to help make them warm.

On the flight out to Portugal I'd been shown lots of images, one had been a keyhole. On the flight back to UK, another keyhole was shown to me, it changed into an outline of Portugal, mmm.

Back in the UK I was straight into routine and went to Debi's circle. One of my hands became very heavy, I asked spirit why this should be, the response was ' Responsibility ', and spirit spoke to me about it the next day. The following night I woke and felt a strange, unusual energy, it seemed to be in my brain and every cell of my body. It was powerful and different to the energies that I was used to, I was also surrounded by purple and orangey-beige colours. I tried to push the energy away, but it was soon obvious that I had no control over it at all.

In bed a few nights later, it appeared as if a light was switched on above me, I then sensed that the room filled with love, I don't know how else to describe the wonderful feeling that surrounded me.

It was at some point around this time that I started looking at flights to Portugal, I was thinking about late May as the most likely time. It was just under two weeks since my return from Portugal and I was sitting at home when spirit came through. They stressed that it was very important for me to return to Portugal, I'd had other similar messages recently indicating that ' I would be educated'. The inference was that would happen in Portugal. A few days later I was sitting at Barbara's and spirit were speaking through me, suddenly a cryptic message was given 'Listen with your throat' , it was then repeated. I had no idea what this meant.

I found myself looking at flights on my computer quite a lot, as if subtle pressure was somehow being applied to me. I was doing it most days and it wasn't May any more, it was April, then March, finally I was searching in February as the pressure grew much stronger. I seemed to have no choice, it was like a compulsion so I had a chat with

M.E. - My Blessing in Disguise

Celia about it. Celia said that she would be delighted if I was to be at their house whilst she was in the UK, it would mean that the house would feel warmer and drier for her return, and the cats would have company too.

That was it then, I booked flight so that I was out there for the second half of February, immediately I'd booked, all the pressure that had built up around me vanished, as if it had never been. I couldn't remember experiencing anything like it before. There was no doubt to me that this was down to spirit intervention, some thing that I've come to call 'acceptance'. I was also getting more thoughts about writing this book, it was as if spirit were saying to me, why not put these recent experiences into your book, it's all good material.

I did actually start to write this book on that trip to Portugal, on February the 24th , it probably seemed opportune, something to do, as there was no tv or radio to turn on. It's now late September 2015, so you can tell that I didn't get very far. Writing has never been amongst my favourite occupations, so it wasn't too difficult to push it onto the back burner. It did cross my mind from time to time to do some more work on it, but it remained buried in a cupboard until spirit gave me a reminder at a demonstration in 2014, that will come later.

As I settled into my friends' house, I began sitting and sending healing, spirit were with me immediately, and sometimes a cat or two on my lap as well. It was a strange feeling being in Portugal on my own, this wasn't the Algarve, there was no guarantee of finding someone who spoke English, it was quite isolating really. I was pleased that Celia was there when I had my first visit, at least some things were familiar.

When the afternoons were sunny, I took advantage and sat out on the terrace, it was a real suntrap. I often closed my eyes whilst there, spirit treated me to some beautiful displays of lights and colours, also shapes such as amazing rotating pyramids. It was so much better than reading, and the nature all around was such a distraction. Their house did sit by

M.E. - My Blessing in Disguise

the road, it was a country road, but it had lovely views all around, and a small river just up the road.

One evening I decided to go into the nearby town of Lousa to eat, Celia had acquired an old van by now, so I drove into the town centre and parked just before the square where the pizza place was. I could have cut across the middle of the square, but for some reason I opted to walk around the side. I'd been in the square quite a few times as it had Celia's favourite Chinese shop in one corner, and a good restaurant near to it that I'd eaten in, I felt as if I was on familiar ground.

The corner of the square with the Chinese shop was in darkness, the street lights were out. I continued to walk through the corner, it was surprisingly dark considering there were lights on all around the rest of the square, but I've never felt threatened in Lousa. Then suddenly hey! I'd tripped over something and was flying through the air and dreading the inevitable crash to the ground. Somehow all that hit the ground was one of my feet, however my momentum was causing me to spin around, pirouetting like a ballerina. I must have completed three or four turns before I stopped and could gratefully put my other foot on the paving. I couldn't have spun around like that if I'd tried.

My pirouetting had been accompanied by some raucous laughter as two or three girls had been standing in a nearby shop doorway and had seen it all. They were doubled up, as I'm sure I would have been had our roles been reversed, it must have looked hilarious to see.

Whew! embarrassed but in one piece, saved from what should have been a nasty fall, I moved on very quickly to the pizza place. I found out later what had happened, there is a small wall that comes out between two shops and I'd tripped over it. This wall is lower on the furthest side, so there's more of a drop, in a way that may have saved me as it gave spirit more time to get a leg down. Yes I've no doubt that it was spirit who saved me from a lot of pain, and no harm done.

M.E. - My Blessing in Disguise

After eating I went back to the van via the middle of the square, jumped in and started on what is about a ten minute drive. Out of Lousa and on through a village as normal, then the van seemed to speed up of its own accord. I took my foot off of the accelerator but nothing changed, I stamped on the pedal a couple of times and changed gear, but the speeding continued. Now we we getting into a section of the road with quite a few bends, one or two are sharpish. The van was holding the road well so I began to think the Spirit was in control, but as we approached a sharp bend without slowing at all, I grabbed the wheel tightly and aimed to get us round this bend. Two wheels were suddenly in the dirt so I relaxed my grip on the wheel, the van was immediately back on line, I then relaxed and let spirit get on with it. A little further up the road I had control back, spirit had had their fun, I carried on back to the house, where I could reflect on an interesting evening.

What was it about? Were spirit trying to prove to me that they can protect me in a variety of situations, or did they just want to amaze me. I was certainly that, it was an evening that I'll never forget.

A few days later I was back in the UK, sitting and healing as before, but my commuting continued as I made several trips back to the 'Casa Do Anjo', Celia and Kelvin's house, the next being in March when Celia was back in the UK again. Whilst out there on another trip, I decided late one evening, on the spur of the moment, to go out and look at the stars. Immediately I stepped outside I could see this bright, white light coming across the sky towards me. It was fairly large and it had a wobble as it traveled right over the house. It was so bright and rapid, I soon realised that I'd seen the Space Station for the first time. What timing, a couple of minutes either way and I'd have missed it, talk about thank your lucky stars.

Late May found me in Portugal for another two weeks, I was beginning to wonder if I should start looking at properties there. It wasn't that I was sold on Portugal totally, but the subject of me living and working abroad had cropped up in many readings, and spirit did seem to want to

M.E. - My Blessing in Disguise

push me in this direction, but what would I do there. It's one thing to house sit as I was, but living full time was altogether a different thing.

I did get in touch with an agent at some point and arranged to view some properties. The agent's properties were mainly south of my friend's house and over some mountains, so not that close. On the way down there I spoke to my guides and said that if we viewed anything suitable could they give me a sign, though as I've said I wasn't convinced about moving to Portugal. The only sign that day was a negative one, I got a peculiar feeling as we drove up a valley to see a property. It was obvious that the valley had been burned the year before, and the land and house was all mixed up with the land and house next door,.that is not that unusual in Portugal. There was one property that I liked the look of and it's situation was OK too, the agent couldn't get hold of a key so I couldn't see inside it, so that was the end of that.

Back at my friend's house and unwinding with a glass or two of wine, it was a lovely evening and some Fireflies came out to add to it all. In bed that night I was shown two lights, why not it's Gemini time after all. The lights were angled north east, was this a hint, when I eventually did buy my house it was roughly north east of my friend house.

A couple of days later I was sitting outside with my eyes closed, I was shown 'East, South, West, NO NORTH', OK then I thought, we'll have no more trips south of here. Shortly before I was due to return to the UK I was relaxing outside again and intending to read, but the distractions of nature got me again. Suddenly a bat was flying about in broad daylight, that's one for the Attenborough chap I thought, then a large moth that looked a bit like a bee appeared, no I hadn't had that much to drink. In the evening it was another night for the Fireflies, one landed on me.

Just before I came on this trip, and during it, I kept getting thoughts on forgiveness, and also on how I must become more non-judgemental and non-prejudicial if I'm to keep moving forwards spiritually. These are difficult things to achieve and will no doubt take a lot of working on, I don't know why these thoughts have come, but it isn't a bad thing to aim for.

I was sitting sending healing on the day before I was due to fly back to the UK, then my left hand felt as if it was inside someone. Another day I had energy flowing back and forth between my palms, then I felt weight on my hands, and the energy seemed to become liquid, I can't explain it any differently.

Back in the Uk and driving one day, Our Friend came through. The next day I was at Shoreham beach and he came through again, first in his own language, then in English, he told me that he enjoys being by the water with me, this wasn't news to me.

The healing sessions kept changing, one day I felt as if I was behind someone pressing against them, the somehow my body was inside theirs! that's a new one. Another day my fingers became rigid and cool, energy then vibrated through my arms and hands, they didn't shake, the energy was vibrating inside them.

At our healing group one of my hands twisted over, so that the back of my hand rested on the client, it's happened a few times since. I think the first time that this happened was with a lady who had breast cancer, I felt very nervous about it, but spirit neatly sorted it out by turning my hand over. I'm sure that with that lady I didn't know which breast was affected, but spirit did and my hands went to the correct one.

Whilst sitting with Debi one day she received a string of numbers that she thought were for both of us, it started with a 7, so it's most likely someone's mobile number. I haven't included it here, if someone is meant to be in touch they'll find a way.

In July spirit impressed me with ' It's not the bad things that you consume, it's the good things that you do that matter '. A week or so later I was again impressed by spirit, ' If you know of someone who is

M.E. - My Blessing in Disguise

abusing their position by misleading others, don't try to show them up or put them down, strengthen your own views and position, that way others will take notice and may change their opinions without any animosity. Don't put down the beliefs of others, raise your own to a higher level'.

One day I was outside watching the acrobatics of some Swallows, white lights and little flame lights were with them. It had been a quietish periods for noises, but one night I was woken by a thud as something hit the bedroom floor, there was nothing to be seen.

In mid July I had another trip to Portugal, I'd had a break as someone else covered for Celia. Whilst out there I looked at some more properties, but there was nothing of interest. I did briefly see a Hummingbird Hawkmoth, no changes this time that I can think of, I have now seen a lot of them here at my own property.

Back in the UK I saw a few shooting stars one evening, lovely to see. There was a day when I was coughing a lot, so it was wonderful to see lots of little gold and black lights coming around me. On the subject of lights, I was sitting in the back garden at Henfield with my eyes closed and I was thinking about healing animals, my eyes opened to see lots of whitish-gold lights dancing around me, beautiful.

Here's a few healing happenings:- At the group one day I had tingles in my hands, they travelled right up my arms, I then felt vibrations throughout the healing of that lady, and for some reason my hands felt as if they were touching her hair, but of course they weren't. At another group session I was feeling very graceful some of the time, what me, ha-ha, before closing a female guide showed her smiling face to me and made me feel floaty, she was a ballerina. At our next meet she was with me again, she returned on a few other occasions. I did wonder if this was the guide who had got me pirouetting in Portugal. Whilst giving healing to a lady one day, my hands felt as if they disappeared for several seconds, later I felt as if I was on a boat that was rocking.

M.E. - My Blessing in Disguise

I continued to send distant healing most days, one day spirit came through and told me to 'raise my belief and trust even higher'. Another day whilst sending, I experienced very strong connections to my head and to the top of my spine, I couldn't recall feeling that before.

A friend of mine asked me to go and talk to someone who was puzzling about spirit in some way, it's not my normal thing to do. However I went and had a chat, whilst I was there I felt lots of healing going through my hands, even though we were just talking.

In September I travelled out to Portugal again. My first evening there was fun as the Space Station came over again, brilliant! Then I saw two satellites moving in parallel, and a single one on the same trajectory. I watched as a near full moon rose through the trees, that was beautiful, and then I spotted a Praying Mantis climbing up the leg of my chair, they are fascinating creatures.

In bed one morning, I was wondering what the time might be, I was shown '7.05', I opened my eyes to check the clock, the time was spot on. Strangely in bed today I was shown '7.25', I looked at the clock and it was 7.25, so a bit of synchronicity again, as I didn't know that I'd be writing this.

I was at some friends' house near the town of Tabua, their youngest daughter Angela has Cerebral Palsy. I was giving her healing and my hands were on her head, I could feel lots going on in her brain. I think that she'll be very bright, if only her communications could be sorted out. Afterwards I went outside and sat with my eyes closed, a glowing, white angel came to me, so beautiful. Sitting later I was shown lots of faces, some of them had things going in and out of their eyes.

Back in the UK and at circle, Annie had a link with my old friend Bazza, he's become very interested in circles and trance, good to know. At home I was on my pc looking at sites that showed properties for sale in Portugal, suddenly my hair stood on end. It was becoming the norm for me to search through these sites before going to Portugal; if I saw a

M.E. - My Blessing in Disguise

property that looked interesting I would contact the agent to arrange a viewing. It often turned out that properties were nothing like the description that was given.

I was still getting lots of those tuning-fork noises in my ears and clicks in my throat, how weird, plenty of noises around the bungalow as well, sometimes very frequent. Perhaps the most interesting were the hands I kept seeing, usually white, most often in pairs.

My lease for the bungalow at Henfield was coming up for renewal, I had to think about it as I was making so many trips. Henfield is a nice village, some decent pubs, lots of little shops, its main problem for me was that it had no train station , and after about 7pm there were no buses either. I was over visiting at Sylvie and Paul's, they had no lodger at present, so somehow it worked out that I would move in with them. There was one condition from Paul, I had to look after the garden, that was fine with me. I had to put most of my stuff into storage, so I found a man with a van to help me with that, and at the end of October I was back in Carden Hill.

At circle one evening I had what I can only describe as a very special energy enter the back of my head, it was so strong and tingly. It came back to me the following night in bed, I loved it and it spread all down my spine, it just felt so special.

At one Wednesday circle there was a link for me with a WW1 soldier, the link came through both Celia and Annie, I took some of it at the time, but had to ask Paul and Sylvie for confirmation. The soldier was wounded and sent back to UK to recover, then Lawrence of Arabia was mentioned, then some one who looked like Hitler. A strange mix, I was right about thinking that Paul's Dad Charlie was wounded, it turns out that at the rehab place he met Lawrence of Arabia, only in passing. The Hitler thing, that was down to Charlie too, apparently he had a Hitler type of moustache for a while, they had a photo of him with it.

M.E. - My Blessing in Disguise

I arranged a three week trip to Portugal in November, Celia was in Portugal for some of this time and had started a development group at Steve and Caryn's, they were Angela's parents. I went up there with her and joined in. In the near future Celia started a healing group there as well. I was shown lots of numbers on this trip, 33 was prominent amongst them, there were also letters and symbols. I've tried looking up some of the symbols that I've been shown, but I very rarely find anything of interest.

One evening Celia and I were in a kitchen, the front door is situated there. We both heard a 'rat-a tat-tat' knock on the door, I quickly opened it, no one was there! It wasn't uncommon to hear unexplained noises around their house. One morning Celia said to me that she had heard voices in my room in the night, I had no idea, so I must have had some visitors I guess. I've heard that story from other friends when I've stayed with them too.

Back in circle in the UK again, Annie had a link for me and Jerusalem was mentioned, I'd been browsing around a bookshop in Worthing earlier in the day, in one of the books I'd picked up and looked at were the words to the hymn 'Jerusalem'.

At our last circle before Christmas Annie had a link with my dad, he told me not to fret, I had to try to be buoyant and positive, someone wanted me to eat more rice pudding, that's no hardship.

On Christmas Day I felt something go into my right ear, it somehow connected to something in the area where the base of the brain meets the top of the spine. Then something went into my left ear and did the same thing, I'm sure it was a lovely Christmas present ho-ho.

A couple of nights later in bed, a bright, white angel flew around the bedroom and landed on my chest, it changed into a baby and I kissed its forehead, it felt real against my lips. What a lovely way to end another interesting year.

More Acceptance

Early in the year of 2007 I was sitting in circle at the Healing Light in Shoreham, spirit spoke through me about the need to be honest and truthful about being involved in spiritual work and what it's all about. One of the sitters, Kevin, was very interested as he'd been reading some books on the subject. Kevin and Don, another sitter, both said that when the guide spoke the darkness changed colour, for Don it was blue, for Kevin it was different colours. At some point during the evening, I felt as if I'd walked halfway around the table that sits in the centre of the circle, turning circles as I went.

Soon after circle I was heading out to Portugal again, I drove up to my sons in Crawley the night before to stay overnight. On the way I was thinking about protection, then a huge, white, celestial figure appeared in front of me, my questions had been answered.
On the flight out I saw a huge, circular rainbow outside the plane. I've seen several of them now, most have been small and sit near the wings, but this rainbow was so big, it was as if the plane travelled inside it, and it stayed with us for most of the journey.

One evening in Portugal I was asked if I wanted to go for a get together with some friends at a bar, a lift was being offered so I went for it. After being introduced to a few people, I found myself talking with a couple, they wanted to know what I did. Bearing in mind what spirit had told me at circle, I told them that I was a healer and hoped to be helping people in Portugal through healing as much as possible. It turned out that the male of the couple had bad knees and other health issues, I also mentioned about Celia and the fact that she was also a healer. After a while it was arranged for Celia and I to go to their house and to give Ken some healing. We went there several times and were joined by Kelvin when he was in Portugal, he was also a healer.

I did quite a few trips that year and saw quite a lot of properties, I did put in offers on a couple, but after initial acceptance, they fell through

M.E. - My Blessing in Disguise

for whatever reason. I was still not totally comfortable with the idea of moving to Portugal though, but again apart from the language issue, I couldn't put a finger on why. With hindsight it was undoubtedly about giving up things like the Pyramid of Light healing group, and the generally easy access to spiritual activities, I'd seen no real signs of spiritual activity outside of what Celia had organised. This is no disrespect to family and friends, who I miss, I would keep in touch with them, but the spiritual side had become so strong, so important, it had taken over a huge part of my life, I didn't want to leave it behind and yet I was feeling as if spirit were coercing me into this change, and I had no idea why.

What I also didn't know at this point was that I'd forgotten something that the property was meant to have, something that had been mentioned to me in readings. I had in my mind the idea of finding somewhere which had a kitchen and bathroom that was ready to use, common sense you might say, but some people's idea of a kitchen was an empty room with a tap.

I was given my reminder about what was missing from my search when I went to a psychic fair in Hove in the early summer. Annie was working there and I had a chat with her until some customers came along, she had pointed out to me someone I didn't know, but had heard about. So with Annie working, I went over to see this chap Adrian for a reading, he was a medium I'd never seen work before. Adrian was an amiable chap and he was soon shuffling a Tarot deck. He worked by going through the whole deck one card at a time, giving me a little message with each card. At some point moving was mentioned, along with my search, and he said that I had forgotten something very important. This was about there needing to be water on or near the property, this was certainly not in the criteria of what I'd wanted up to that point, but it did help to explain why my offers had come to nowt.

Adrian went on to mention about the fact that I was being pushed into this by spirit, I asked what would happen if I refused, apparently I would be pushed much harder, I had to accept that spirit needed me to

M.E. - My Blessing in Disguise

be somewhere, I had no choice in the matter. He told me that there was this huge, brown horse who walked with me that was doing the pushing, the horse could push so much harder if it had to, but he was also there for me to lean on when necessary.

There it was then, whatever I felt I was being told in no uncertain terms that I had to go to Portugal, but I didn't know why. The suspected coercion I was feeling was really compulsion. Many involved in spiritual work will raise their hands in horror and cry that we all have free will and can therefore refuse to do something. I now know more about the Law of Acceptance, this is something I believe that we sign up to before we incarnate, once we agree we have to stick by it. I don't know if this happens in every incarnation, perhaps not, but if you have specific tasks to achieve then you probably have to sign on the dotted line. I look at it this way, free will relates to earthly things, acceptance to spiritual tasks.

I was soon back in Portugal and this time looking at properties with a new criteria in mind. After contacting some agents I saw some which said that they had streams or rivers on the land, but in summer they had dried up, so I couldn't see how spirit would be happy with them. Strangely I received an e-mail from someone who I hadn't contacted, they sent me some property details, I arranged to see some that mentioned rivers and streams. At circle one day, I received a message through Lin, 'I will find what I need, but not necessarily what I want', mmm.

In the run up to my finding the property I was to buy, I began seeing a large, white, celestial being, I think this went on until I found it. Just before the first viewing I was sitting on the terrace at my friend's house when I heard wings beating, I was impressed that this was from the celestial being.

It was now the beginning of August, very hot, so I wasn't really looking forward to driving anywhere, but I went off with my new perspective. The other strange thing was that these properties were in

M.E. - My Blessing in Disguise

an area that I hadn't wanted to look in, had actually avoided for reasons unknown. I met the chap in the town of Arganil, parked up and he drove me around. One of these properties had a very peculiar set up, one large room on its own with just one door, but outside steps so that you could use the flat roof. Close by was a mostly outside kitchen, it may have had a small bathroom, then the largest building, which was again not linked to anything, and looked to me like some kind of miking shed that was full of cobwebs, though I'm no expert in those matters. It had land which was mostly on the other side of a quiet road, it was very long but not too wide, and it stretched down to the river. It would take a lot of imagination, patience and money to turn this into some sort of home, some new buildings would certainly be needed, it was either that or knock the whole lot down and start from scratch.

We moved on to the last one to view, it was just two kilometres from the centre of Arganil. We turned off the road into an untidy area, then down a short steep track, a bit like a little black run I thought, then parked on a grassy area at the bottom of the track. Though it was baking hot I decided to walk across the overgrown field to view the river that was at the end. Wow, what a river, it was the Alva and it was big and looked beautiful, with lots of trees on the far bank and mountains off in the distance in one direction. It felt wonderful standing there on the bank above it. Yes I've stood on river banks in the UK, but this was in an entirely different context.

A little reluctantly I left the river and walked back across the field, wading through the long grass and weeds, but I had to see inside the house. The kitchen and bathroom were usable, all there in other words, a bit dated, but with cupboards and sinks in the kitchen, a shower, basin and loo in the bathroom. A promising start, this part of the house was an extension so now I went into the original building, the old stone part of the house. It was in a bit of a state, the floors and wall plaster looked to be in quite a bad way. However, before I knew it there was some strong and beautiful energy filling my head and making me feel as if I was floating across the floor, detaching me from all the negative side of the house. It was as if spirit were saying that it's all cosmetic and easily

M.E. - My Blessing in Disguise

sorted, it doesn't matter you just fix it. The roof space was also in need of a new floor, it was very patchwork at best. The room down the other end of the house had a little balcony, there's a lot of these in Portugal, they are tiny. The roof to that room had lots of gaps in the tiles, I think some Redstarts had taken up residence in there. That energy was still with me and if anything had got stronger, so I'm surprised that I'd noticed as much as I had, so I left there with something to think about, and the energy was still with me.

I was a bit confused for the rest of the day as I mulled over what I'd seen, the only one with any chance was the last one I'd seen. However, it was a bit of a mess, but the energy that poured into me when I was in the old part of that house was something else, surely that was a positive sign from spirit. I decided I'd have another look at in in a few days time, that would be the best plan, so that's what I did. The energy came in strong again as I entered the old part of the house and it transported me around as if my feet weren't touching the floor. All the problems were in front of me but the energy in my head seemed to make them dissipate. The river still looked wonderful.

When I was back at my friend's house I went onto the pc to see if any more properties had been mailed to me. A Portuguese family, who had taken me out before on my search, sent me some properties to peruse, strangely amongst them was this house that I'd now seen twice. It felt as if spirit were ganging up on me a bit. Celia and Kelvin were in the UK, so I called up some other people I knew, to see if I could get someone to come and view the house with me, I wanted a second opinion, but no one was available.

That evening I heard the sound of a bicycle being wheeled around in the kitchen, that 'spokey' noise. Was this spirit telling me to get on with it, as in it's time to get on your bike. I sat and had a hard think, listing all the negatives, the untidy and steep access, the state of the old part of the house, the fact that I didn't really want to live in this area at all. Yet weighed against all that was the river, apparently a must, and that incredible energy that spirit had brought in to me. I shouldn't forget the fact that now the Portuguese family also wanted to show me the property, as if spirit were giving me another push. I felt as if I'd been backed into a corner, that word acceptance was looming large once again. I'd had messages in different guises that had told me that some things I could change, other things I just had to accept, I had no choice, it seemed as if this was the crunch.

I went to see the house for a third time, I'd decided that if the energy hit me again there was no choice, I would have to put in an offer. The energy was at least as strong, it could have been stronger, I left there having put in an offer. Within a few days I'd signed a promissory contract and paid a deposit, the process was in motion. I sat after making my decision but spirit didn't come through at all, I expect that they were satisfied that things were going to plan.

I was soon on my way back to the UK, I had to make arrangements to send the balance out to Portugal, at some point I was advised of the date for completion, which was September 10th. I hadn't expected things to move so fast, several people that I knew had said that their buying processes took a long time, and it was now August, when everything shut down. It seems that someone up there was pulling strings in order to get this through.

So the whole process was completed in a little over 5 weeks, and on the day of purchase I went to view what was now my property. It was disappointing to find that there was still some cats and a dog there, and quite a lot of other stuff. I contacted the solicitor and it was gone within a couple of days.

A few other things had gone too, the boiler, the shower screen, the old cooker and other bits and pieces. I didn't realise that this sort of thing is apparently common practice in Portugal, I know now. I wasn't going to move in straight away, but it was an unsettling start.

I was back in the UK for a while, and thankfully still welcome at the Pyramid of Light and at a couple of circles. Annie gave me some

M.E. - My Blessing in Disguise

names one evening and then a bluebottle, well there had been a fly buzzing around me earlier in the day when I was in the garden. During another circle, a WW1 soldier who was suffering from shell shock entered my body. I was impressed with an explosion and how he became totally spaced out afterwards. He wasn't aware at the time what had happened to him, he was given no sympathy at all. He said that 'no one should rush to judgement of others'. I was then impressed with 'there are none so blind as those who cannot see'. Annie had a link with my dad that night, after some evidence the message was 'failure is not an option', I wasn't sure in what context I was meant to take this.

On one trip to the UK I went up to London to meet up with several old friends at our old haunt the Rose and Crown, near to Blackfriars Bridge. It was a good evening, I think I left the pub about 9:30, having had a good watering. I walked back down through the back streets to the side entrance of Waterloo Station. I turned a corner to then cross the road to go into the station, but the police had cordoned it off, apparently someone was up on the railway bridge that crossed the road, and was threatening to jump. I made my way around to the main station entrance and duly got on a train to Clapham Junction. My Brighton bound train came in and was crowded, I found a seat at a corner of one of those tables. The guy on my left was reading, the one in front of me had headphones on, the chap diagonally opposite me was slumped down and looked as if he had the world on his shoulders, his eyes were fixed down, staring at the table.

Then spirit began what was a totally unique experience for me, it hadn't happened before and hasn't happened since. They began speaking to the chap who was down, the voice that came through was loud and very clear, I think everyone in the carriage must have heard what was said. Spirit told this chap that they knew what he'd been going through, how tough life had been for him, they then began to tell him that he was going to get out of this situation, he was going to get better and recover completely, not only that, but he would be helping others in the same situation once he was fully recovered. Spirit must have spoken for about five minutes, they ended just as we approached East Croydon,

M.E. - My Blessing in Disguise

where the chap got off. Whilst they were speaking to him, he slowly came up from his slumped position, then sitting upright, and finally looking full of self belief whilst wearing a beaming smile. He walked tall, getting off the train as a new man, no doubt about it.

This was an astonishing experience for me, I could never have done that, never spoken so loudly and so positively in front of a carriage full of strangers. To think they used me when I'd had a bellyful of beer too, it's incredible, that chap needed help and spirit were determined he would get it. Lots of people got off at that stop, the guy sitting on my left looked at me after, I just shrugged my shoulders and said 'It's nothing to do with me, I don't know where that came from', then I walked down the other end of the carriage and sat down to reflect. Was that could-be-jumper situation setting me up for this, perhaps our chap was contemplating the same idea, he surely was a long way down, but what a transformation in him, I don't think that spirit paused to let me draw breath, they just spoke non-stop, convincing him that his life was going to be worthwhile, well done to them.

At some point Debi asked me to go along to her development circle to see if spirit would do a question and answer session. I was nervous, but it went well, having her lovely energy around helped me through it. During the circle I saw lots of faces appearing on Debi's face, several had facial disfigurements, there was also one face that was Jesus like, and I heard him say 'love'. We did two of these sessions about a week apart, one guide said to me 'Keep on to the end of your pathway, follow your heart'. Towards the end of one of these sessions I heard the sound of something dragging across the carpet going away from us.

It was in between these sessions that I received the sad news that my friend Murrey had been diagnosed with Motor Neurone Disease, a dreadful condition with which the body slowly loses control of its muscles, and therefore movements. I sent healing for him and Pauline and felt cold throughout, though it was August.

M.E. - My Blessing in Disguise

I did my best to keep in touch with spirit despite all the travelling, here's a few examples of our connections:- I was shown a map of Continental Europe, it scrolled across from east to west and a large, white, semi-circular wall appeared on S.W. Brittany.

I was impressed with ' A wise man is calm and reasoned with other people's problems, and also with his own'. I was thinking about my friend Sheila when I saw a white telephone, it must be time for a chat then. I was shown some different images which indicated that I must keep my connections going with those in the UK. Some of the images included lights and lines that were pointing roughly north east, which is approximately where the UK is in relation to Portugal.

I was shown a compass pointing N.E., and a line of gold lights pointing in the same direction. I also saw a white bird in flight flying in that direction, as it did I somehow seemed to hear the door of my heart being opened. The message was very clear, some white chevrons and white arrows drove the point home.
 I went to Shoreham Beach for a walk along the shingle, it was empty as usual, twice a guide named White Owl came through to speak.

I was hearing lots of sounds in Portugal, near the front door and in the lounge, voices and coughs were common, but there was never anyone there. One evening in the lounge it sounded as if something had fallen onto the floor and rolled across it. The noise woke up White Tip, one the cats, he looked surprised as he stared across the room in the direction of the sound, I could see nothing. I was often being woken by knocks and bangs, and I was continuing to see white keys and locks. I was walking around Lousa one day when a beautiful, large, white, sparkly light appeared in front of me. At this time I was reading a book about Leonardo da Vinci, the pages often got colours on them.

I had taped some sittings during the year, a message was repeated four times on one tape, it wasn't in English, but I seemed to be impressed with the meaning, 'I have been waiting'. This was repeated at the next day's sitting too. The following day I was reading a mail from Debi, as

M.E. - My Blessing in Disguise

I did someone pressed into my back and hugged me. It happened again the next day and filled my back with wonderful tingles, wow!

One day I saw a scene in which an old friend appeared, Chris, he will get some more mentions later in the book. I heard Chris say 'Oh but he is the one, he's going to deliver our message'.

At the Pyramid of Light one day, I felt the ballerina was with me again, for a short time my hands parted, as if playing piano. That day one of the clients thought that I'd moved closer to her, another thought that the couch had moved two to three feet across the room.
Whilst sending distant healing one day, I was twice shown a face that had ectoplasm coming from its nose and mouth.

M.E. - My Blessing in Disguise

Big Moves

During January 2008 I was making preparations to move my stuff to Portugal, I still wasn't sure about this, it almost didn't seem real. Leaving family, friends and all the spiritual connections certainly didn't feel right at all, talk about having mixed feelings. Yet I'd had so many messages from spirit telling me that this was something that I had to do, but no explanation as to why, other than I had to accept some things, it appeared that this was one of them. I'd come out to Portugal originally to support Celia and Kelvin, this was something else entirely.

I made the most of my spiritual activities in January, as best I could, I wasn't sure when I'd work with the healing group again, or sit in the circles, speaking of which, I was given a message from Charlie, Paul's dad, 'The dark days are over', I had no idea what it meant.

Towards the middle of January I squeezed in a few days in Ireland to see Murrey and Pauline. I gave Murrey some healing on most days, in the hope of stemming the tide of his 'Motor Neurone Disease'. The only noticeable change was that he had feeling return to his lips. His condition was quite advanced, he was getting trouble with his walking and his hands and arms were just starting to be difficult to control. They treated me wonderfully and we went out and about a few times, Murrey had always been one to make the most of things, he didn't want to stop now.

I remember that we went to Galway one Sunday lunchtime, there was a band playing in the pub, after every couple of songs they'd stop and pass the hat around. Then they'd get a round of drinks in and sup for a while, play a bit more music and so on, all good fun though, it got me wondering if the Corrs or U2 got started this way.
It was good to see them both, but sad to see Murrey's plight, he's always been a fit guy and liked to live life to the full, he was very competitive, how he would cope with what was to come I don't know. I left them with mixed feelings and wished the best for the pair of them.

M.E. - My Blessing in Disguise

It would be a trial for Pauline as well as Murrey, this horrendous condition doesn't relent. I continued to send healing for them both, Murrey moved onto a better place in 2010, Pauline continued caring for him until his passing.

Back in the UK spirit gave me the name of Williams, he'll keep cropping up from time to time, he also passed with an unusual condition. On the 31st January I was off to Portugal, initially staying at Celia and Kelvin's house, before moving to my own a week later. My furniture was still en route, but I had a fold-up bed, a chair, kettle, corkscrew, fridge and cooker, so I could get by.

I felt desperately lonely for some time, no one spoke English around here. This is the middle of Portugal, the Algarve is about six hours drive away. It took some time to settle in, I began painting some of the rooms as they were all white, not my colour at all. I soon had a red room and a yellow one, that really helped a lot. I'd spent lots of time on my own at my friend's house, but it was different now, being alone here felt horrible.

Spirit on the other hand, made themselves at home here in no time at all, they came through after a couple of days when I was sending healing. A couple of days later I was chatting on the phone with Sheila and something was placed on my head, normal service was being resumed. Incidentally, as I was sending healing to Murrey and Pauline my chair was tipped a long way forwards.

My furniture had arrived 7-10 days after me, there was no way that the lorry and trailer could get down the track, so my estate car was used a lot to bring boxes and the smaller pieces of furniture down to the house, it sure saved a lot of walking and a lot of time.

Now in my own bed I was seeing lots of images, including a group of celestial beings which circled overhead. One night I was shown several aircraft, one was huge and had many engines and wings that curved forwards.

M.E. - My Blessing in Disguise

Early sittings here were leaving me woozy and shattered, so I guess some intense work was being done by spirit. One night whilst watching tv, something flew past me and into the hall, it was golden, beautiful and seemed to have filigree wings. A few days later I saw the image of Kirsty McColl. As the year went on these beautiful beings, or whatever they may be, have flown past me several times, either gold or silver, sometimes they seem to be angelic and sometimes more like butterflies. I don't mind what they are, they're so beautiful they can come and show themselves to me any time. I was shown the image of lots of people sitting at a table, one of them turned and looked at me, it was Kirsty McColl.

One day in early March I went to get some stuff at the local supermarket, as I parked I changed my mind and went down to Lidl instead. I went to get a trolley and bumped into Clare, a lady who I knew from Celia's groups at Tabua. We had a brief chat and she asked about having some healing, so once the shopping was done, she followed me back to my house for a healing session. It felt very cold after Clare left, but it seemed obvious that our meeting today was arranged by spirit. I sat that evening, spirit came through to say that 'You've been on the B roads long enough, now it's time to get on the motorway'.

Shortly after that encounter I was on a plane back to the UK. Friend Steve met me at the airport in his sports car, good lad I thought. We drove to his place with his sun roof slightly open, as I had a big case on my lap and I was holding my skis, luckily it was only light rain and drizzle. I was staying at his house for a couple of nights before our usual crowd were off skiing to Bacqueira again. Steve is Sheila's partner, we all used to work together in the dim and distant past.

On our flight to Spain I could see a rainbow outside the plane. I was carrying an injury this trip so I skiied one day then rested one day throughout the week. On one of the days I didn't ski it was thick fog all morning. We went up the first lift to hang around the mountain

M.E. - My Blessing in Disguise

restaurant, lots of others did the same. Suddenly the sun burst through in just our small area, it was beautiful, and the crowd reaction was wow! Everyone enjoyed it, but our magical moment was soon gone. It had felt so hot and bright for thirty seconds or so.

On landing back in the UK I spent a couple of days with my son before heading back to Portugal. On the plane to Portugal I was shown a purple ball that became a heart, then two hands came in and joined behind it. I was also shown a man who seemed to have ectoplasm coming from his mouth.

For reasons unknown to me the number 33 has become quite prominent in recent times. Our first encounter was when Celia was looking to move her shop in Shoreham, I was one of the people who told her about the empty shop in East Street, which is where she moved the shop to, it was no 33.

In Portugal it's cropped up a few times now, I first got it as part of my Fiscal number, then when I bought my property it was in my landline phone number and in my postcode. The whole area of Arganil is allocated with 33 postcodes, so perhaps it was all totally predetermined that I would have to be in this area. The flight numbers with the airline I use between Gatwick and Porto mostly start 33, so something is going on. I understand it's what is called a master number in numerology, but I don't know any more than that, other than I seem to have a connection with it.

A week or so later Clare came over for some more healing, suddenly during this session I could feel other hands, solid hands, were between mine, that was interesting. Later that day my hearing became a bit peculiar as I seemed to be getting extra hearing in my right ear, as if a mini speaker was in there. This happened for a few weeks on and off, before it stopped as suddenly as it started. In that time spirit worked on my ears quite a lot. As well as healing with Clare, we sat several times, during which spirit would quite often speak to Clare.

M.E. - My Blessing in Disguise

Many of the images I get shown by spirit have a touch of the surreal, so should I have been surprised to see a house moving along and towing a car, I know those huge Winnebagos can do that, but a house! The next day something white and gold flew around and landed on the floor by me, I looked down to see more of it, but there was nothing there.

There were lots of sounds being made in the night, knocks were common, the sound of a blind going up, keys turning in locks. One of the key in lock noises sounded like the front door's lock, even though the sound was in the bedroom. I tested this out anyway, with a friend's help, you cannot hear the front door being locked or unlocked from the bedroom..
One evening I was watching the Corrs on tv, suddenly lots of white lights were flying around, one went around my empty wine glass. I was seeing quite a lot of white lights outside the windows at this time. I was driving one day when a strange voice came through the cars speakers, the radio was not even turned on.

Two sisters, Barbara and Pauline, came out to stay for a week in April. I'd dug out a small bed in the land for planting, they wanted to help so we went to the local garden garden centre and bought a few plants and some Sunflower seeds to put in. Whilst they were here the weather was mild and mostly dry, we walked into Arganil for meals some evenings, I think they enjoyed their stay here. A few days after they left the heavens opened, we had torrential rain on and off for three days. Nearly all the seeds we planted were washed away, two Sunflowers survived, one became enormous and had masses of flowers, it kept flowering for ages.

Over time I cleared and dug more small areas, planting shrubs, trees and herbs and lavenders, I've had to go over each area about three times, sifting the soil to try to get rid of the weeds. Some of the grass roots grow like corkscrews and clump together, they're very difficult to get out, it's hard work.

M.E. - My Blessing in Disguise

The torrential rain created a mini lake on my land; remember the steep slope for access, rain just poured down there. I was worried about my car, so I drove it back up to the road and parked in a nearby side street. As I walked away from it I noticed I hadn't parked straight, but it was raining, the street was wide, so I left it with the front sticking out. In the morning I went to drive into Arganil, I only got a short distance and I stopped, it was like driving a different car, very strange. It turned out that someone had taken advantage of my bad parking and had swapped my front wheels for some old ones. I now had almost bald tyres and they were totally out of balance. I had to buy two new tyres and get the wheels balanced, a lesson learned the hard way.

Celia's development and healing groups at Tabua continued for a while, but they eventually dissipated, sadly there just doesn't seem to be the commitment out here. Most who attended were non Portuguese, they were Dutch, Belgian, German, British and from all over the place, it was tough for Celia as she'd put a lot of work in to it, but as they say 'You can take a horse to the water, but you can't make it drink'. It is a shame when you can see that some people do have abilities, but just can't be bothered to make the most of them. Somewhere along the line Celia did have a group going in Coimbra, almost all Portuguese, the language was a challenge for her, but she stuck at it.
This reminds me of a message that spirit have given through me, they were saying that it's important for mediums to keep up sitting for their own development, no matter that they are running groups and working on platform. The reason for this is that they may have more abilities to develop, if they don't do it then they may well have regrets when they get back to the other side.

I was carrying on sending healing and giving healing when asked. Whilst sending one day, spirit spoke to me about changes, and how I need to accept them with a positive attitude to ensure that I fully integrate them, that way I can get the most out of them. Wise words I'm sure, but not always easy to do at the time. I was sending healing on the anniversary of Mum's passing and I felt pressure on the left side

M.E. - My Blessing in Disguise

of my chest, Mum had passed with a heart attack. I was also shown a white pair of arms and hands.

My friend Clare continued to come regularly for healing, and it wasn't unusual for experiences to happen whilst she was on the couch. One day it seemed to me that the couch was breathing, the energy was so consistently strong throughout, possibly the strongest I'd experienced up to that point, though it's impossible to tell. On another day with Clare, my right hand seemed to signal to my left hand to stay still. Several times I heard sounds near the French windows, it was a bit like a curtain rubbing on the walls or floor, I could see nothing there that could've have caused it. I was shown a bald headed man in a Doctor's coat.

Another healing for Clare gave me index fingers as cold as ice, the cold went up my arms and spread throughout my body. I then saw myself sitting in the corner as someone else came and got onto the couch, I stayed put on the chair as spirits got on with the healing. Now that would be a way to work, I've been given hints about Spirit Surgeons before, it would be brilliant if things can develop that way. It would mean that I'd be fully in trance and would probably need other healers helping with the energy requirements. At the end of the session Clare felt spacey for the first time. I was still being used by spirit for sending distant hands on healing, quite regularly I was feeling someone's pulsing and breathing.

In July, Jan the psychic artist/medium came out and stayed for a few days, I think Celia had lined up a workshop for her. Jan also had to check out a property that she was interested in, unfortunately there were one or two legal issues and it fell through. While Jan was here I showed her some photos I'd taken, one was of the Fig tree that was close to the house. I'm pleased I did as she spotted a face on the tree. I'd heard about these type of things but had never seen any, but now I'd taken a picture of one without knowing. I copied the photo for Jan to take back and show someone in the UK who was up on these type of

M.E. - My Blessing in Disguise

things. The face was recognised as being Pan, who I've previously mentioned, I think he had the Ram's head, quite a turn up.

This opened up a whole new world for me, as I can now see faces on trees, shrubs, rocks etc. and many show up in pictures now. Sometimes I see them before I take a photo, sometimes I get surprised and only spot them when I look at the photos.

Whilst she was here, Jan convinced me to try some drawing, she thought that spirit might want to work with me that way, she recommended that I start with blackboard and chalk. I bought a couple of small blackboards and tried drawing, I think I soon decided, or perhaps was impressed to close my eyes and see what happened. Lots of scribbly doodles happened, but somewhere along the line it seemed I wasn't moving my hands, but equally I didn't feel any particular energy in them, or in me, just a little around my head is all. I'm not sure how it works, perhaps it was more like spirit moving the chalk, I also began sitting in the dark to do it, well it's very tempting to open your eyes in the light. I've really only felt energy around my head when drawing, there doesn't seem to be any obvious influence on my hands.

I don't know how many more scribbly doodles there were, and there may have been one or two tiny faces amongst them, but sometime in August I was looking at something on a board that I didn't recognise. I put it down and walked away for something, I came back at a different angle and I was now looking at it upside down from how it was drawn. Wow! There was a drawing, it was either showing the skull of a Gorilla or a Neanderthal. Amazing, I couldn't have drawn it if I'd tried, well I might be able to do a rough copy, but that would take some time, this had taken less than a minute. I was over the moon as they say, delighted, what's more this picture was drawn upside down! The obvious conclusion was that somehow spirit wanted to try and draw through me, although how it worked, was beyond me. There was another conclusion, I needed some more black boards, no way was this board going to be cleaned off, I still have it today. I've never had any pretensions of being an artist, I loved drawing aircraft and ships as a

M.E. - My Blessing in Disguise

boy, but faces, people, animals and trees have always been completely beyond me. I had to keep on drawing now, slowly more drawings appeared, so it wasn't a fluke, one drawing looked like the beat up Coyote from the Roadrunner cartoon, another was like a Turtle swimming. They were outlines, not fully detailed, but I was more than happy with this development.

A few months on and I had to have another chat with Jan as I now had thirty or more boards with pictures on. Jan suggested that I try soft pastels on paper, that's what she uses. Well spirit certainly seemed to like that medium, forgive the pun, quite a few pictures were produced by them, lots of nothings as well, but the pictures seemed to be in several different styles and on different subjects, most were way beyond my imagination.

These pictures have given me a great deal of pleasure and fun, I could never have dreamed of pictures like these coming through me, I'm so glad that Jan told me to try, and that I listened to her advice. I've no doubt that to any critic they'll be rubbish, but what do they know ha-ha, I only buy pictures, books, music etc. for my pleasure, I don't think of anything like that as investments. I like some of them so much that I have them on my walls. One or two people say they can see certain styles in some of them, I don't know enough about art to say.

Many of the drawings are nothing to me, some look childish, but I don't know whose working through me. I did go through them and threw a lot away, I still have a boxful, it's only rarely now that I try to draw, as we went through a period where no pictures of note were being produced, maybe we'll try again one day. Whatever, I feel I owe Jan a debt for pushing me in that direction, and also for helping to open my eyes to the elementals too.

Examples of some spirit drawings follow.

M.E. - My Blessing in Disguise

M.E. - My Blessing in Disguise

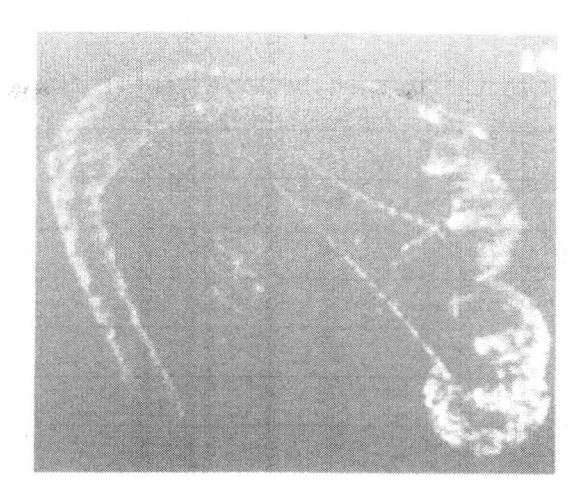

The picture above is the first recognisable drawing produced and it was drawn upside down.

Before we leave the drawing, I was shown an eye on the paper a couple of times, I should have thought more about that before pressing on. I say that because I think that's how Jan works, so it's not impossible that spirit may want to try and use that method with me. I think there are several methods used by spirit through different psychic artists. When I next get around to drawing I'll have to have a chat with spirit first, maybe they'll want to change something.

Annie once gave me a message about there being a stash on my land, well I think it must have been about elementals, as I've dug and planted in so many places across the land and nothing else has come to light.

I was still being shown many things clairvoyantly, in one sitting I saw an angel with uplifted wings, then in front of it came a male angel with uplifted wings, which were also outstretched, it was so close and looked so beautiful. At another sitting I was shown the amazing white image of a circle of angels, all with uplifted wings, then in came a golden flying bird, wow! There were more colourful images especially

M.E. - My Blessing in Disguise

one of a 7 which has several coloured lines joining it, I've seen this image many times now, it's often in a beautiful blue.

I continued to see some images with my eyes open, including a beautiful, white bird above the tv. I was reading a Gordon Smith book when I had a tuning-fork noise in my left ear, something made me look up, astonishingly I could see a group of faces looking back down at me. Another day an area of brilliant white appeared on a wall, there was a sparkling pyramid in it, beautiful. I was shown a man with a white light, he had winged creatures around him.

On a different day I saw something silver and gold flying around the kitchen, it kept catching the light. I also had several of them flying in the hall, they're only there for a few seconds so I can't make out what they are, apart from beautiful that is. One evening a blue light appeared three times on the wall behind the tv, then a golden light appeared.

Twice I've been shown 'PAT' this year, nothing else with it, I've known males and females by that name, but I have no idea which one it could be. Sitting one day a lady said 'hello', then there was a man tapping on my right shoulder, I was impressed that he was saying 'no, no, Sombrero'. Another man gave me an address of Byron Road in Whitechapel, I could find no trace of the road. At another sitting I felt incredible strength in my arms, then my fingers splayed. During a different sitting my chair seemed to be pushed forwards, then my legs felt as if they were moving through long grass or water.

In bed one night I woke to feel powerful energy pouring into my head, it felt a bit like an electric current, and I wondered if I'd been plugged in. I thought my hands were together, but I couldn't move them, then I found that I couldn't move at all. The energy went down as far as my coccyx.

I had a trip to the UK and was sitting on the sofa when I heard my heart beating so loudly that my torso began to vibrate. That night in bed my heartbeat raced at an incredible speed. During one flight I nodded off,

M.E. - My Blessing in Disguise

on waking I began to rub my eyes, clairvoyant images appeared. The gentle rubbing of my eyes intensified the images I was seeing. This became a habit with me and it would often cause the images to change dramatically, with colours becoming even more beautiful and stronger. I also found that this happened when I went back into my house, after I'd been working outside. Those images were often celestial beings and so beautiful, golden angels, guides, birds and butterflies with rainbow coloured wings, impossibly beautiful.

One August day, I arrived back at my property and was driving down the track when I had to stop the car. There in front of me was a beautiful Hoopoe bird, I'd heard their calls many times, but had never seen one. It proceeded to walk very slowly down the track in front of me, I managed to park my car and I'm pleased to say that it stayed around for a while, they are a delight to see with their crest and their unusual colouring.

One day I was reading Findlay's 'Edge of the Etheric', a part of the book where Arthur had a sitting with Bertha Harris, very strong pressure grew in the middle of my chest, accompanied by a warm, loving feeling. Bertha had been a regular visitor to our Shoreham circle, and has made several visits to Celia's circle in Portugal.

One night I got up to visit the loo, I opened a door to find a light on, it was one of those push Led lights, I have a few dotted about the house in case of power cuts, I certainly hadn't put it on. Just before New Year I returned from a UK trip on a late flight, I opened the house door and one of these push lights was on, I said a quick thanks to spirit for being helpful.

I continued to hear things when I sat and also when I was in bed. At one sitting I seemed to feel that someone was very close to me, then I heard a voice say 'alright'. One night in bed it got quite noisy, a lady said 'hello', a man said 'Pat', later a man was speaking into my left ear in a foreign language. The rest of the night was filled with noises in the bedroom.

M.E. - My Blessing in Disguise

Another night I was woken by the sound of someone clapping, the next night it was the sound of curtains being drawn that roused me, there are no curtains hanging in my house. And so it went on, noises from the wardrobes, which included a voice saying 'sort it out', and the sound of a key turning in a wooden door. For a while I had an echo in my ears, as if a speaker was in there, it was as if the speaker was switched on two or three days running at about 7pm. A few weeks later it was back on again, this time for a several days, spirit had been playing with my ears before it was turned on.

Back sitting I heard some grunts, which at first I thought might have come from me, then they seemed to be next to me, I also heard a cow 'moo'. At other sittings I heard ladies singing in the distance, also a conversation in a foreign language, yes I know this was in Portugal, but it was in the house. Another day I seemed to be on the phone to my mum and heard 'The best thing about being here is that we don't have to get up', then the phone was cut off. I'd gone off during one sitting and I seemed to hear some knocks on the window, I was eventually brought back by my chair rocking.

In bed the fun continued as I was treated to some harmonica playing one night, my dad and his friend Ernie both played harmonica, so who knows. I had more noises in my left ear one night, it was of course the one on the pillow, but I still heard a door bell and various types of phone rings in that ear. Another night in bed I was shown a scene in which three people said to me that I had been reborn, one of them said that he had seen me reborn.

In bed one night I was woken by metallic noises, this was followed by some Morse Code. Another night I was woken at 3.33, then 4.44, I also heard some loud sneezes, but they weren't mine.

Towards the end of November I was woken a few times, there were soft knocks on the door and some tuning-fork noises in my right ear, which became a four part harmony. It started with the highest, then the

M.E. - My Blessing in Disguise

others came in in turn. It sounded really beautiful and was totally new for me to hear them like this, later I heard a low whistle. The harmony was repeated about a week later.

On day as I walked into my healing/sitting room there was the distinctive smell of honey. In May that year I watched the Cup Final, I can't remember who played now, what I noted though was that I was surrounded by beautiful spirit energy, and I went all cool and tingly as 'Abide With Me' was sung. Over the years there have been several occasions when I've felt energy with me as I've watched various sporting events, especially Rugby. I do know a lot of people who are now in spirit who had strong sporting interests, one or two did play rugby.

Whilst sitting I've received some messages from spirit, one was 'The road ahead is open and welcoming, you only have to journey down it to find what you seek'. Another message was 'Our task is to help you on the Earth Plane by influencing those who might distract you and cause you difficulties, we work with their guides, even those people who have no spiritual interest'.

Now we must talk about Stonechats, these birds have made an impact on me this year, I'm not sure if I even ever saw one in the UK, but I sure know now what they look like.

On September 1st I was sitting with spirit in the afternoon and we kept being interrupted by some knocking on the house windows. Eventually I had to investigate and I was very surprised to find that a small bird was the cause of the disruption, The knocking had started on the window of the room in which I'd been sitting, then it went to the next room. It move to the French windows and only left there when I opened them up. It continued all along the windows at the back of the house, giving each of them a good bashing in turn. What could this be about I wondered, I don't need reminding that the windows need cleaning.

M.E. - My Blessing in Disguise

The next day I was sitting to send distant healing when the Chat began knocking on the windows again. This was again repeated the following day and carried on until the French windows were once again opened. It's now September 4th and the knocking began immediately I started to sit for spirit, it was on the window next to my pc. Somehow in the room where I was sitting the blind was rattled and the window was knocked from the inside. I was determined to sit that day and did actually go off for a while, but it was knocking that brought me back.

A few days later Clare was on my healing couch, it was a lovely day and the French windows were open. The Chat appeared and was soon knocking on the side window before it moved on to the French windows. Clare absolutely loves birds and she found it very funny, she told me straight away that it was a Stonechat, it then did its thing by going along all of the windows at the back of the house.

There was of course a pair of Stonechats, I think it was the male who'd done all the knocking. Over time this moved on as the Chats would greet me with their raucous 'clawking' sound, my description, every time I went outside. They would fly in front of me, flying from pole to pole or tree to tree as I walked down the land. It seemed to me that they were encouraging me to come outside, and possibly this was the first part of a plan to get me to plant further down the land, as my initial idea was to plant trees and shrubs and herbs on just half the land. They're still around now, but they don't tend to take so much interest in me, so I guess that they served their purpose.

So it was a year of big moves, I could now spend time in Portugal at my own place, my eyes had been opened to elementals, and also to the exciting fact that spirit were happy trying to draw through me. It sounds as if things should carry on being interesting in the future, though I still wasn't sure that it would be here.

M.E. - My Blessing in Disguise

Rainbows

Another New Year dawns, I was in the bedroom and felt someone press against my lower back, then higher up as my head went cool and tingly, it seemed as if someone was hugging me. What a way to start the new year, lovely.

My old friend 'white bird in flight' was around early in the year and showed itself as I sat for spirit. It was flying close and low and it looked like a Dove. Then the Dove was on the ground eating, it soon became a plane and took off. I was still sitting for drawings, but one evening spirit came through for a talk, a little unusual. A few evenings later there was a smell of lemons as I went to start drawing.

One night in bed I woke up to hear the German National Anthem in my head, the top half of my body seemed to shake severely. Spirit continued to wake me up by various noises as the year went on, including the sound of a push bike's wheels whizzing round, the sound of water dripping into a metal tray happened a few times, a chair scraping across the floor, loud scratching and gnawing, the sounds of a child that was too young to talk, door handles rattling and keys turning, doors knocking, loud cracks in the bedroom, a high pitched noise outside the bedroom, creaking doors, harmonicas playing, electronic sounds, phones ringing, as you can see a whole variety of noises, let's not forget the musical knock 'de de de de de de', they never finished with the de de, perhaps they expected me to.

A noise from the kitchen or bathroom got me out of bed one night, as I turned on the bedroom light I saw that the key to the door was not in the lock any more, it was hanging vertically from the lock surround, impossible of course.

M.E. - My Blessing in Disguise

One or two more noises one evening were sneezes in the bathroom and door handles and keys turning, there was no one else around. I was driving in my car one day when the cassette player came out with a sawing sound for a few minutes, there was nothing wrong with the player or tape, music soon resumed playing.

Spirit were coming through regularly when I was sitting and also sometimes when I was sending healing, one forceful voice brought spells of intense cold that had me shivering. Spirit spoke on a variety subjects and also came through with a lot of encouragement for me. There was a long chat form one who said he was an Ancient One. Here are some other messages from spirit:-

'The message can be in the unsaid', 'The door is open, you should go through it'.

Spirit spoke about free will and its spiritual meaning 'accepting the will of God', this sounds to me like the Law of Acceptance.

Spirit for me 'I must stay patient throughout this incarnation', that was painful to hear. 'Everything in the universe has cycles, we should tune into them when necessary'.

Spirit spoke to me about drawing 'Seek to feel no one, lest you fool yourself, and in doing so expose your own life's shortcomings for all the world to see'.

' Stay aware as things can happen quicker than expected, go with the flow'. ' True love is unconditional'.

' Changes can happen very quickly once they start, too quick to plan for, fear and logic must be set aside'.

I was often finding a press light on when I got up in the night, the most common one was the one that sat on the table where I ate my meals. Having them is a legacy of staying at Celia and Kelvin's first house,

M.E. - My Blessing in Disguise

when almost any amount of rain would bring a power cut with it, it hasn't been anywhere near as bad here, but it does seems that spirit like to play with them.

One morning I looked out of the window and something looked different, I realised that I could see the water in the river, this was the first time that I'd seen it from my house. There had been a lot of rain lately and it had obviously raised the river level. There are lots of hills and mountains in this area and some of them will drain into the Alva, incidentally the Alva's source is in the Serra d'Estrella, the highest mountains in Portugal.

From the house it was looking as if the river would burst its banks, but I didn't go down there to see, I went into panic mode as my basement door is much lower than the main door. Fortunately the rain had stopped, so I went outside with some plastic sacks that I would use to fill with earth, then I could sandbag the door. The earth was of course sodden, so heavy that I couldn't put much into each sack, consequently I soon ran out and had to go into Arganil to get some more. I eventually got the barricade up to between two to three feet high, and in doing so I'd made the space for another shrub bed on the land.

At some point I phoned Celia and told her of the situation, and I asked if I could stay at her place for a couple of nights. Celia was off to the UK later that day. She said it was OK and told me where she would leave a key. I packed a bag as I kept looking out of the window, the river looked as if it had stopped rising, but we were still getting some rain on and off, so I didn't want to spend the night there.

I couldn't go to Celia's immediately as I was waiting to call my daughter Alison, she said that she would text me when she got in from work. Whilst waiting I looked out of the kitchen window at the tree filled hills around Arganil. Suddenly there seemed to be a fire on one of the hills, it didn't make sense as everything must be absolutely saturated. I tried to figure it out what could have caused it, a logging

M.E. - My Blessing in Disguise

lorry crashing, or someone spilling a load of fuel, but they weren't logging in the area anyway.

The blaze had spread out, yet it still seemed impossible for a fire to start, then after only a short time the scene changed as the fire became a beautiful rainbow. It grew upwards and then seemed to lift off the ground, whilst that was still in the air, another one was growing in the original spot, wow! How incredible to watch this happening, phenomenal. The second rainbow also lifted off the ground, then a third one began growing, I think we reached five rainbows, it was looking like a ladder going up towards the sky. I don't know how long it lasted before the inevitable fading out, if only I'd had a digital camera, or even a film in my old camera, but unfortunately I didn't, what a shame.

I'd never seen a rainbow born before, let alone such an unusual one that looked like a ladder. I began to think that this must be spirit's doing, perhaps their way of telling me that I was safe and protected. It was one of the most truly astonishing and incredible experiences of my life, and spirit have given me a few of those. Thank goodness that Alison hadn't got home early, else I'd have missed it. I do hope that some other people saw this wonderful sight. .

The other thing about it was the fact that the sun didn't come out at all, nature usually puts the sun and moisture together of course to make rainbows. Writing this book has reminded me that a couple of years or so before this happened, I was shown a rainbow that looked like a ladder laying on the ground, well now I've seen it standing up..

In due course Alison texted me and we had a chat, then I was off to Celia and Kelvin's where I had some cats to feed for a few days. I came back to my house during the daytime. The river level dropped down, when I eventually went to have a look at the river I soon worked out that what I'd seen was the river going over onto the far side, and it had gone in amongst the trees over there. The bank on my side was four to

M.E. - My Blessing in Disguise

five feet higher, so there was still some leeway, the only way to know for sure was to go and check.

One evening I was outside taking some pictures of the full moon, I try to line things up so that the moon is amongst the trees, it gives some unusual images that way. On this particular evening, I must have had some strong influence around me as I couldn't keep the camera still even when leaning against a wall, my hands were shaking.

I was sitting one afternoon when I started getting the songs from the Elvis film 'Jailhouse Rock' singing in my head, as 'Young and Beautiful' was sung my body filled with incredibly, beautiful energy. I then became cold and tingly, this went down my spine and spread. Another day I was listening to Gene Pitney and reading the cd cover when blue lights came around me. One evening I was watching the Carpenters on tv singing 'Help', blue light came near the tv.

One morning I had an upset stomach, I found myself looking at yoghurts in the supermarket, something I normally never do. I picked up one and was trying to read the ingredients as I have a soya intolerance. With one type I felt a hand on my stomach and it became tingly, yes I bought some of those.

I was woken one night by a strange noise which made me think that someone was trying to get into my house, before I could get up, I seemed to be lifted up by strong arms and held secure. I don't know how long it lasted, but it was a wonderful and reassuring experience.

I was in the UK in April and I sat with one of Debi's circles, spirit spoke through me and also for a question and answer session. I was also able to help at the Pyramid of Light with healing. Not long after that I went to Debi's where she was trying out crystal healing, I was a guinea pig. I found it very calming, and it seemed as if some old injuries were being worked on, I was so relaxed that I was drifting off.

M.E. - My Blessing in Disguise

All too soon I was back in Portugal and being woken up to feel someone inside my hands, I could hardly move my fingers or thumbs, it was a strange feeling. On reflection it reminded me a little of the morning when I awoke to find that I had ME, and struggled to move at all. I've had similar situations where I've been prevented from moving, or parts of me have, but it had never felt the way this did, an unwanted reminder.

Back in 2008 I'd done a fair bit of planting on my land, trees, shrubs, herbs and flowers had all gone in on the half of the land that was closest to my house, I was happy with that, intending to leave the other half to nature. Spirit had other ideas which manifested in two ways. In the first I was up at the town's weekly market looking for a particular tree, there was still room for the odd extra planting. I checked out all the stalls selling trees and soon found what I wanted, so I had a wander around the rest of the market before going back to get the tree. I picked up the tree and was about to go and pay for it when it was as if someone was shouting in my ear 'Peach Tree, Peach Tree, Peach Tree'. It was being repeated non-stop so I sent my thoughts up to say 'OK we'll get one', that stopped it and I went home with two trees.

Having put in the one I wanted, I had no idea where to put the peach. After much pondering I moved my imaginary boundary down the land and planted the Peach. I'd been try to think of how I could separate my two halves of land, the piece that I'd look after from the wild one. Somehow 'hedge' was dropped into my mind, that's a good idea, I liked that, but what could I use out here, this was spirit's second way of course.

I had an idea for a shape for the hedge, gentle waves, I didn't want a straight line. I mentioned the hedge to Clare when she next came over for healing, Hawthorns would be prefect she said, and she knew where I could get them. They were growing all over the place where Clare and Chris lived, and every year there was more, so I went over there to dig some up. it's not that easy, the roots seem to spread out a lot. I must have come back with a dozen or so, probably a foot or so tall, Clare

M.E. - My Blessing in Disguise

also gave me a few Cork Oaks and ordinary Oaks, only inches tall, but I'd plant some in the hedge and the rest elsewhere, I also bought some red Robins to add colour to it

I dug out a spot to start the planting, then did some more to get the shape going, mmm, somehow my wave shape changed into something much more resembling a horseshoe. The spade I was using just would not do what I wanted it to, it just turned in the ground when I pushed my foot down. After a couple of attempts to correct it I decided not to fight it and just let it happen, of course for a while I had no idea of what shape was intended, but it was OK. I was lucky enough to find that the local garden centre had a stock of Hawthorns, so I bought some taller ones. I didn't do the hedge all at once, and spirit spoke to me a couple of times about finishing it, well when you've got some land it's so easy to get distracted as there are so many things to do. However it did get finished and now it's grown and is beautiful, so it provides some seclusion and privacy. There's also a Maple Tree in it, providing some lovely Autumn colour. The Hawthorns have all grown very well and have their own beauty when the white blossom is on them in Spring, and lots of red berries to follow later in the year.

In May friends Sheila and Steve were renting a villa with pool down near the Algarve, they asked me to come down for a few days, it's a fair old drive to get there, but they're good company so I made the trip and relaxed nicely.

I was outside strimming here one day when I felt a tap on the head, it made me stop, and just in time as I was about to swing the strimmer, if I had I would have chopped down some wild Scabius flowers, so thanks for that spirit. There are lots of wild flowers growing amongst the tall grass, I don't know the names of them all, but Evening Primrose and Camomile are two, there's also Shamrock, mostly white flowers, but there are a few clumps with pink flowers. I try hard not to chop the flowers, but it's sometimes very difficult to avoid them.

M.E. - My Blessing in Disguise

One lovely sunny afternoon I went out with a beer to sit under the Cherry Tree that's near to the house, I nearly took my camera, as I often do, but for some reason I didn't. A short while later a Mongoose walked across my land, all I could do was watch, if I'd moved to go get the camera I think it would have run, so I had to content myself with just watching it have a leisurely stroll. It was the time of year for Fireflies, most evenings there were some about.

I came into the house one day and saw big bug of some sort on the floor, I got the dustpan and brush and gently swept it up, I looked at it outside and it was a beautiful gold colour, I put it amongst some vegetation. I looked it up, it was a Golden Beetle. More creatures then, at Circle one day I had a Shield Bug on my arm, whereas outside one day a Grasshopper landed on an arm and wouldn't go away, so I stroked it.

I was standing outside looking around one day when someone came and put their arm through my left arm, that was lovely, whoever it might have been. Many times I would see areas of spirit colour in front of me as I watered the plants.

During my planting of the hedge and some more trees down nearer the river, the Stonechats did a lot of clawking, everytime I came outside they were at it. Occasionally they came close, as if to make sure I was doing it right, but usually they'd be watching from the top of a nearby small tree or a bamboo pole.

I was in the UK in September, whilst there a few of us were going up to Hull to a séance where the medium would be Stewart Alexander. Jan organised it for nine of us, it was only a small room they sat in, and with three or four of his circle as well, it was quite cosy. Stuart is a well known physical medium, it was a cracking evening with Walter coming through a lot, he is Stuart's main guide. The trumpets were flying about a lot as we all did our share of singing. The highlight of the evening was when Walter's hand was materialised in red light for us all to see.

M.E. - My Blessing in Disguise

Lucky Barbara got a grandstand view, as she was called to sit right next to the table where the hand appeared.

On our journey back we called into a little spiritual church in Mansfield, where a chap called Richard Smith gave a long talk about the wonderful mediumship of another physical medium, called Isa Northage; it was her church we were in. If you know nothing about her, as I didn't, there is a book called 'A Path Prepared' about her. She had a spirit doctor who worked through her, well more than that, he materialised and performed operations and healings, amazing. Richard who was giving the talk, was lucky enough to sit in Isa's circle for several years, I think he also had an operation from the doctor. He made it a very interesting afternoon for us and was passionate about his subject, so it was an excellent trip which I think we all enjoyed.

Whilst reading books, especially spiritual books, I often see spirit lights or feel touches or energies. I was reading Micheal Bentine's book 'The Door Marked Summer', when out of the corner of my eye I saw some light or energy moving at the bathroom door, it seemed as if the door had become a curtain and was blowing about. In bed that night I saw my brother-in-law Paul looking much younger than his years, I think this may have been around the time when he was diagnosed with Prostate Cancer. That night I also heard what sounded like a broom handle falling onto the floor.

I was reading 'Every Wall A Door' when my hands started bouncing about, it makes reading tricky I can tell you. Some times the pages would go coloured and lights would appear on the book.

At circle a few days later I was astonished as my eyes were opened by spirit, and there right next to my mouth was a hand, wow!

A couple of times in the summer I saw a white, diamond light flashing in the sky, it wasn't moving and it was there for a few minutes both times. Then when sitting one afternoon, the white, diamond light appeared, it became a planet with rings, like Saturn.

M.E. - My Blessing in Disguise

Clare was still a regular visitor for healing and sitting, she would quite often get messages from spirit. One day whilst giving her healing I took my hand off her head, the top of her head seemed chaotic and bubbling, almost erupting you could say. Later it had calmed down and was pulsing regularly in an orderly fashion. More than once that day I saw some sort of movement by the door. At the end Clare said that she felt that she had been moved around a little.

More Happenings In 2009

Here are some more happenings from 2009, we'll start with images I was shown, some were with my eyes open and some were when they were closed.

I woke to see a man who was in a white robe, he was standing and talking in front of a huge rock.

Whilst in bed I was shown a glass falling, as the glass hit the table there was a loud crack in the bedroom.

Another night in bed I saw white light and shapes on the ceiling, they began moving and spreading out until the whole of the ceiling was covered. I saw three white birds in flight, then two, then one, then I saw a white dragon.

I was shown something that looked like an animal with a man's head, it turned towards me and smiled.
I saw a man who opened his mouth and let a crescent moon out. I was also shown numerous scenes in which people have white lights or shapes that go into or come out of their eyes.

I saw myself amongst a group of people, a white shape was in my right eye, either a pyramid or a near full moon. In another person's face, their right eye opened to reveal two white eyes, and in someone else's face when their right eye opened it had three white eyes in it.

I saw a white dog with a golden eye, it also had an owl upon its head.

I was shown a tree that became covered in silver foil, then somehow I began using the tree as a steering wheel.

I saw myself being taken to a Hall of Worship, lots of people walked past me, my guide, White Bird in Flight, was showing me around.

M.E. - My Blessing in Disguise

I saw a large white figure who held out a quiver of arrows to me.

I saw lots of white lights come floating down on parachutes, one was attached to a balloon. There was a large white bird in flight above the tv.

I saw a man with a staff, he became a huge, white bird.

One day in my basement I saw a light that was flame coloured and black and flashed, it spread out and became a cluster of blue lights and blue and white lights.

I was shown lots of pyramids, several were made of white crystal, some had pyramids inside them in clusters, others were white framed and transparent, there was also a golden pyramid. They were all very beautiful.

Over the year I was shown several signposts, usually white, when they had writing on them I couldn't read it.

I saw a white dodecahedron, then three of them joined together, they were sticking out horizontally from a rocket, which was on top of a mountain.

One day I saw Arthur Conan Doyle, a little white being appeared and went into his left eye, as ACD faded out, a large, powerful, white bird appeared. I experienced some moments of surprise and delight in this sitting.

I saw myself planting three seeds into some dark, rippling energy, instantly there was light in it.

I was watching tv one evening, three times spirit took me off, each time I came back the light was golden, like sunshine.

M.E. - My Blessing in Disguise

I was shown someone who had six or eight rods that came out of their neck, the rods were golden and had light on their ends. I then saw two naked, little people in a huge, glass cylinder, which had two holes in the bottom of it, they were looking for corks. None were found so they compressed some sand and used it to fill the holes.

Spirit closed my eyes, but my right eye still seemed to be open and had a golden circle around its outside, with wine coloured light pouring in.

I was reading a book by ACD when a shadow came onto the book, then some white lights followed.

I was shown a beautiful, starburst tree, it became an enormous bird, then the tree again. I saw my white, feathered shape going across the ceiling, as it did in 2004.

Driving up to Porto airport for my Christmas trip I saw a shooting star. On the flight I could see a round rainbow for ages, there were others behind it.

At my friend Sheila's a week or so before Christmas I was shown a pathway lit by golden lights, then a white door with silver lights on it. I saw a crowd of people, amongst them was a man who was glowing white, and two people who were sleeping, white bird in flight visited them.

Now for some sounds I experienced, often linked to scenes.

One day I was seeing black and white lights, there was a sound in the healing room, as it happened the lights all fell to the ground.

On another day my right hand rotated anti-clockwise for a minute or two, after it stopped I had a thought, 'now that's a wind up', ho-ho.

In bed I woke to hear a bird's wings flapping, then someone said 'morning' in a phoney French 'Allo, Allo' type accent.

M.E. - My Blessing in Disguise

More sounds happened on another night, I was being shown a long shotgun when boom! Then I saw a flower vibrating, as it did so I heard a loud sound in the room, as if something was vibrating on wood.

I was having a cuppa when I heard someone stomping their feet in the basement, the door was locked and of course there was no one there.

Sitting on a chair I heard the sound of a chair spring go boing across the room, I have no chairs of that type.

One day whilst relaxing I heard the sound that's made when someone runs their finger around the top of a wine glass, perhaps spirit wanted me to have a top up.

I was listening to a playback of a taped sitting, on it was a slowed down wolfwhistle, mmm.

Some instances when healing.

Whilst healing one day, spirit spoke to me, as they did I found myself shaking, this was new.

Several times this year I have had instances during which I've felt incredible strength come into me, it's usually in my arms and hands and only lasts for a minute or two.

Whilst healing, I was talking to spirit about my pal Murrey, I was stopped in mid-sentence, but the healing carried on.

More experiences with music playing.

I had a Roy Orbison dvd playing, he was singing 'Crying', during the song there was golden light around the tv, and the room lights dimmed, I have no dimmer lights.

M.E. - My Blessing in Disguise

It was similar, but to a lesser degree when Johnny Cash was singing 'A Boy Named Sue'.

There was a second occurrence with Roy Orbison singing 'Crying', as there was golden light around the tv and also down the hall this time.

Other happenings.

In circle one day I saw myself in Gibraltar, I've never been there, a lady with a child came to visit me. We went to the gondola so that we could go up to the top of the rock, as the gondola started up, I felt my right shoulder go up in the air, as I seemed to become the gondola.

Sitting one afternoon I heard three knocks on wood, no not on my head, I suddenly felt surprised and the song 'Sunny Side of the Street' was playing in my mind.

After reading one of ACD's books I felt impressed to put my hands over my eyes, I saw a beautiful pair of white hands that seemed to be in an impossible position.

In bed something was placed over my right ear and the surrounding area for a while, then I heard some bits and pieces of a bluesy harmonica.

After a taped sitting I listened to the playback, there were some loud noises and knocks and some electrical noises near the end, de de de de de de de de de de, all very quick, I didn't hear them at the time.

I was shown a signpost whilst sitting, there were some names on it, one on top of the other, then a white tap appeared in front of it.

Whilst watching tv it felt like some hands were clamped around my head for a while.

M.E. - My Blessing in Disguise

I was shown this in bed one night, a large area of pale green, it had dips in it, like an egg box. There were balls in the dips, half were turquoise and half were golden.

In bed I woke to see a bright, white and orange light flashing on the wall, a little wow. Another night in bed I was shown an image several times, it was of Jesus with his arms open.

In circle at Barbara's I saw a young girl appear between two of the other sitters. She had long, brown hair and wore a yellow dress, she began playing around and went to the spare chair, then she was gone.

Whilst staying at Barbara's I heard noises in the bedroom at night, then a child's voice said 'you can listen to us if you like'. Then a mass of energy came down on me, then I heard children's voices and giggling.

During an afternoon sit my hands were held and my brain was squeezed.

In bed I awoke to see a large, white bird in flight with my eyes open, lovely.

At Debi's I saw a white key turn upside down and go into a green lock. In circle I saw this scene, I was with a lady who drove me to a village where she lived, we were there to meet someone. The village was by a lake with a steep hill behind it.

Writing some notes in my diary and a large area of it went gold, then there was bright, white light.

I had my hands over my eyes and saw a golden lit area, in it were several spirits. It reminded me a bit of the Bohemian Rhapsody video.

I felt pressure grow around my left eye, as if some one was pressing a pen or pencil into the eyeball. Then someone was in my cheeks and lips, making them feel fatter.

M.E. - My Blessing in Disguise

Near Christmas I was reading, a full moon appeared on the book.

Another interesting year, that trip to Hull and Mansfield, lots of surreal happenings and experiences, and the amazing sight of the rainbow being born, wow!

M.E. - My Blessing in Disguise

An Arrival and a Departure

It was a quiet start to the 2010 and then I went to Portugal on a late flight, if everything went to plan I'd be home about 01:30. At the check-in desk I was told that we had a two hour delay, oh well I thought, getting back by 03:30 wasn't a real problem as I had no schedule for the next day, c'est la vie.

Shortly after I left check-in, I was being impressed with a time of 5 something, I thought surely not. Sure enough though we had a further delay, I finally got back at 5:25am. I'd asked spirit for help so that I would stay awake during the drive from the airport. They duly obliged by playing with the volume of the cassette player, they kept turning up really loud, it did the trick and I arrived back at my house in one piece.

A couple of days later I was sitting again, what a welcome I was given as I was freezing from the waist down, even my skin felt frozen, I couldn't recall that sensation before. My brain was squeezed a few times, this carried on over the next few days and sometimes it was hard. I've no idea why it's done or what it can achieve, but its not unpleasant at all. When I wrote the notes on this sitting, spirit froze me again.

Tuning-fork noise carried on throughout the year, an early one began high-pitched, then took on a lower tone, before it ended with me having the feeling of having cotton wool in my right ear.

About a week after getting back spirit began waking me up with all sorts of sounds, the first being the sound of a heavy, wooden door clunking shut. Another trend was the continuation of lights appearing as I read spiritual books. I had a band of light cross the page as I was reading about Jack Webber, it seems that he hasn't lost his touch then. One night I woke to hear voices outside my bedroom door, 'Comms is back on', someone said, I then heard a lot of incredibly low sounds, which I can't remember hearing before.

M.E. - My Blessing in Disguise

I'm writing these notes from the 2010 diary on July 30th 2015, a very muggy day, so I decided to get to the end of January and stop. I was feeling as if I needed to go and lie down, I went and had a drink of water and the feeling grew stronger so I did. The next day I was back making notes, the first entry I looked at in the diary read:- 'Afternoon sitting – I saw a man with a Native American in a headdress standing behind him, the N. American put his hands on the man's shoulders and made him lie down', now that is good synchronicity to me, after my experience the day before.

There can be no doubt that being in this location puts me right into nature, as I look out of the French windows there are lots of Swallows gathering on the telephone lines. The adults keep coming and going as they feed their young ones, though how they find them is difficult to say, they all look the same to me. A lot of the ground is now browning in the summer heat, but there's still lots of greenery in the trees. It would be lovely to be able to write this outside, but I know that my concentration would be absorbed and distracted by all the nature here.

I'm reading Ursula Robert's auto biography at present, it does make me question why spirit want me to write mine. Ursula was in her seventies when hers was written, after fifty years or so of spiritual work, I've come into this knowledge so much later in life and I don't feel as if I've made any meaningful contribution yet, apart from helping others with some healing. There have been some small burst of spiritual philosophy but the main flow hasn't begun yet, it all seems a bit premature to me.

Now on to an arrival, my first grandchild, Aidan was born at the end of May, Noelle and my son Brian being the happy parents. I can say he's turning into a right, cheeky chap, but lovable with it.

As if to balance the books, my friend Murrey passed away in August, leaving me with mixed feelings. He'd been inflicted with Motor Neurone Disease for a few years. It's one of those progressive conditions, which in the end takes away any control you have over your

M.E. - My Blessing in Disguise

body, and ultimately strips you of your dignity, as you cannot do anything for yourself.

I was sad of course, especially for his wife Pauline, his two daughters and his grandchildren, a massive loss for them all. My thoughts were tempered as I realised that Murrey had been released from the relentless, ever-tightening grip and horrendous lifestyle that MND imposes upon its sufferers. He is in a much better place now and no doubt restored to full health.

I received the news about Murrey the day after he died, but on the day of his passing I had my eyes closed and I was shown a date '1985.1.--', I can't remember the day of the month. However, January 1985 was the month of my first skiing trip, this trip was arranged by Murrey, so on reflection it seemed quite astonishing that I should be so visibly reminded of it on the day that he passed.

Thankfully Clare was still a regular visitor for both healing and to sit with me. She was good company and often received messages from spirit. She was always willing to share her knowledge of plants and birds with me, and if the opportunity arose she loved to give me the needle, she is an acupuncturist.

At this time I was receiving a lot of encouragement from spirit when I sat, but sometimes I was given some in circle, as when Lin brought through my Uncle George, 'Your efforts have been recognised'. I'm not really sure what it meant, but it was nice to receive it.

Spirit can be very helpful at times, whilst sending healing one morning, I was trying to remember what I'd been shown in the night. I was soon impressed with the word 'HAND', so there it was, that's what I'd seen. At one morning sitting I'd just sat down, spirit came through immediately to say 'lock it'. I quickly realised that I'd left the French windows open in the next room, once shut we got down to business. I got out of bed one night in the dark, and before I could find the light

M.E. - My Blessing in Disguise

switch a torchlight appeared on the wall next to it. The next night the light switch was lit up by a luminous white light.

During an afternoon sitting with spirit I kept hearing what sounded like noises around the house, I had to get up to try and locate the cause of the disturbance. For a while I found nothing, and the noises had stopped, I'd checked all of the living floor and was about to return to sitting when something made me look in the roof space, though a noise from there shouldn't have been heard, unless it was stamping or banging. I walked through the upstairs and a Sparrow flew out from behind a beam and went to a window, aha we have it. I opened the window at the other end, then walked towards the Sparrow, it instantly flew past me to the open window and was gone thank goodness.

One of my kitchen windows is large and for some reason attracts birds and a few have crashed into it, sadly some have been killed on impact, but several others have survived and lived to tell the tale. I've helped a few stunned birds recover by holding them for a few minutes and asking for healing for them. They are then put into the bowl of an apple tree, so that they can recover. Some take quite a while, most have been Sparrows, but there's also been a female Bullfinch and a juvenile Waxwing too.

One morning I woke up and saw a bird hovering in my bedroom by the open window, it quickly turned and went back out. I think it was a Redstart, but it could've been a Chat. I'd literally just woken up and opened my eyes, still, what a surprise.

Throughout the year I've often found my solar plexus acting very strangely, almost a nervous feeling, I could think of no reason for it to be so. Somewhere along the line I noticed that it was coinciding with earthquakes and such like in South America. I've no idea why this should happen, it doesn't happen when earthquakes hit other continents. I do ask healing for our planet from time to time, I believe it is a living, breathing entity in its own right, and obviously one that is still evolving.

M.E. - My Blessing in Disguise

One Sunday morning in summer I was hoping to lay in bed for an hour or so, I don't know why, but every time I think I will I seem to wake up early. Anyway, it was hot so the windows were open, I was dozing nicely when I heard something like a rapid drumming sound. It seemed to be close so I got up to have a look. I soon spotted the culprit, a Black Woodpecker was hammering away at a Cherry Tree, Ah well, it's time to put the kettle on then.

I had a reading with Fleur at Ditchling this year, she picked up that a Chinese guide is waiting to come in and work with me, it's not the first time that he's been mentioned to me, and he has a Unicorn with him, I'm not ready for him yet. He will eventually want me to be in a trance circle with sitters who have some experience, a settled group who I'm comfortable with. It will move on so that I won't know what is said in circle, unless I listen to a recording after.. The teachings will need to be made available for a wider audience. Sitting in circle in the dark was also mentioned. Then my situation, I cannot move yet as something is holding me here, I am meant to be here for a longer time. I was told that part of my land was sad, Fleur is into earth energies, I've been neglecting it, I must get it energised. This was true as one side of the land I hardly ever used to walk on, so that had to change. Overall an interesting reading with quite a lot of confirmations about the present and future.

There were quite a few happenings with regard to music during the year, I've said before that music plays an important part in my life and has brought me much enjoyment. A couple of singers have turned up several times, namely John Lennon and Roy Orbison. Yes I loved their music and I'm sure that I always will. I saw them both on the same show in 1963 at the Brighton Hippodrome. The Beatles were top of the bill, it was of course the time that Beatlemania was in full flow with girls screaming throughout. The only time there was quiet that night was when Roy Orbison was singing and he sang beautifully, receiving huge applause at the end of each song.

M.E. - My Blessing in Disguise

Recalling these never to be forgotten memories always makes me realise how lucky I've been to reincarnate at a moment in time when there has been so much music to appreciate, and of course it's been easily accessible to many of us. So on to some of the musical experiences from the year.

At one circle I saw John Lennon when he had long hair, he was speaking into a microphone. Then the angle that I was viewing from changed and a white light appeared in his left eye, the light became a 'J', then an 'L'.

Roy Orbison singing 'Crying' has brought several experiences to me over the years. Whilst sitting one day I could hear Roy singing it in my head, I realised that my head was slowly nodding in time to the song. After sitting I played the song, as I did a pair of dark glasses appeared on the blank tv screen. Another day I played it to finish the sitting, as my eyes opened there was an area of white on the door in front of me. Later I was playing a Roy O cd, when it got to 'Crying' I felt that something had been placed on my head.

At circle one day we had 'I Got You Babe' playing, and probably being sung along to, beautiful energy came into and around me.

I was watching a documentary about Freddie Mercury, very strong energy poured into my brain and body, it made me feel very woozy, there were also lots of white lights around.

I saw Bob Dylan and Eric Clapton singing 'Don't Think Twice It's All Right', four white lights appeared, like the corners of a square, they were just to the left of the tv.

I had Eric Bibb singing 'Needed Time' on the cd player, as he sang the fingers of my right hand were moving of their own accord.

One evening I was watching a tribute to George Harrison, a white key appeared on the wall above the tv, moving from right to left. Another day whilst sitting, spirit came through with a brief message. The message started and ended with spirit singing George's 'All Things Must Pass'.

At circle one day I was shown a group of people in hats and coats, we zoomed in on one, it was me with a moustache and beard, John Lennon was with me, and as I looked around I could see lots of singers and musicians that I recognised.

On December 8th I was reading and had a John Lennon cd playing down the hall. My eyes seemed to drift to the hall where several tiny, white lights were flying around. It was of course the anniversary of his passing.

Some different experiences here:-

In Mid-September I was watching a programme about the Battle of Britain, I suddenly began getting extra sounds in my right ear. They were the sounds of aircraft propellers, it seems that spirit were adding to the soundtrack as the sounds didn't come from the tv.

I've received some brief messages from spirit this year:-

In bed a lady had a chat with me, the gist of it was 'build slowly'.

At circle one day I was impressed with 'Sometimes less is more'.

One night in bed I was shown some unusual cards, the last one was mostly blank. I asked spirit what it meant, I heard 'He will be buried here'. Again I asked what it meant, I was then impressed with 'Your old self will be left behind'.

Spirit have continued to show me lots of surreal images this year, these first ones are while I was sitting in circle:

M.E. - My Blessing in Disguise

I was shown a purple elephant, then a hamster wearing glasses followed by a group of Extra Terrestrials.

Another time a beautiful, white, Celestial being was beckoning to me.

I was shown a man whose left ear was highlighted in white, inside his ear was a circuit board and a white line zig-zagged through the board, as if connecting things.

I was shown a bride and groom with their guests sitting around a table, a beautiful, white bird hovered above them, then a white horse and rider leapt over them and remained above them in mid-air.

Now some examples of when I sat on my own:

I was shown a child sitting in front of a grandparent, little white angels were flying around in front of the child's face. This was repeated with other children.

Another day I was shown a circle, I was above it and I saw a beam of light was connecting two of the sitters.

On a different day I saw two white lights were moving around, a white face appeared and the lights became his eyes. He drifted slowly to the right and became a full body which laid down. Later I saw a white tap, a pipe then appeared with hands on it, the pipe was by a table, a face came out of the pipe and was then on the table. More faces followed until the table was full of them, the faces then grew into people.

Here's some examples of things shown when I was in bed:

I was shown the white hand of a man, a white ray was coming from his eyes. Then I saw a head from the front, I could see inside the left side of the skull and into the brain.

M.E. - My Blessing in Disguise

One night I saw a sky full of milky, white stars, a huge spaceship appeared which was in the shape of a cross.

Another night I saw a magnificent, white angel, it was very close to me and there was lots of white mesh around in which several celestial images appeared.

Late July and I was in bed, I saw a large, white 11, it was close to an area with lots of lit, white candles. There was one large group and the others dotted about in smaller numbers.

On waking just over a week later, I was impressed that with ground Zero in New York. If these two are linked to September 11 then the timing seems to be a bit awry.

One night I woke up and saw close up, large, white bird in flight with it's wings outstretched, so beautiful. Then a huge pair of white, semi-transparent hands appeared underneath it, wow! The hands showed themselves in different positions, then a pair of semi-transparent feet appeared.

I saw white shapes on the ceiling one night, then two circles of white hands, it felt very special.

Now some examples of images received when my eyes were open:

Looking down the hall an area of rose-pink appeared, a white shape flew out of it.

Christmas morning and I'm sitting on the sofa having a cuppa, to my delight there suddenly appeared lots of gold and white lights flying around the room. That was a lovely surprise present that didn't need unwrapping.

M.E. - My Blessing in Disguise

With this example I had my hands over my eyes:

An angel flew towards me and looked at me for a while, its wings were transparent white, like gossamer.

An example shown whilst healing:

I saw a huge area of white, a cross was laying over it.

It has become a common thing for spirit lights to appear when I'm reading, and not just reading spiritual books, but with all sorts. Another thing that can happen if I allow it is for spirit to show me faces clairvoyantly on a nearby wall. This happened as I read D.D. Home, some of the faces were huge, and a light mingled amongst them.

I was reading a book about Unicorns when my eyes were dragged down the hall to where a white scene was waiting. Transparent horses head shapes appeared, people were kneeling down and looking up, then the head of a Unicorn appeared, it was white with black eyes, a really beautiful image, wow.

Whilst reading Estelle Roberts story, strong energy surged into my brain, it briefly made me feel woozy.

A couple of evenings running I was reading a Doris Stokes book, on both occasions I had the smell of cigar smoke. I have no idea whether she smoked cigars or not.

Here's some more happenings:

How many ways can spirit wake me up, here's some:

M.E. - My Blessing in Disguise

A finger whistle, a toolbox being put down, a high-pitched alarm, light switches going on and off, doors opening and closing, beep-beep and an engine running, piano notes, voices, an electric drill, harmonica playing, sound of a bird flying around the bedroom. Well I guess it's always good to have variety.

A lady with an Irish accent spoke my name, then a phone rang, a lady spoke and said her name was Purple.

One day I heard a 'boom-boom' in my ear and simultaneously felt a double blast of energy.

Sitting one day with Clare, I saw a scene in which someone was throwing clothes about, each throw was accompanied by Goonish sounds.

Whilst watching tv one evening and my eyesight was dramatically improved by spirit for a couple of minutes. In that time I could read everything on the tv without my glasses on. It soon went back to normal and left me with aches tightness in my eyes and around my temples.

One day I heard in my head 'Does this mean that you can hear me Brian', It was Chris, who I've already spoken about.

One day in early September I turned off the tv and a huge, white 'T' appeared on the blank screen. Later that day I felt energy moving in straight lines in my brain, that was new.

The next night I woke up at 4.44, in the following late afternoon I received an e-mail requesting healing be sent for two people, the mail was also timed at 4.44.

Sometimes trends do occur with what spirit wish to show me, this year I've seen quite a lot of celestial beings, Pyramids and Unicorns.

M.E. - My Blessing in Disguise

Here are some of the pyramid scenes:

In January I was shown a huge pyramid rising slowly from the sea, two days later I saw a large red pyramid, it became cone shaped and slowly sank into the sand.

I saw a pyramid which was soon surrounded by a glass cube, then a robed magician was in the pyramid talking to a crowd of robed people, they all had their hands in the air later.

In circle one day I found myself in a pyramid looking down on people seated around a large group of tables, in the centre was a 3D model of a city, which was all pyramids, it was computer generated and kept changing. I was impressed with 'Don't let others impose their limitations on your ideas and plans'.

I was shown some interesting things when I sat in the afternoon of July 10th, I saw a white horse with a white rider, then the rider was standing on the horses back as it ran around. Lots of other white horses appeared and a flying Unicorn as well.

I then saw a white road and soon there was a fork in the road, a white arrow appeared and pointed to the left fork, so no chance of going straight on then. I read that as spirit had taken a decision for me, or it could have been reiterating that I was still meant to be in Portugal.

A couple of weeks later I was sitting outside, I seemed to see a wave come towards me.

Not long after that, I was sitting with Clare and saw this scene: A group met in a pretty and secluded park with lots of trees and flowers around. Everyone wore white robes, though mine was yellow, we'd all arrived on bicycles. After a while I decided to leave, I was told which bicycle to take, it was a different one from which I arrived on.

M.E. - My Blessing in Disguise

Over the years I've seen lots of scenes where eyes become highlighted in white, here's one:

I was shown a face in which the right eye was highlighted in white, it became a white, twinkling, four point star, I was given a close up of it, so beautiful.

A year mixed with happiness and sadness, but also with some interesting musical experiences.

M.E. - My Blessing in Disguise

A Bit More Music

A quietish start to the year, but one evening somehow a mouse had got into the house, oh no, but it was true, and aren't they hard to catch. I think it must have come up from the basement as I opened the door, sneaked under my feet, and then totally ignored the 'No Mice Allowed' sign. I had it cornered but it disappeared, dematerialised perhaps, there was no sign of it anywhere. It was a tiny mouse and very furry, but they can be destructive, so I wanted to put it out. It was getting late so I went off to bed.

The next morning I was racking my brain, yes that hurts, I felt strong pressure on the top of my head and seemed to be impressed to look under the Halogen heater. I carefully tilted it to look underneath it, yes there was the little, furry ball half asleep, thanks spirit, now to safely move it. I managed to get it outside in one piece, I'm sure it'd be happier out than in. I must have picked up the heater when trying to catch it, and somehow put the heater over the mouse without squashing it, the heater's base is raised, so hollow underneath.

I made a trip down to the Algarve when Sheila and Steve came out in May. Driving down the A1, I felt a hand on my shoulder as I approached what I thought would be the Algarve turn off, however, the sign had gone. I decided to carry straight on and eventually came to another junction which did have the Algarve signposted, so I took that and duly got to the villa. When I get that hand on my shoulder it's usually reassuring, it was this time too.

One night in bed in the villa I saw a lady medium sitting in a small circle. They linked hands and a much larger circle appeared around them, lots of energy was moving around and some ectoplasm too. I saw a man whose white shirt glowed, then another man with a white light on his shoulder. This then became a white area and guides appeared behind him, including a Native American.

M.E. - My Blessing in Disguise

On another night I was in a scene and going to a house to meet some people interested in spirit, it was then switched to a house around the corner. All the people were men, business people or leaders of some sort, it seemed that spirit were going to speak to them through me. On a different night I had white light and heat coming down onto me.

On one trip to the UK I went to the Banyan Retreat to a séance with David Thompson as the medium. We experienced some wonderful phenomena, I do enjoy these evenings and attend when I can. In December I was back at Banyan again for a Christmas Tree séance with Scott Milligan as the medium. In the middle of the circle was a Christmas tree and lots of wrapped up presents, everyone had to bring one. The presents are opened by spirit children, after the séance they are sent to a nearby children's hospice. It's a lighthearted evening with lots of noise and with a little chaos thrown in. towards the end of the séance I was shown a pair of hands together, pointing up in prayer, then another pair came in and the two pairs together made a four sided pyramid, beautiful.

Spirit were very communicative through me this year, quite a lot was spoken in circle, and lots more when I sat at home. At some point in time I began playing music to start my sittings, and to close them. Towards the end of the year there were bursts of song from spirit through me, the first song was 'Keep Right on to the End of the Road', 'We Are the Champions' was another, a couple more were 'All Things Must Pass' and You Are My Sunshine'

Family and friends figured several times over the year in various scenes, I saw myself giving healing to my mum, oh what a lovely thought, she told me that I'd be able to help lots of people. My dad and Aunt Edith, were around, my son too, I saw him helping people in Africa, and Squeaker(Porky) the old family cat made himself known on occasions. Chris was through again, making sure that I could hear him, and I saw Trish behind a bar. There were also childhood friends and their families, Mr and Mrs Smith in particular, old work colleagues who are still around showed up, I'm not sure how that works.

M.E. - My Blessing in Disguise

Numbers, letters and symbols were still being shown to me along with keys and arrows, mostly white. Spirit have been showing me signposts for a while, I'd love to know more about the when and where of my future, so I'm wondering if there's a bit of teasing going on, as none of them have been helpful yet.
I'm still sending healing of course, but the 'hands on' aspect is mostly gone now.

One of the most common occurrences this year has been the feeling a hand on my left shoulder, a very reassuring gesture for me. I believe it is William, an author who wrote a lovely book about his own experiences with mediums, I've had the name given to me twice. Sometimes the sensation has spread from my shoulder into my chest.

Spirit have given me some messages in Celia's circle through Lin this year, 'Embrace the day, things will happen in their own time, you can't bring forward the future'. Lin had a link with my aunt Edith who gave me this message, 'A Cricket ground, someone knocked the stumps deep into the ground, only a few inches were left showing, then someone comes into bat with a Tennis Racket, it's about thinking differently, going with the flow of the river's meanderings'.

Here's some things that spirit have said through me at different sittings:
'It's a shame it's got to be Brighton'.
'Seldom is the storm that passes unnoticed, Yet frequent is the calm that lies unfelt'.

'Some say an upwards pointing sword is active,
A downwards pointing sword passive,
But the truth is that swords are only made active
By the minds of the holders,
It's they who determine the swords mode,
This applies to all weapons and objects.'

203

M.E. - My Blessing in Disguise

I continued sitting with spirit most days and consequently I was shown many celestial and surreal scenes, here are some of them:

I saw a large, beautiful, white, winged creature, it was on the ground, but its long, graceful wings were moving.

I was shown a white eye, then a dark eye, a white hand rose up and partially covered the eye.

I saw a group of Native American faces, then I saw the shelves in the room where I sit, the ones with the larger crystals on. There was a crowd of angels on top of the shelves around the clock, then a large angel joined them and was in front of the clock, a beautiful image.

I saw a scene in which I dropped something, as it hit the floor there was a loud clink in my right ear.

I was shown a crystal ball with a framework around it, a white bird landed on the framework, then a golden bird. The golden bird flew off, many white birds came in.

There was a white pyramid and some other structures, some were white and some magenta. They had golden rays of light coming from them, they all appeared to be upside down.

I saw myself searching through some plants looking for one with lots of seeds on it, twice I found one, then lost it quickly. Then I found a third plant that had lots of good, large, mature seeds, I kept it safe.

There was a man's face and it began changing and he closed his eyes, then ectoplasm began coming out of his mouth. In the ectoplasm appeared a young lady holding a baby.

I saw a circle of celestial beings, all were in white gossamer, they took turns in the middle of the circle. Then magical lights appeared as they went into a glass and were swallowed.

M.E. - My Blessing in Disguise

I saw a picture on a red wall, the room I sit in has red walls, someone came in and took a large, grey feather from behind a picture.

I saw an angel with uplifted wings sitting on a large yet graceful animal, other white angels were around.

I was shown an upside down light bulb or a hot air balloon, a 7 appeared in the round part.

There was a scene in which there was a pinky, purplish area with an eye in it, this became a cave with a door, someone went in through the door.

Twice I was saw myself in scenes where I threw things, the throwing made my body jerk and it brought me back. This has happened during other sittings as well.

I saw someone sitting, then someone came behind them and laid them down to give them healing. I then felt some liquid in my mouth, it had no taste.

I saw three crossroad signposts in a row.

There was a scene in which I put a finger on a flat spring in order to make it 'boing', as I did it I heard the noise to my left.

During an afternoon sitting I was shown a white, wooden, crossroads signpost, there were some words on it but I couldn't read them. Then there was an outline of England and Wales. I was playing some music at closing, the second song was 'Let It Grow' by Eric Clapton. The song starts with lyrics about trying to read crossroad signs, a nice bit of synchronicity.

I saw an upside down, white triangle or pyramid, it became a white heart that seemed to give off bubbles of love, then it began spinning.

M.E. - My Blessing in Disguise

I was shown some beautiful, white images including two groups of pyramids, amongst them was Eros firing an arrow.

I saw two guitarists with a drummer and a keyboard player, they all had white lights around them.

I saw a lady in a long dress, it looked like a waterfall, then a white robed figure appeared. I was shown a beautiful, large Swan swimming, then a white bird of prey on a perch.

There was a scene with four or five Penguins flying as a group across a clear, blue sea, one peeled off and dived into the water. I then saw a small, white ball thrown into a hole in the side of a plastic bag.

A man in glasses came forward and shook my hand, there was something unusual about his hand.

I saw a beautiful lady, then another, then I felt someone kiss me. Soon a lilac parachute was coming down with someone under it, they landed safely.

Someone with a card, then bacon or similar was wrapped around the card and it was eaten.

Here are some examples of scenes shown to me when I was in bed:

I saw several groups of white lights arranged in geometric shapes, they all became white birds in flight, I was given a close up of one flying. I then saw a large number of white circles in an oblong shape.
I was shown a large area of white, then a pair of white hands, they became part of a circle of white hands, there were two people sitting down in front of the circle.

M.E. - My Blessing in Disguise

I saw a key with a white celestial around it, someone was given the key, and with the celestial went to find the door.

I was in a large room or hall, lots of happy people were queueing up to thank me as they left. Then a lady led me to a table for a chat.

I was shown a White Christmas tree, it's June!

I saw waves of rippling white light, some purple and gold also.

I saw a white, young lady and she jumped into a sun or a flower which had a face and an aura.

I was driving in the UK with passengers on board, it was a long drive from the north to the south. We all fell asleep and spirit drove the car a long way for us. We woke to find that we were near to our destination, and we were all safe and sound.

I saw the white image of an angel which approached someone, a white net or similar was put over them to protect them.

I was shown the fretboard of a guitar, it had two large, golden circles on it, they seemed to radiate joy, harmony and light.

I saw a white hand in a white heart.

I was shown a crossword grid, 33 was filled in and some symbols too, most squares were blank. I saw 77, then a whole row of 7's, then a row of T's.

I saw a white hammock with a large 'M' on it.

I was shown a beautiful image of the Earth rotating, the lower half of South America was covered in an unusual, thick, milky cloud. Nothing was visible through it.

M.E. - My Blessing in Disguise

I saw a white key which had white angels and celestial beings going around it, after a while they offered me the key.

I was shown several scenes and images whilst my eyes were open, some of these were whilst in bed, others not:

I got out of bed in the dark and white bird in flight appeared in front of me, it stayed with me even after I put the light on.

I woke to see white shapes and symbols on the walls and ceiling, then a white cross and white bird in flight. Lots of triangular, white flags were dotted about behind the cross, as if on a map.

I got into bed and was immediately shown three white, crossroad signposts, one at a time, they all had lights above them and the second one had five directions. A beautiful, young lady swapped my coat for hers and she ran off. Later I saw her and caught up with her to retrieve my coat.

I was up at my brother's house for dinner with Bob and Saci when a large pair of eyes appeared, then a Tiger's face filled in around them, wow!,

At my daughter Alison's place I saw several large faces.

In bed I was shown lots of images on the ceiling, some were animals, including a Tiger, then some peoples faces followed by four white aircraft in close formation. There was a bi-plane, a jet airliner and two other aircraft.

On waking one day I was shown a series of wonderful, white celestial images, a huge jet airliner with white light coming from it. These images were beautiful but were topped by a truly, wonderful, feathered image.

M.E. - My Blessing in Disguise

I was walking from the hall into the diner/lounge, something large and white went behind a chair, I couldn't find anything.

Sitting on the sofa when a carved, wooden post briefly appeared next to me.

I was reading one day when I saw a child's face, he closed his eyes. I then saw a bearded man and a white light shone from his third eye.

I was making a cuppa when a crystal ball appeared between me and the kettle!
I was writing some notes and a white light appeared on the page, it became an arrow, a star, a 7 and then white bird in flight.

I saw a white case handle for a while, then a bluish-white, neon light was on my jacket.

In bed with my eyes open I saw a gold light by the door, a pyramid then appeared and floated around. Then a tiny, white key went into a lock and turned.

Again in bed with me eyes open I saw golden lights like stars, then there was a crescent moon near one of the stars (we'd just had a new moon). Later on waking a bright, white bird in flight appeared.

A large area of burnt yellow appeared at the top of the tv, it then spread all around the tv frame.

I was reading a book when I noticed a blue light on the tv, then white faces on the blank screen, one face was wiggling its tongue.

Now for some examples of images shown to me whilst travelling:

On a plane once I was shown a flock of white birds in an area of purple, they were all flying and beautiful. I was also shown lots of

M.E. - My Blessing in Disguise

fluorescent colours, so alive to me. I saw lots of white, celestial figures playing guitars and other instruments. Then there was a white, wooden, 4-way signpost with a white bird flying around it. These images do help to make time fly.

On another flight I saw a passage with magenta walls, at its end was a golden door, the door opened and a lady was standing there.

I was on a train with my eyes closed and I saw a man with long hair flying around.

On a different journey I saw a white bird on a white tree, white bird in flight came around it, then several more white birds turned up.

Here are some examples of what I've seen in circle this year and some happenings:

I was shown a pair of hands that looked ready to applaud.

At an August circle I saw lots of people looking at me, I was trying to communicate with them. I felt myself slumping down, spirit then lifted me up by the elbows, no it didn't hurt. This happened two or three times, spirit also shook me to prevent me from drifting off. These were new experiences for me.
At one circle I experienced lots of cold, this is not that unusual but something made me move a little. When I did it seemed to trigger massive tingles all over. Later something tapped me on the head and made me duck, too late I thought.

In another circle I saw John Lennon, then a glass dome. There were lot of people looking like string puppets in the dome, and lots was happening with my hands too.

M.E. - My Blessing in Disguise

At a circle I was shown a beautiful, diamond shape. At closing a large heart appeared, then a beautiful screen of magenta, in its corners were magenta coloured hearts which were trimmed with gold.

Some more unusual happenings:

I was outside pruning branches off of a dead Apple tree and I could smell smoke, there was no sign of any anywhere. Incidentally I've left the main trunk in place, it's a nice piece of natural architecture.

I was sitting on the sofa and could suddenly smell smoke, the alarm also went off. I searched around and found nothing, no cause at all. The next morning I woke up and felt absolutely wonderful, I can only describe it as a feeling of being full of love, spiritual love I suspect.

Many time this year I've seen these little angels or celestial beings flying around the house, they disappear when you try to look for them, they're usually silver or gold. This began last year and has thankfully carried on.

There have also been occasions when clusters of golden lights are flying around, a real treat as they're around for a minute or two. One day something made me turn around, and there they were, lots of beautiful lights zooming around, most were golden.

After I'd finished a sitting, I kept feeling someone or something resting on my left thigh, just above the knee. There was one squeeze from this friendly spirit.

Happenings related to music and musicians have continued this year, here's some:

There was a tv news item about Michael Jackson's passing, it brought in lots of cold energy which surrounded me and tingled around my head.

M.E. - My Blessing in Disguise

Whilst watching a programme about Elvis, there was a cluster of blue lights to the left of the tv. There was also an area of yellow moving around the tv frame.

I was listening to a Gary Moore cd when I noticed an unusually, bright, white shape, then a pair of black lights, they were all on the blank tv screen.

At circle we had Sarah McClachan's 'Angel' playing one day, the music suddenly speeded up, I shouted at spirit and it then played normally. Another day I was playing it at home and it kept speeding up, I could see nothing wrong with the cd, so it must have been you know who.

I had the Pretenders 'I'll Stand By You' playing, cold energy filled me for a while, then it came again. Since then I nearly always get that reaction when I play that song.

At circle one day Kirsty McColl and Roy O both showed themselves to me, they were both singing into microphones, sadly I couldn't hear them.

Eyes closed and I saw Elvis, then I saw him with some friends in a Limo.

I was listening to John Lennon's 'Mind Games', beautiful energy poured into me and filled me from head to toe!

I was playing a Nils Logfren song, 'Shine Silently' as I closed a sitting session, someone came into my body and I became cold and tingly, they stayed around.

Listening to a George Harrison cd, strong, cold tingles began in my face and then spread all over me.

M.E. - My Blessing in Disguise

Whilst watching George H strong energy came into my brain and third eye area, then I had pressure across the centre of my chest.

Another day I was watching more George H and a yellow hue was on the tv frame, as they talked about the passing of Roy O. It disappeared but came back as George's wife talked about him. I was seeing images of George quite a lot around then.

Got up one morning and the song ' Has anybody here seen my old friend John' was in my head, it was the day before the anniversary of JFK's passing

One way or another you could call it a musical year.

A Special Year

During 2012 I was shown an abundance of numbers, letters and symbols, words and parts of words, keys, clock faces and hands and digital clock times, the whys and wherefores of this are unknown to me, though I believe that '7', the most common number relates to showing me that I'm on my Pathway. 'T' has been the most common letter and I think that I now know what that relates to. I am still having doubts about how I can ever move forwards and how my role can grow into something more useful, and also why I'm having to spend this time in Portugal. I still making regular trips to UK, but I'd much rather be there on a full time basis.

During a circle at Celia's I was shown the name Doreen Lang, no one could take it so I investigated to see what I might find. Doreen Lang was an actress who had small parts in several films including 'The Birds', 'Almost an Angel' and believe it or not 'Brian's Song'. I've only seen 'The Birds' out of those three, but the titles of the others are interesting, mmm. 'Brian's Song' is about an American footballer who has terminal cancer. Doreen also had parts in television series, and I've recently found out that she was in 'North by North West' too.

This year brought in two new arrivals to my family as we welcomed Mia in February, courtesy of Alison and Pete, then Roisin in November, courtesy of Noelle and Brian. Roisin was a whopping 10lb 4oz, they're both growing up nicely.

Life carried on with healing being sent most days, along with sitting at home, and in circle when I was out here. In the UK I was taking in the odd demonstration and a reading when it was due. Of course nowadays you can have readings on the internet, and I think this was in my mind when I sat one day. During the sitting I was shown a white feather so after I decided to look up white feather to see if it had any significance. I soon found that there was a medium who did online readings and had

M.E. - My Blessing in Disguise

White Feather as his principal guide, his name is Robert. With Celia's help I duly had a reading with Robert over Skype.

I taped the reading and then reviewed the tape, writing a list of bullet points as I went. I realised that I'd had a lot of good evidence and ticked off lots of items on the list. As part of preparation for this book I went over the list again, I now ticked quite a few more items, some I wasn't aware of at the time, and some other things that have since happened, so all in all it was an excellent reading. One thing I've literally just found out is that Harry Edward's main guide was White Feather, how about that. I found it out as I'm reading a book about Harry Edwards, it's by Paul Miller and called 'Born To Heal'.

Spirit lights continue to often accompany me, they're a joy at the best of times, so imagine how I feel when I'm driving through foggy conditions or through heavy, lashing rain and they show themselves, it's very reassuring to see them or white bird in flight. Driving home from circle one day I had a tower of blue light with me, then a blue light was inside the windscreen.

I think it was during this year that I decided to have a sort through of the spirit pictures that we've drawn. I've said how amazing some are to me, but then there are the others which just seem like doodles. Hundreds of them got thrown away, rightly or wrongly, but I did discover a few that I really enjoy, so I added a few more to those on the walls. I've pinned some to blank canvasses, that way it's easier to get more up on the wall.

One day in early January I was sitting at my pc, the halogen heater was on a few feet behind me, if anyone doesn't know, they give off a bright light. Suddenly a shadow passed across the screen and the wall behind it, for this to happen, it meant that someone came out of the room where I sit and walked behind me. The door to that room was shut and did not open, and there was no one else in the house, so I must have had a spirit visitor.

M.E. - My Blessing in Disguise

Another day when I was at the pc looking at the PM4U site, I had a George H cd playing, the music was being messed about with but I was ignoring it, then I got a whiff of tobacco smoke.

I have a woodburner in my lounge that gets a fair bit of use in the winter months, it's a cheery thing to have around. I'm not the only one who likes it. One or two Lizards are frequent visitors to my house, I don't know how they get in and out normally. One seemed to have set up home as it could be found lying on the shelf in front of the woodburner when it was lit. Lizzie started getting braver and came onto the rug between my feet, a dodgy place, then it climbed onto my foot and made itself comfortable. When the weather warmed up, Lizzie made it up into the roofspace and would lie on the sunny window sill. They generally disappear from the house in the summer, preferring to race around outside.

Twice I've rescued baby lizards in the house, one got itself caught in a web on the stairs, the other was in the Summer room, making its way towards a large spider, I put these tiny creatures safely outside.

On August 22nd I was sitting as usual, now hang on, I'm writing these notes on August 22nd, there we go, start again. I was sitting in August and I heard 'Larry' whispered. I've known at least three chaps called Larry, one is in spirit. I can't remember when he passed, but I think it's got to be Larry the pool/snooker player, loved all sports and was one of those larger than life characters whose nearly always up and happy, lots of chat and very gregarious. The odd thing though, Larry didn't whisper unless he had laryngitis.

The sitting carried on and I went off for a while, I was brought back by a noise to my right. The noise happened a few times so I got up to see if I could spot what was going on. There is a low storage unit in that corner, but I couldn't see anything likely to cause the noise. It must be spirit playing I thought, so I sat back down and hoped to go off again, but spirit ended the sitting soon after.

M.E. - My Blessing in Disguise

I was just about to leave the room when I heard the noise again, still nothing on the floor though. I'm off for my cuppa then I thought, but as I was leaving that corner the noise was repeated. This time I realised that the noise was coming from the little inset cupboard, halfway up the wall which contains the fusebox. I opened the door to the fusebox and what a surprise I found, there was a lizard in there, and it wanted to come out. There's two ways into the box, the door I opened, which had been firmly shut, and through the corrugated plastic tubing which is used to carry the cables in from outside. Lizzie had got a bit too adventurous and must have come all the way down the plastic tubing, I bet it won't do that again in a hurry.

Whilst it was nice of Larry to let me know he's around, at the end of this what came into my mind was the name of a children's cartoon character from I don't know when, 'Larry the Lounge Lizard'.

Having two granddaughters born made this a special year, but there was also something else memorable too. I went to the Banyan for a séance in October, Scott being the medium in the cabinet. At some point in the evening a man came through direct voice, it was his first time and he did struggle, but he persisted and said two or three things that had a few people interested, I was one. Then he said that he was here for his son, still three of us in, but then a clinching piece of evidence as the Red Cross was mentioned, so it was my Dad, wow. It felt so wonderful, it's very difficult to put the feelings into words. He couldn't speak for long, but I got another piece of evidence that I finally corroborated about a year later. That was to do with a photo which had my godfather and a crew in front of a Lancaster bomber, I couldn't recall ever seeing it before, but it turned up in a cupboard at my sister's. Dad had been in the Red Cross when he was an ambulance driver, it was voluntary work, but sometimes we would get some complimentary tickets to various events. So well done Dad, you made it a very special evening for me.

Another thing I was happy about was finding 'A Path Prepared', it was a new version of the book about Isa Northage's mediumship.

M.E. - My Blessing in Disguise

A month later to the day and I was sitting with spirit, there were lots of images that day, and I was also impressed with the name 'Blue Wing'. After sitting I was reading A Path Prepared and Blue Wing was mentioned in the book, he was at a séance.

During the summer, Jim, an English neighbour, was talking to me about India, it's his favourite subject, probably because he spent a lot of time there when he was growing up. He told me about a place on the India/China border where there is a lake, the people around this lake have mixed with each other freely, unhampered by any border restrictions. The outcome is that you have Chinese looking people who have Indian accents, and of course Indian looking people who have Chinese accents. This interested me because I've been told a few times now about this Chinese guide who is meant to be coming to work with me, I, on the other hand, have been expecting Rashid who sounds Indian, and from time to time I've asked spirit how come the Chinese guide is hanging around. Only time will tell, but it's not impossible that spirit have answered my question through John, even though he has no time for spiritual things at all. His parents were missionaries, so he was put off of a lot of things.

A cold day in December and I was back sitting on the sofa, after I got frozen hands whilst sitting with spirit, even though I was wearing gloves, it was mostly spirit cold I should add. Later there was a programme on the tv about Egypt. As I watched I felt someone come into my lower legs, and began to move up into my stomach and chest. I asked spirit who was with me, at that moment the word 'Rashid' appeared on the tv screen, wow! There is a town in Egypt called Rashid apparently, some coincidence there, or not. I've waited a long time for news of Rashid, so I took this as reassurance that I've not been forgotten. I was soon taken out of it for a while, then brought back by a loud bang.

In the course of the year I've received lots of messages from spirit, some through circle and some at demonstrations, many direct through

M.E. - My Blessing in Disguise

me, and also some from the White Feather reading. here's a few of them from circle:

Messages given through Lin often come in phrases rather than sentences:

Lin had Coral Polge through more than once for me, Coral had a blackboard and easel, she drew lines to quarter the board, she wrote one word in each quarter, 'Home, Coast, Motor, Future'. No real explanation was given..

There was also a golf analogy given, no not by Coral, 'Don't think you'll always find the rough, it also doesn't matter how many shots it takes to get the ball in the hole, it's a life's work'.

Through Lin again, 'Don't react to others, stay calm and things will happen step by step, no rush as you will be guided, the future may seem muddled, but it will become clear and work out'.

My Uncle Bert gave me a message through Lin, 'You can't make an omelette without breaking eggs', that was about something that had been on my mind. He also said that he was happy with what I'd done with my land, but told me not to force feed my plants, as they'll flower in their own time. 'When you deal with people who have strong connections, don't just defer and don't charge in, take the middle road'.

Lin gave me a message about gold coming for me. I arrived home after circle and parked my car in the usual way, as I reversed I saw a large, gold light fly from the back of my car and into my house!

Celia had a link for me in circle with some lovely evidence, she then brought a message through for me, 'You're interested in healing and its history, you should do it your way, how you are comfortable, don't follow others, the best healers have been individual, including psychic surgeons, don't worry about organisations and certificates, people will come'. Then Grey Owl spoke and said, 'I will bring windows to you'.

M.E. - My Blessing in Disguise

He also told me 'You must keep in touch with nature, it gives you uplifting energy and is very important for you'. He said that 'he was not my main guide', as he spoke white bird in flight appeared as if to confirm this. It's interesting because I had been on the net looking at healing organisations in the UK, spirit had obviously picked up on my thoughts, and given me theirs.

Another message through Celia, 'Williams, he is around you and helping you to build your ship and to rig it out, so that when the time is right you can sail away. He's organising it so that some kegs of beer go on board, he's generally helping me at this time'. Thanks Chris, that was a very encouraging message, as was the one about healing.

There was a brief follow up to this a few months later, 'Boat connection, don't fret, be patient, it's all under control'.

I went to a demonstration at Barnes Healing Church with Sheil, Betty was the medium on the platform, I received a message, 'You will find what you're looking for', and again 'spirit like what you've done with your land'.
Lin had given me a lot of names, one was a paratrooper, a chap I knew from the sixties, they are part of a supporting network for me.

There was also a brief message from Mo, it was a cricket analogy about using 'yorkers'. I'd sat with Karen and Mo a few times at the back of Karen's house, in her shed a few years back. Karen lives near the football stadium. I've heard that Mo had passed, the last time I saw her was at the Banyan, we were both there for a séance.

I've continued to receive messages when I sit at home, often they're forgotten before the sitting ends, but here's one or two that were remembered:

'That's mudwater in there from the river Brian'.
'Doors will open, doors will open'.

M.E. - My Blessing in Disguise

'It doesn't matter how well you can cook if the recipe is wrong or some ingredients are missing'.
'There's a need to bring spiritual ideals into your everyday lives'.
'You must keep an open mind as Spirit can cure anyone and any condition, unless healing is refused or it's a pathway condition'.
'Brian you are a Jack of all things'.

A message was given to me one night in bed, I saw a man laying on the ground with a blanket over him, as I got near to him he said 'You're one of those global healers'. I sat down next to a man who was trying to help him.

Another night in bed I was given a very clear message, it was an answer to my thoughts. I'd put my house on the market due to feeling continually unsettled here, it was obviously a premature action as it's now 2015. I was thinking about a couple who'd viewed the day before, wondering if they'd make me an offer as they'd seemed very keen. Then a black cat appeared and began shaking its head vigorously, that'll be a no then.

I do ask spirit questions, it's a rare thing to get an immediate answer, it could be weeks later when an answer comes through, yes, I'll have forgotten the question by then.

I'm still getting noises when in bed, I've had a couple of metallic doooing noises from the wardrobes, and also the ruler flicking noise as well, unfinished knocks on the bedroom door, as in 'de de de de de', I do wish they'd finish them, or perhaps they expect me to do that bit.

One day I woke up feeling shattered and could hardly keep my eyes open. I crashed out on the sofa for a while, suddenly wow! There were lots of beautiful spirit lights floating just above my head, some moved around quickly, most of them were golden.

M.E. - My Blessing in Disguise

Another day a single, beautiful, golden light came floating down, another wow! Shortly after I went to the bathroom and more golden lights were there floating around, so beautiful.

Later in the year I was sitting on the sofa having a cuppa, several beautiful golden lights were flying around in front of me, it gave me such an amazing feeling. They are only occasional visitors, I guess that's why they seem so special to me. Most spirit lights I see are still, and often on their own, though sometimes in clusters.

I've been shown a few more hands recently, usually white or partly white, one white hand was holding out a telephone to me, I also saw a pair of white hands. One unusual occurrence was when I got out of bed one day, I seemed to see a hand on the window blind.

Some unusual things occurred as I was healing or sending healing. My hands were moving in a circular action, individually, yet somehow together. Another day my hands were put into the prayer position for closing, I've since adopted this as the normal to start and to close my distant healing sessions. It's something I used to do, and I seem to remember Don was shown me doing it in a circle at Shoreham many moons ago.

Another day my hands were shaking vigorously for a few minutes in an up and down motion. The next day brought lots of unusual hand/arm movements for several minutes, the session ended with my hands making slow and circular movements, beautiful energy was around me. One summer's day whilst healing, my hands and arms seemed to make a heart shape. An old favourite, but rarer these days, was to feel my left index and middle fingers to be as one. Feeling someone's aura is also a more occasional occurrence now, as is the anaesthetised feeling in my left cheek. It did happen one day though and it spread across across my left eye to the bridge of my nose, it then went to my left ear, seemingly joining up with the point at where it started. I am still feeling as if someone gets into my hands, and sometimes there seem to be hands

M.E. - My Blessing in Disguise

over mine. It does help to make the sessions more interesting, and I'm sure the healing keeps flowing regardless of whatever sensations I feel.

I was fortunate enough to be able to help some friends with their healing clients when on a trip to UK. In one session my stomach kept on somersaulting, at another I saw a pair of eyes looking at me as I gave healing to a lady. With another lady, I was drawn to her jaw and throat, my fingertips felt as if they'd gone under her skin when I sat at her head. I could feel things moving between my hands and there were also strong vibes coming up through my feet and into my body and hands. When the background music changed, it seemed to alter the energy in me.

So what else has been going on this year, well I've seen quite a lot of owls, both in sittings and in life. I've also seen a lot more Native Americans when sitting, nearly always in a full headdress, sometimes singly and sometimes in groups.

Aunt Elsie and Uncle George have showed up a few times, my old neighbours the Smiths too, also Nell and Ernie.

I saw several scenes with old friends and colleagues, they mixed the ones who are still here with the ones who have passed for some reason. I saw myself talking with Chris as well, but I have no idea what was said. It is good seeing the likes of Bazza, Murrey, Norman and Trish, the world's a poorer place without them, well that's how it is for me, but of course they're all in a good place.

Spirit have kept the musical connections going I'm pleased to say, Phil Lynott has been around quite a lot.

Here are some of those surreal images that spirit showed to me when I was sitting this year:

M.E. - My Blessing in Disguise

My old friend White Bird of Flight was flying around, then there was someone strapped underneath him, as they sometimes do with hang gliders.

I saw several images of spirits who had areas highlighted in white. I also saw a man slide up a rope.

Part way through a sitting my eyes were opened, I saw a blue bag to my right, something else to my left. Later it seemed as if someone was to my left, they got up and crossed the room to pick up some bags and things from the floor. Also in this sitting I saw something white and wooden with names on it, a white key was behind it.

In another sitting, I twice saw a face and another face appeared in its right eye.

I was shown an unusual van moving very slowly down the track behind my house, it is narrow. The van was green and silver with perhaps a little black, it hasn't turned up yet.

I saw a white door with a black, square panel near its right edge. There was a white keyhole in the panel which then became different shapes, including a key.

I saw a man talking, he began looking at me and then he became a Tortoise. I saw the profile of a Native American, a bright, white light appeared behind his ear, it became a fairy. I was then shown some aircraft, Superman appeared underneath one. The next thing I saw was some white pyramids, white bird in flight was above one.

One day I was shown a huge, heart shape, there were two white keys inside it at different angles.

In another sitting I saw a doorway with the door half open on my side, then the door was pushed through to the other side. There was a big

M.E. - My Blessing in Disguise

clock and a fireplace, and a bride was waiting in her white dress. There were lots of people around and a party started.

During a sitting I saw a small, white ladder, then a group of people sitting down. Butterflies and enormous flowers came up behind them. A lady in the group was speaking about a canoe factory.

I was shown a face and spirit seemed to be trying to show me where the third eye was, then another face appeared where the third eye was situated, strangely it was over the left eye.

I saw a bright, beautiful, white bird in flight which rose upwards, wow! Then I saw a chaotic looking Heath-Robinson type of machine, it somehow became orderly with a large wheel which revolved perfectly. Then my beautiful, white bird in flight was back and rose up again, yes another wow sight.

I was shown the white image of a Native American, two lit candles started moving around him, a beautiful scene, then I saw two moons and a golden sun in the night sky.

A Native American appeared in full bonnet with a white bird on his hand, he was talking to another white creature. Then he laid down and was surrounded by lots of small animals.

I saw a young man who appeared to have something like paper growing at the bottom of his back. You could tear it off to read the sacred prayers that were written on it, then more would grow.

I was shown a man's face, he closed his eyes and two black, diamond shapes appeared in his right eye, then a white Tepee came in behind them. The diamond shapes then became jumping deer.

Here are some images and scenes that I saw whilst in bed:

M.E. - My Blessing in Disguise

I saw a room with a sofa and an easy chair along two walls, on the floor by them was lots of white energy dancing around, it was like mini whirlwinds.

I saw a man in a business suit walking on my land, he seemed to fall down a hole and disappear.

I was shown a tall, tiered cake, a bride in a long, white dress appeared next to it, lots of golden stars shot out of the cake and went all over the bride.

I saw a purple robed figure, then a huge, long-haired, black bear, which began coming towards me. I put my palms up to face the bear as I looked at it. The bear stopped, turned around and went away. I then went into my house and found our old cat Porky was on the sofa.

I was shown a lady with a white face, beautiful jewellery appeared on her, a butterfly and a necklace then sat on top of her head.

I saw a scene in which I'm driving along a straight road on the right hand side, a car then overtakes me on my inside, the right. He turned across the front of my car and went around behind me, I followed him round until we'd gone around in a complete circle, so I was facing the way that I'd been driving. I put my foot down and sped away along the straight road, leaving him behind. I now found myself driving on the left hand side of the road.

In this scene I'd woken up, so my eyes were open. There was a big screen going across the ceiling and down a wall, two life sized people were shown on the wall. One was John Lennon with what looked to be a mobile phone. We zoomed in as he was pressing buttons on the phone, I was so amazed that I didn't think to look to see what numbers he pressed. Then there was a man in a convertible, wind in his hair and laughing, it was Paul McCartney. I think it may have been Paul with John at the start, well what a team they were. The image changed as lots of angel wings and white feathers appeared across the ceiling.

M.E. - My Blessing in Disguise

Here are some happenings whilst I was in circle:

I saw several faces who had something that made their right eyes prominent. I suddenly had something in my mouth and had to swallow it. There was no taste or discomfort.

I was shown some faces, one had ectoplasm streaming from the mouth and nose.

I was shown a vase or a long-necked bottle, some liquid was pouring out of it in a controlled way. Below it was a huge dish collecting the liquid, there was no splashing. I then saw some unusual faces, one winked at me, there were some more sitting on a sofa playing a long, box shaped guitar. At this point I could feel energy being taken from my solar plexus.

I saw an enormous cross and I was flying above it, I then saw a circle with a medium in trance. I found myself with some people sitting in a glass dome, masses of stars were all around us, one appeared to come into the dome and roll around the floor.

I was shown a white boomerang and was then impressed with Charlie Drake. I saw a man playing piano, a word appeared on the keys, it was either 'bang' or 'bash'.

I saw an area of white light that seemed to grow and light up what was around it, there were some faces with unusual conditions. One man's lips were highlighted.

I saw lots of faces that looked normal, but had hidden conditions. I saw Louis Armstrong with his trumpet amongst lots of spirits, some of them had something over one eye which apparently enabled them to see me.

Later in that same circle white bird in flight lit up an area for me near the doused light, so that I could see some spirits.

M.E. - My Blessing in Disguise

I was reading a small booklet written by Roland, a lovely chap who I've mentioned previously, and I was shown the white image of a man's face, then white bird in flight came in front of him. Another day I was reading his second booklet and a lady's face appeared in the hall doorway, I also saw some figures on the floor. Roland is now in spirit.

2012 turned into a special year for me, two new grandchildren and hearing my dad speak to me, of course that means two more reasons to be full time in the UK, that feeling grows stronger.

M.E. - My Blessing in Disguise

A Not So Good Friday

2013 began with a longish and very wet winter, only slowly melding into spring. Several times the river was high, and a little way down river a huge, beautiful tree was washed away. Several of us lost a few feet of land as the river made more space for itself. The wet weather continued right up until Easter, being very wet in the week running up to it. Good Friday it wasn't, with the river high from the start of the day and rain falling until about 6pm, but the river stayed in its bed. I spent the day driving around, there was water everywhere. It was a relief to see that my land was still green when I got back, some patches of water, but it wasn't from the river.

I think that this was the year that the Hawthorn hedge really took off, and so did several of the shrubs and trees that I'd planted, they all grew so well.

Brother-in-law Paul was continuing his fight with cancer, and along with my sister Sylvie, they were now well established members of the local bowls club, it kept them out of mischief and in a way returned them to a former lifestyle, when Paul played cricket and Sylvie would help out with the teas. There was some bad news to come in September or October, as my daughter-in-law Noelle was diagnosed with breast cancer, a tough time as they now had two little ones to look after.

There was a family occasion in the early part of the year as Roisin was christened, all went well apart from one mishap. I'd taken my jacket off and left it on the back of a chair, when my ex-wife's brother-in-law came past the table with a tray full of drinks. Ted had a wobble and tipped the tray, so we had our second christening that day, my jacket, it was saturated, I'm so pleased that I wasn't wearing it at the time. Ted had been unwell on and off for sometime, but he'd been in good spirits that day.

M.E. - My Blessing in Disguise

One thing that has come in is what I call sending calm, I raise my hands so that my palms face away from me, facing whatever direction calm is needed in, and ask spirit for help. This came in handy one Sunday afternoon during a hot spell, as a fire started by a village just the other side of Arganil.

To begin with it was heading towards Arganil and that meant this way, I raised my hands and asked for help, in a short time the wind changed direction and the fire went in the opposite direction, towards open country. It grew quite big as everything was dry, and we had planes and helicopters dropping water on it for a few hours until it was under control. I've also used this in situations with neighbours, well there's no harm in trying.

Spirit were continuing to work with me and spoke through me a lot at home, and a few times in circle. I saw a lot of clocks and clock hands this year, no explanations were given. As with last year I saw past and present friends and family all mixed up in some scenes, I can't figure that out either. I expect quite a few had no idea that life carries on, so maybe spirit are just being supportive to me.

Having just spoken about helicopters, I had a bit of synchronicity one evening. I was watching a program about the Sea King helicopter, part of the way through it a helicopter came over and literally hovered over my house for a few minutes.

Now onto healing, there was a lot of control when I was sending healing this year, some days my hands were shaking a lot, sometimes vigorously, and also there were lots more hand movements, as in up and down, back and forth, circular movements, on a few occasions all of these movements would happen in one session. One day the shaking of my hands was so strong that my body was jerking. The energies changed quite a bit, often it was the, what I'll call, usual energies, but there were days when the incredibly beautiful energies would come in, they do feel special. I can only presume that other healing guides are

M.E. - My Blessing in Disguise

required at that time, and they have these different energies to help out those in need.

In one session beautiful energy came in and then I couldn't feel my hands, but somehow I could feel the energy that was going around them. At another session, something touched one of my hands and it totally changed the energy. There have been several times when my hands have circled each other, and others when they were drawn together, as if by magnets, with the fingers interlocking sometimes. I've also had occasions where my hands have suddenly felt so heavy that they literally just flopped down into my lap.
I've mentioned before about feeling heat and cold in my hands; at one session my fingers became very cold after cold energy had come around my hands, somehow my thumbs and palms remained warm.

It was different one session when my body felt as if it was being hugged by some cool energy as I was sending. At another session my arms were held above the elbows for a while.

Here's a couple of things I was shown whilst sending healing:

A lilac pyramid with an arc of yellow lights under it.

I saw a white key go into a lock, then a young lady in a lab gave something to a young man, he was standing and looking into a microscope.

One day three different spirits came through, then I saw an unusual shape which became a white, Victory sign. I saw a dark shape which went into a white building, when someone was taken into the building, white protection appeared around it.

When closing one session I heard some wind chimes tinkling. I do have some, but they're still in the box.

M.E. - My Blessing in Disguise

I received some healing from Barbara one day and I saw a white sailing ship on the ceiling, this was next to a large, white hand.

Moving on to circles this year, I received some good evidence early in the year through Lin, it came from an osteopath who had treated me for a back problem in 1982, it was in fact my first ever visit to one. I was given some advice about looking after my back when I'm digging or gardening. Then it was mentioned about a hole in my land near the river, about how it needed fencing, it's a collapsed well. I only found this well by chance as I was strimming my way through some brambles then a sudden reflection from the water caught my eye and warned me that I was on the edge, a close one.

On another day Lin had Charlie for me, there was a good description of him and his characteristics, then the message was 'He wants me to walk in my own shoes'. Then Charlie showed himself in the rain, but keeping dry by holding something over his head. He also said that he wants to help guide me along, to light my way, then he gave me a trophy for the work I've done and said that I've lots more to do. That was lovely encouragement Charlie, thanks.

A couple of weeks later Lin brought another message through for me, it mentioned Simon standing by a small harbour with lots of boats, he takes everything in and embraces life. Lin saw me with new soil under my feet, then new grass and new footsteps to walk in. I've been going around in circles, I have to walk down the land in new footsteps and then branch right, I'll come to a welcoming shed/cabin, all I need is there. It may rain or snow but I'll have the right clothes to keep dry and warm.

I received a message at a demonstration at the Brotherhood Gate in November from Trish, good to hear from her.

I heard a lady's voice say to me 'Having an audience is wonderful'.

I think I was impressed with this, rather than me hearing it,

M.E. - My Blessing in Disguise

'Your life is not about to turn upside down, but is in fact to be right side up'.

I made a few visits to the Banyan Retreat for seances and for a couple of workshops with Scott. At one workshop spirit spoke these words through me,

'The truth is inside you, Spirit is truth, Truth is love, Love is all'.

Spirit have continued to encourage me and said such things as 'Focus on the will be', 'There is light at the end of the tunnel'. I've heard spirit say a couple of things, this one was when I was sitting, 'He's the number one surgeon'. I also heard this, 'You could be part of his daily team'. In bed one night I heard, 'Isn't there some manky wine downstairs', and the answer to that was yes, there was some, ha ha. I'd given my grapes to someone one year who'd wanted to try wine making, I was given a dozen bottles of wine, well manky was a good description, it just didn't work out. I have now got rid of it, poured it away. I did taste it, but then I wondered why.

At a circle in April I was impressed with a couple of verses, I was going to give it off when spirit came through and beat me to it,

'Sometimes you must fail,
Sometimes you may cry,
These are the times to remember,
The beautiful sunlit sky,
For the clouds must surely fade,
And the rain must surely cease,
And then you can look forward to,
A restful, blissful peace.'

This came through a few days after my 'not so Good Friday'.

M.E. - My Blessing in Disguise

Hands have appeared for me a few times this year, I was in bed when I saw a sky full of grey cloud, beneath it was a strong arm with the hand going up into the cloud, white light was emanating from where the hand was up in the cloud. On another occasion I saw a white pair of hands, one of the index fingers was beckoning to me. I later saw a hand on the ceiling.

There have been a few occasions where I've felt incredible energy rubbing over my hands. It's happened in circle and when I've sat at home, and also when I've been sending healing, it's such an amazing feeling.

I've been shown a huge range of images again this year, many of them white. We've had keys, some of them in locks, spanners, pyramids, white birds, sometimes in groups, three lights looking like Orion's Belt, a space station, and several times I've seen Apollo Capsules, there's many more.

There's been a lot of Native Americans showing themselves to me, sometimes in groups, nearly always wearing headdresses, sailing ships keep popping up, sometimes more than one at a time.

In bed one night I could feel something going on in my right ear, which was on the pillow. The next thing I knew was that someone had blown a couple of Raspberries in my right ear, it seemed as if they were blown from the inside out, don't ask me how I figured that one out. A little bit later I'd turned over and so now had the left ear on the pillow, yes they now blew Raspberries in that one, darn clever eh. Strangely I'd just put a card in the post for my son's forthcoming birthday, it was a Spike Milligan card, now he did like to blow a Raspberry. It's been a while since that happened, but it did recur a couple of times during the year. The night before this I'd heard the 'Ying Tong Song' somehow.

During one afternoon sitting I saw some WW2 aircraft, seeing aircraft is not uncommon, but as they faded I saw WF, it quickly changed to

M.E. - My Blessing in Disguise

MF, the initials of Murrey, now in spirit. In bed that evening I saw myself walking with Charlie, who'd brought some messages to me. He was very happy and jumped into some shallow water for a paddle and a splash, just like a kid. I never saw him like that when he was here, but then I knew him as an elderly gentleman.

One day I felt what I can only describe as a ball of energy in one side of my stomach, a concentration of spirit energy inside me. It happened a few more times in coming weeks, including more than once when I attended a workshop to do with developing physical mediumship at the Banyan Retreat with Scott.

One hot August night I was shown an e-mail in bed, it said 58 days left. The only thing of significance that happened when winding forwards 58 days was that during an afternoon sitting I saw a white tv, its screen on and a child on the screen. The child looked like someone who has been missing.

The following days sitting produced a lot of images including scenes with a séance trumpet, the scenes were mostly in white. Earlier that day I was sitting on the sofa when a very strong influence came in, I suddenly felt as if I was lifted and tipped to the left, then tipped to the right, the influence then disappeared as quickly as it had come, I was woozy before this started and after.

A couple of days later I was outside sitting in the shade, it was a hot August day and I closed my eyes, spirit seemed to show me different ways to water and feed my plants and trees, it was interesting to begin with, but then it became too complicated for me to follow.

A week or two later I was again sitting outside, this time my eyes were open as I was watching my white bird in the sky. A white rocket or plane joined it and both rose higher before coming down lower, much closer together. The somehow they became a kind of heart shape, really beautiful, and together they then both rose back up into the sky holding that shape, a wonderful sight.

M.E. - My Blessing in Disguise

I was walking around my house when I was shown a white bottle laying down. Then there was a glassful of white liquid with a lit candle behind it.

Another day when I had my eyes closed I saw white bird in flight and two white spanners, one large and one small. Then one end of one spanner became another white bird in flight, then another white bird in flight appeared, so there were three.

More than once this year I've seen myself doing things in scenes, in which something happens to bring me back, an example: I saw myself going up some stairs, then I tripped, as I did, spirit brought me back by jerking the foot that tripped.

One scene was repeated two nights running, it showed a white nail or screw being put into place to hold two things together, it was probably going into my brain, ha-ha.

Spirit continued to wake me when they thought it necessary, using a wide variety of noise. There were keys turning in locks, door handles being tried, knocks, bangs and door slams, an aerosol being sprayed, footsteps in an ear, voices in the basement, bird flutters, plastic pen clicks, and of course the blowing of Raspberries. There's been quite a few noises when I've been sitting including a throat clearing, the sounds made when some one gets up from a leather chair, musical notes, and the sound of energy moving around.

One morning I got up and saw two, large, white birds gliding down to the river, Geese I imagine. I've had so many of those Golden Beetles in my house this year, they're usually on their own, but I was sometimes getting two or three in a day. They are harmless, it seems to be the year of the Beetle. I don't think it's the same one getting back in, but who knows, I've never tried to ring them to find out.

M.E. - My Blessing in Disguise

Here's a few examples of some more surreal images that were shown to me in circle:

I saw a man's face, a white line went into his left cheek and came out of his right eye, then it went back in at the bridge of his nose and came out of his mouth. I then saw some one holding out a white key.

I saw a white heart and a series of white clock hands, these became celestial beings. Then I saw lots of people at an open air cafe, the celestial figures then came and lifted up some of the people there, and flew them into large, cereal type bowls. They released them so that they slid gently down into the bowls, with between four to six people to a bowl.

I was shown a huge dog, when its right eyelid went up I could see a room in there, inside it were lots of people and also a white dog that looked like Grommit. Amongst them was a lady swinging on a rope, she was wearing a small hat and a jacket and she looked like a Ringmaster, she was very relaxed.

Now for some surreal examples of when I was sitting at home with spirit:

I saw a man in an upright armchair, the chair seemed to have white wings at shoulder height, it looked as if they were the shoulders of the man in the chair. The man got up and another took his place in the chair. This man looked like Leslie Flint, and I then noticed that the wings on the chair moved.

Spirit followed this up the next day as I was shown a room with a mantelpiece, and things on its shelf, the upright armchair from yesterday was also there. A Native American with a full headdress then appeared and went behind the chair. A man looking like Leslie Flint came and sat in the chair, he then left and another man sat down.

M.E. - My Blessing in Disguise

I was shown some unusual plants, big and roundish, on top of a shallow, ornamental pond. Someone came and peeled back the large, top leaf, underneath were some tiny fish swimming around.

I saw a funnel with a long stem, it became a Martini type glass, then the glass was filled with liquid and something added to it. Three or four different types of glass appeared, they also had something in them, then for a few seconds I could smell Basil.

I saw a man with a white shape in his left eye, it came out of his eye and became a bird. Then I saw a throne on a raised platform with a figure in a white robe sitting on it, all around the throne were huge, white hands. There was a man on the steps of the platform who was also in white, lots more people were all around, all were in white.

I was shown some drinks and a white bird appeared over the top of them, one of the glasses was a straight, pint glass. A white, spirit figure appeared at the bottom of the glass and made an umbrella, this he pushed up to the top of the glass. This was then repeated in another glass.

I saw a huge, beautiful tree, it was multi-coloured in green, light green and brown, the colours were arranged in alternate, triangular shapes.

I was shown a white, séance trumpet and then a glass ball with a long neck, similar to a yard of ale glass. Then I saw some white faces, including a man with a thick, white moustache. He had a white, séance trumpet on his shoulder, it moved to be near his mouth.

I was shown a large room whose wall were lined with books, several people were in the room and there were some names on the walls. You could push a button to speak to those whose names were on the walls, I heard a warm, female voice say 'You've got to play Arsenal's best'.

M.E. - My Blessing in Disguise

I saw a bright, white key, then a smaller one, the keys were pointing at each other. The small key then turned around so that both keys faced the same way. I seemed to be seeing one key with each eye.

I was on a moving pavement, a man was standing by it and he spoke to me as I went past him. Then I saw an open book with a lady reading from it. There was something about her presence that I felt meant that she could turn a flag upside down. Spirit impressed upon me that she'd spoken a word in Latin that meant upside down.

I saw a scene with a sofa and a white rug or carpet, white mist began swishing around over the carpet, then it all became purple.

I was shown some large pictures on a wall, then a large, sailing ship came in front of them. There was a misty building behind the ship which looked like the Royal Pavilion in Brighton.

Here's a few surreal examples that I was shown whilst in bed:

I saw a white golf flag on a green, there was also a large, white golf flag across the green. Behind the green was a white, naval ship, white bird was flying around.

I saw a scene outside my house in which an old car or strange buggy was on the track by the wall near the main door. Three black wolves appeared by the car and were looking at me, there was no threat from them. I had a belt in my hand as two of the wolves moved out onto my land.

In bed with my eyes open I saw a lot of black lights floating around, then they all suddenly dropped back down to land on a set of Dominoes, all in the right places.

This was a year with a lot of communication with spirit, they do like to keep me interested.

Kicks Up The Backside

2014 turned out to be quite a mixed year, I was given reminders by spirit that they wanted this book to be written and to be out there, which is a positive message, although it's led to lots of hard work. Sadly my brother-in-law Paul lost his fight with cancer and passed in November. Before the year was out, my ex-wife's brother-in-law, had also passed with cancer. Both of them were good people whose company I enjoyed.

Paul was a very outgoing chap, not shy of being the centre of attention, a life and soul type with a generous nature, I'd seen a lot of him in the past two to three years. Ted was quieter, but had a good sense of humour, and I hadn't seen much of him at all in the past few years. Even with what I now know about life being eternal these are difficult times for me, so for non-believers it's all magnified. They leave a hole in our hearts, they're bound to when we've known them for so long, I'm just glad that I know we'll meet up again. Death still shocks me even though it's a temporary finality, but my beliefs help me. How I wished I'd had this knowledge way back when mum died suddenly.

I had many trips to the UK this year, if anything I was spending even more time there now. I was lucky enough to be able to sit with Debi quite a few times, Sue joined us when she could, these sittings were growing in importance I felt. I was generally feeling that my time in Portugal was coming to an end, it would be great to stop this commuting and be full time in the UK, I just felt as if my energy was drifting away from Portugal.

In March after sitting with Debi in the morning, I found myself at Three Bridges Spiritual Church for an evening demonstration, the medium was Lesley, someone I'd never seen work before. There was a good sized crowd and I found a seat near the back. I think Lesley is a bit of a throwback in the way she works, it's about getting messages to people, and as many as you can, the audience were certainly very warm towards her.

M.E. - My Blessing in Disguise

Most of the messages she gets are shortish, not the long drawn out ones that seem to be the fashion for many mediums today. A lot of people got messages, her delivery is quick, I'd say on average that the messages may be short on time, but not on substance. Towards the end of the demonstration she came to me, Lesley gave me some good evidence and the book got a message in passing. There was also something about my work changing in the future, and also that there is a teacher in spirit who will work with me. I closed my eyes when the closing prayer was said, I was shown a white hand which then gave me the thumbs up.

At the end of April I went to Crawley Spiritual Church to see Lesley on platform again. I didn't expect to get a message this time, but I did, and it was probably the longest one of the night. Again I was given lots of good evidence about family and friends, and also that spirit know what's going on around me. Lesley was just moving on to the next message when she turned back to me and asked if I was the one writing the book. I think I replied, 'well sort of'. Then came the kick up the backside, 'spirit want it written, they want it out there'. Spirit then told Lesley that the book was about my spiritual experiences, and followed up with 'they want others to be able to read this book, you must get on and finish it'. It was a lovely, positive message, albeit with a sting in the tail.

I did get back to writing after the message, but perhaps not as much as I should have, so I probably shouldn't have been surprised to get an even stronger gee up. This happened towards the end of the year when I went to a demonstration at Barnes healing Church with my friend Sheila. I don't have the medium's name, but she had a link with my Aunt Elsie who gave this message 'I've been putting something off, I need to get on with it, I should put my foot down to finish it, then I can relax'. It had to be about this book and I have put a lot of time and energy into it since and now I'm nearly there.

M.E. - My Blessing in Disguise

Since then spirit have spoken to me many times about this book, the overall gist of the message is that I can't move forward on my pathway until it's done, changes can't happen, the key is inside me, as I've been told before. Spirit have also said that it doesn't matter if no one buys it, it's about making it available. I haven't sat very much with spirit for sometime now, they say that the book is the priority, so the point has been rammed home.

I attended some more seances at the Banyan, most had Scott as the medium, but David Thompson was the medium for one. I hope both of these mediums can make further progress, it would be fantastic to see them able to work with red light so that some phenomena could be seen in the light. The mediums have no choice in this, it's all down to the guides, what they'll allow, they set the limits.

My feelings of returning to be in the UK full time grew stronger as the year went on, perhaps it's not surprising when Paul and Noelle's health is considered, Noelle after all is the mother of two of my grandchildren. This was on my mind one day in Portugal when I did an internet search on something, an advert appeared at the side of the screen, I usually ignore those, but this offered a free 3 card Tarot reading. I expect they hope you'll go for a full reading, which you have to pay for, I went for the free one to see what came up.

Three cards appeared and I had a question in my mind, I can't remember what the first two cards were about, but the third card was interesting. It was about my 'present position', and the message was 'You're in the wrong place as your future lies overseas'. Now that's what I call a clear and emphatic answer, so I'd best get on with the book then.

During my frequent trips back to UK I'm always looking out for books, especially spiritual books, I do love reading about mediums from the past. On one trip I was fortunate enough to find three or four books, one was a small paperback by a man called Tom Pilgrim, a healer. I

M.E. - My Blessing in Disguise

hadn't heard of him and I nearly didn't buy it, even though it didn't cost much.

I had Tom's book for several months before I read it, I just kept letting it slip to the bottom of the pile, or did I? Eventually it was the only book left that I hadn't read, so it was time to read it. I do love a good bit of synchronicity and I found some quite early on in the book. Tom had lived in Brighton, my home town, and the area in which he lived for sometime is just a few streets away from Debi's house, where we sit, so that was a good start.

Now at the time I'm reading Tom's book, I'm also pressing on with my own, gathering notes as I scour through my diaries for tales and happenings.
 There was a note entered in 2003 about circle, when Annie brought through a message from my Dad. It all made sense to me apart from the last thing said, 'Egremont Place'. I knew it was a street in Brighton, but I had no idea where it was. Shortly after I'm reading some more of Tom's book, and he mentions 'Egremont Place' and an experience he had there, which was hearing his name called out as he walked up this street. It wasn't his usual route I might add, but there he was trying to spot who was calling out his name. He couldn't see anybody and found himself looking up to the sky, up there he saw a beautiful cross above his head.

That message from dad was at the end of 2003, so I've moved on to the 2004 diary, and in an early 2004 circle I was shown a beautiful golden cross, wow! The reason this synchronicity had such a big impact on me was because of it's timing, I'd had Tom's book for a few months and it could have been read any time, but somehow it was pushed aside until the very time that I was searching my diaries and spotted those entries which related to Tom's happenings. This was astonishing, if I'd read the book earlier I'm sure I'd have been pleased to know of the similarities, but it wouldn't have seemed so important, the timing here was everything.

M.E. - My Blessing in Disguise

Twice when sitting around this time, spirit had used a certain phrase to me, it was the 'proof of the pudding is in the eating', this phrase appears in Tom's book as he was giving healing to a well known actor.

Earlier this year I'd read a book about another healer, Alan Bacon, he lived close to Brighton when he was healing. Incidentally, he was raised in Putney, not far from where my friend Sheila now lives, and Sheila is now also a healer. I often get spirit lights on books when I read, especially spiritual books, I think that there were more around when I was reading Alan's book than is the norm.

One afternoon in mid-October, I wandered around my land in the sun, as I approached the river two large birds that I took to be Geese landed on the water. As they were swimming about, I realised that they looked different to Geese, just then an adult Heron came over and landed on the opposite bank and the young ones headed over to it. The adult spotted me and immediately took wing, closely followed by it's offspring. I didn't realise that Herons swim, I see them quite often here, but I'd only ever seen them flying, wading in the river or on a bank, and occasionally on the top of a tree, but never swimming.

During the year spirit spoke to me quite a lot when I sat on my own. There was quite a lot of talk about the book, this seemed to start after I'd read Tom Pilgrim's book. I remember spirit asking me what I enjoyed about his book, after I answered, they told me that I should be aiming more along those lines, rather than the way I'd been thinking up till then. I thought about it and it made sense, so I had to change tack, but that of course meant that I'd have to go back over all of my previous notes. At some point after that, it's been emphasised on several occasions that the book has to take priority over sitting and other things.

Earlier in the year I had a croaky throat, when I sat spirit still managed to come through and speak very clearly, regardless of how my own speech sounded. I also had instances where two spirits seemed to speak simultaneously, sadly I wasn't taping. There was another time when

M.E. - My Blessing in Disguise

four or five voices were through in rapid succession, one was in a staccato type voice.

I had a series of messages from spirit in September and October, all short and sweet:
'The light has changed from amber to green'.
'The light is green for go'.
'The lights are still green for go, they cannot change back.'.
'We're in this together' (this was shown to me in writing).
'The gun has been fired, we're go, the plane has taken off and the wheels are up, there's no stopping things now'.
'The waiting is over in all but name'. 'Focus on the future'.
'We are the ship about to enter port, we are moving forwards as the tide rises, a berth and unloading awaits us'.
'A year of change is fast approaching'

In amongst these encouraging messages were some others as well, some were interesting to me:

'We are taking control for a while to ensure that certain things take place'. 'When spirit needs something to happen, it will happen'.

The most intriguing message was this one:

'The next time you hear my voice it will be through another medium'. I don't think it's come through yet, the guide who spoke had been through many times, so hopefully I will recognise the voice when it comes through.

Spirit have been very helpful on a few occasions this year, one day I heard what sounded like material tearing, I got up to investigate and it stopped. I looked everywhere, but couldn't find anything, however I notice that I'd left one of the sliding windows open a little, so I might have gone out without noticing it.

M.E. - My Blessing in Disguise

There was one occasion when my old friend the Stonechat was making a lot of noise at my bedroom window. I think it wanted me to go outside for a while, once I did it went quiet, it's been a while since they checked on me.
I was painting my Summer room this year, using up some old cream paint, the new coat was looking a bit anaemic. On two or three occasions as I neared a corner, this room's corners are lilac stripes, an area of yellow appeared on the wall near the lilac. A few days later in circle, Lin brought me a message from Uncle Albert, part of the message was that I needed more colour around me and yellow was mentioned. The yellow spirit had shown me on the wall looked kind of dirty, so I ignored that but took up the big hint and brought some yellow paint for the Summer room. The paint looked nice and bright in the pot, but when I put it on the wall it looked a dirty yellow, I was not impressed and told spirit so. However, once the paint dried it became a beautiful, sunny yellow, and there's no doubt that it's changed the character of the room, so I said thanks to spirit.

I had some viewings of my house during the year, one was with a chap and his daughter, they also had a friend in tow. He really seemed to like the place, but he was an elderly gent and I'd thought he'd struggle to manage the land. We got on really well and had similar taste in music, it would have been good to have had him as a neighbour. No offer came as he still had somewhere to sell in the UK.

The upshot of this story is that I felt a tremendous sense of relief once they'd gone. I put some music on and found myself doing some crazy dancing, very unlike me. The relief reminded me a bit of 2006 when I booked those February flights to Portugal and a massive weight was lifted. It was a strange feeling to get in this situation, but obviously it wasn't meant to be sold to him.

I've had several messages in circle this year, mostly through Lin. I referred recently to a message from Uncle Albert with yellow paint, well in the same message he showed himself to Lin doing some crazy

M.E. - My Blessing in Disguise

dancing. He'd obviously got that from me after the viewing, the rascal, so I had to own up, the message was a couple of days after the viewing.

There was also a part of the message about me having difficulty in contacting a friend, 'keep trying' he said, I did and eventually I got through. My age was also given during the message.

During one circle I felt a muscle vigorously jumping about in the left side of my chest, interesting as I'd recently been writing something about Buqi, the non-invasive acupuncture that started my recovery and healing process. At the original demonstration and talk about Buqi, I'd had a muscle jumping like crazy behind my ear in similar fashion.

At another circle Lin had some evidence about a boy who used to sit next to me at Junior school, the message was brought through by Gordon, he's visited our circle on a few occasions, and brings lovely energy. It's possible it's the same Gordon who spoke through me quite a bit a few years back now. Lin brought a message from Betty through, ' I should be on the platform doing clairvoyance'. Well if it does happen I'd expect to be in trance, going by what's been said in the past.

Charlie has been a regular visitor for me in recent years, and he gave me some interesting evidence through Lin. He was talking about Glastonbury Tor, he wanted me to remember what happened up there. I have described this earlier in the book, I was shown a beautiful symbol and I couldn't understand what it was. I went and found what I'd drawn after the Tor, this message from Charlie prompted me to solve the mystery. The penny dropped as I looked at the symbol, it was a combination of 'T' and 'P' pushed together, it was so obvious, but I couldn't see it at the time. I now associate these initials with Tom Pilgrim, I can't think of anything else. If it is Tom then that's another tie in with his book, and I'm amazed all over again. I showed a few people the symbol I'd drawn and no one spotted what it was, I'll have to try to draw it and include a picture of it in the book. There was one last part of the message from Charlie, 'eat bigger dinners', I don't see that as a good idea Charlie.

M.E. - My Blessing in Disguise

Later in the year Lin brought through a message from an old work colleague, he spoke about the past being behind me, and that changes will come into most areas of my life, including development. I must not attempt to interfere, just let things happen. My Pathway went on what seemed to be a deliberate diversion, now I'm going to be doing what I agreed to do before I left spirit to incarnate here, it's my purpose now. He also wanted me to write in chalk on a blackboard, I can't see that happening at present.

Another old work colleague has brought messages through Celia a couple of times, Pete, who was one of my old bosses. I really appreciate those who take the time to find out how to get messages through to us, we have no idea what it's like and how the system works. I expect that they have to learn as much as we do.

One message from Spirit I want to include I thought came from a book I read, but I recently read it again and didn't find it, here it is anyway, 'Love from Spirit calms, and conquers fear'. It's one that has stayed with me.

On one of my numerous trips to Porto airport a white key appeared in front of me whilst I was driving, it was there for a short while. Keys, white ones in particular, are shown to me a lot.

I was in the UK in November when Paul passed, I flew back to Portugal a few days later At the airport car park my car wouldn't move forwards or backwards, there was no obvious reason for it and I got out and checked around the car just in case. I decided to give it a go using a lot of wellie. It worked and I backed the car out of the parking space, but as it first moved one of the wheels on the driver's side went over something, even though there was nothing to go over. It reminded me of the chocks that they put around aircraft wheels, now Paul of course had been in the RAF, but I thought it was a bit early for him to be playing jokes. I made the sad journey back for his funeral a few days

M.E. - My Blessing in Disguise

later. Many of us chaps who were there wore lairy waistcoats for the day, Paul had a couple of prize ones, and he took one with him.

I had my share of being woken by spirit this year, many of the usual ways and some new ones as well: filing metal, gnawing, chain saw, coins being dropped, paper crumpling and cellophane, my name called and resounding on, log stacking and a gong. One night I woke to feel as if a pneumatic drill was hammering away around my heart, it happened again the following night. Another night I was woken by a loud noise, it was as if someone had opened my bedroom window.

When sitting this year there was also a mix of sounds, gargling was new, snoring and a muffled sneeze as well as the usual selection. One sitting I was brought back by a loud crack or a shot, and I saw something snap and smoke. Another time I distinctly heard breathing, I held my breath to make sure that it wasn't mine.

One summer evening in my kitchen/lounge area, I heard the sound of dripping, it seemed to move around the room and then return to a corner. I looked all around and could find nothing, not even a Lizard. It then occurred to me that I'd been gathering notes from an earlier year's diary, there was an instance of dripping sounds one night when I was in bed. I began to wonder if someone in spirit was having a laugh with me, or calling me a drip, whatever , the dripping was gone and I never found a cause, just another bit of synchronicity then.

I had a couple of noise instances at Sylvie and Paul's, in bed one night the head board was banging on the wall, but the bed wasn't moving at all. An evening after Christmas I was sitting on the sofa when someone blew a Raspberry from behind the sofa, well I think that's what it was, who knows, Paul had been good at making noises.

I was shown a few words during this year: Paul, Love, MINT, Angel, Train, intriguingly 1-33 and 1st PRIZE.

M.E. - My Blessing in Disguise

I continued sending healing as much as I could, there were several different happenings. More than once my hands were moving a lot, incorporating up and down, in and out, forwards and backwards, and sometimes circular movements as well. Quite complicated when put together, but I'm sure there are reasons for these actions. One day I felt as if someone was sitting on my shoulders, then the contact extended down my front and back.

There were three or four sessions this year when it all felt so beautiful, with my hands touching someone as they used to, and also feeling weight on my hands. This beautiful feeling was with me when my hands seemed to enter someone's aura, my hands were then pulled together.

On one trip to the UK I had one of my lower back niggles, I went up to London to see Sheila and have some healing from her. When she started I became all cool and tingly, lovely energy worked its way down my back, my niggle was gone the next day. I nearly always ask for healing when I finish sending for others, one day spirit gave my right wrist a thorough examination, it had been hurting for a while, in a few days it was fine. Another time receiving from Sheila, my lower back was pushed in and slowly the top half of my back was pulled backwards, as if correcting my posture. Sheila's hands stayed on my shoulders throughout.

One day after circle with Debi, she needed some healing. Strangely we hadn't been healing for very long and it seemed to switch off and my hands moved out a foot or two. Then I felt very cold, and the cold travelled up my arms and down my body, a short time later my hands again moved further away from Debi and the cold energy process was repeated.

Whilst healing I've felt my hands pulled together as if by elastic, and I've also felt my hands pushing against something. I had a tingling touch on the back of my right hand, it travelled up my thumb and felt wonderful.

M.E. - My Blessing in Disguise

I had a lot of finger movements one day during distant healing, it was almost as if I was playing the Harp. The day after this I went into the room to send distant healing and there was a smell as if a candle had just been blown out. I took the hint and lit a candle for that session. In another session my body was rocking backwards and forwards as if rowing, then my body laid flat on my thighs, then upright. This was all repeated a few times, seems like someone wanted me to do some exercise.

There were a couple of occasions where my hands were pulled in quickly together, with one hand supporting the other, it's also happened where the hands come in and my fingers interlock. One day whilst healing, a bright, white shape became a crown, then a bird, the bird in flight soared upwards and sparkled, a truly, beautiful image. A new feeling was when something seemed to be brushing the skin on the right side of my stomach. In one session everything felt different, there was weight on some fingers only, then it was on all the fingers and the thumbs as well, I can't explain why it felt different. Towards the end of 2014 there were more occasions when my hands felt as if they were in spiritual gloves or spirit was in my hands. I felt a finger trailing around the centre of my left palm whilst sending, and I've also felt someone take a deep breath.

During the summer I had a reading, the first full reading for two or three years. It was a chance thing as I was walking around on my way to a second hand bookshop. I spotted a sandwich board outside a shop that was advertising that readings were available. I went into the shop and got lucky, I could have a reading in about ten minutes, so I went for it.

The medium was Cathy, and she picked up most of what was going on around me, I've had to be where I'm at, and had to have lots of time on my own so that I can develop as a person in a certain way, as well as the spiritual development that's happened. This was all confirmation of things I've been told before. Then I was given an analogy of my present position. 'I'm in a hurdle race, I've just jumped the last barrier, but I'm still in the air, when my feet touch the ground the changes will begin'.

The medium was excited by the changes that were coming in, big steps forward in healing and mediumship, more confirmation for me. Then she had a look of real disappointment on her face as she said to me that I wanted to move to another country. I think she asked me why would I do it when all this is about to happen, I didn't respond then. There was more about it not being a mistake to be where I am, it was necessary. She thought that my healing was moving towards psychic surgery, we'll have to wait and see about that.
When the reading was over I could see that Cathy was still feeling disappointed about what had come through, so I told her that the move to another country meant that I'd be back full time in the UK. I'm pleased to say that her smile came back. It was a positive reading for me with confirmations that things are heading in the right direction.

This year was no exception for being shown surreal images, here's some that I received in bed: I was shown a huge, beautiful, rainbow-coloured '24'.

Another night I saw myself in a shop looking at crystals and stones, I picked up one that I liked, on one side it had '2'.

I was in a scene with friend Barbara and we met Sai Baba. He was in a car with another man and several children, he looked my way and we had a chat.

One night I was shown a large, white 'Y', then I saw an angel with uplifted wings, then the 'Y' again. I then saw a ladies' football match, after which I was in a locker room when a small horse or pony came in. It came over to me and rose up on its back legs and placed its front legs on my shoulders, as if it wanted to hug me.

I saw a pair of beautiful white birds in flight, they seemed to be on the edge of a Butterfly's wings.

M.E. - My Blessing in Disguise

I was shown a huge, white map of Australia, something strange happened in the south west corner. After that a white arrow dropped into a bow and was fired.

I saw a small, white pyramid which became a light. I was being held by a white, robed figure who was making it shine down.

I saw a golden shape, then it was over a child's bed, it became a golden star and a child appeared in it.

A few night's after his passing I saw Paul, he came out of a lift and go through a door, he was looking round as if he was unsure of where he was, but he was OK.

One night early in December I saw a blue screen with some writing on it, written in a cartoon style was 'Thanks for everything'. I'd recently written that as part of a message in the condolence book for my sister.

I found myself on a water bed, there were bushes and trees around it, a young lady and man came towards me. The whole of the image was white.

I was shown these images when my eyes were open in bed:

An area of wall was lit up, in it were some white propellers, like modern windmills.

On waking one August morning I saw a white, Christmas tree. It lifted up and became horizontal, then it became a parasol.

After getting into bed one night, an array of slightly golden, white lights were above me, beautiful light was pouring down on me. I saw a torso with a tie on, and a tenpin motif on the tie.

M.E. - My Blessing in Disguise

One night in the corner by the door I saw a white shape that looked a bit like angel's wings.

Here are some examples of images received whilst sitting:

At one sitting I saw a couple of white spaceships and a white sun which sent out a large solar flare. Then there was a map of the UK, a gold light flashed somewhere in the south east.

I saw a large, white, celestial figure who was about to cut a big cake with a knife, then a group of celestial beings appeared in front of the cake.

White bird in flight became a jet plane, then a white, celestial figure came and sat by a wall, small birds and animals soon came around the figure.

I was shown a series of white images, it began with a collection of tools or odd looking golf clubs, then there was a white table with celestial beings on it, then the table became covered with brides and grooms.

I saw the beautiful image of a white celestial on a swing, there was a white circle around the swing.

I saw some drinks, one glass fell with a loud thud onto a wooden floor. The glass didn't break, a cat came and licked up the spillage.

There was a room with no windows, a red, patterned carpet covered the floor. There were lots of things on the floor and I saw a white rider on a white horse, an E.T. face. Olive Oyl was there and she became a beautiful lady in a white dress.

At one sitting a beautiful white bird appeared twice, it looked fabulous.

I saw the open end of a white spanner, other white images followed, I also saw Paul.

M.E. - My Blessing in Disguise

I was shown a white shape that had sparks coming from one end, it grew smaller like a firework, there were people at the end of it, possibly behind a curtain.

I saw a face with a cone or trumpet to its mouth.

I saw several Native American ladies holding their babies, some white energy was moving back and forth between one mother and her baby.

I was shown what looked like an eye, in it were guitars and guitarists, then a bright, white diamond joined them.

I saw some WW2 aircraft, some had lots of spirit people sitting on their wings as they flew.

I was shown a white room with a fireplace, there was a cream rocking horse and something else cream in front of the fireplace. I was out of it for sometime, when I came back there was someone in my legs. I don't know how to explain this, but my legs felt beautiful, they've never felt like that before, and I've had them a long time now.

Now for some examples of images from circle:

I walked up to someone who was stacking logs, they sloped down and away from the wall and were looking as if they would fall down at any minute. I picked up a log and threw it at the pile, nothing fell down, I was amazed. I threw another and everything still stayed in place.

At Debi's I saw two male faces, one had a white cover, the other had a large hole in his left cheek. Someone else appeared and took both pieces of the cover and pushed them into the hole in the cheek.

I was shown a clear glass jug which was being filled with a clear liquid from some glasses. Then some of the liquid was poured into a cup, it became instantly hot like tea.

M.E. - My Blessing in Disguise

At one circle I saw a choir who were all in white, they were joined by a Harpist. There was also a white key on a cushion.

Another day I was shown a column of men in uniform coming towards me, they were in two lines. I was up on some rocks and they couldn't see me, they stopped next to the rocks that I was on. Their hats were the flat style, I stepped onto the nearest head and ran along that line. Near the end of the line I jumped down so that I was between the two lines. I then quickly ducked under the other line of men and was gone before any of them could react.

Here's some instances of images seen whist my eyes were open:
I was looking out across my land when an Owl flew across and landed on a post, whilst it was there white bird in flight appeared next to it.

I was on the sofa when a large, yellow light appeared on the wall opposite me, there was something like a clock with it. The image grew smaller and became a couple of small faces.

I saw white bird in flight, it became a jet plane which turned upside down and flew backwards, a black jet plane did the same. Some golden faces appeared, they were followed by some white images including 'T's', angels and a white key that became enveloped by an angel. I also felt as if I was wearing an oxygen mask that covered my face from forehead to mouth. I also saw a white chalice on several occasions around this time.
 One day in June to my delight, there were golden lights flying around, some went up like rockets. Another day I had golden lights coming and going.

I saw two spirits in my house by my front door, they disappeared as I tried to get a closer look.

Looking out of a window I was treated to my large, white bird in flight. The next day I saw a white circle with white bird in flight inside it.

M.E. - My Blessing in Disguise

One day I saw a fast moving, golden light in the hall.

I saw a series of white images, first some ladies, then three birds in flight, then came a man's face and a white bird went into his left eye.

I saw a large snake or serpent, some golden birds and then a face with golden birds on it, lastly a golden fish.
I was shown a golden crown, then golden arrowheads on a compass, images began overlaying each other. There were angels and cupids throwing and shooting, they went from golden to white.

I turned the tv off one day and a ring appeared on the blank screen.

I was in my car in a car park, on my way to circle, suddenly lots of faces of people and animals were showing on a wall.

Now for some of those instances when I have my hands over my eyes:

I saw some incredibly, beautiful, white images, there were two, bright, white angels with uplifted wings, then a pair of much larger, angels wings came in accompanied by several celestial figures. This was repeated, but this time some of the celestial figures had glowing, white hoods, the others had dark, blue hoods with white stars on them. These scenes were truly magical with a wonderful feel to them.

Another day I saw two words '----- Becky', then two people were standing on the edge of a large, white, spotlight circle, a bright, white angel with uplifted wings appeared, and two white birds were flying around.

There was a period when I stood on the basement steps, it's very dark there and I received images with my eyes open. It first happened by chance, but then I often would do this after I'd been working on the land.

M.E. - My Blessing in Disguise

I saw lots of amazing, white images, birds, keys, faces, then the astonishing image of some judges in gold, black and white, wow!

I saw a white crown, lots of white birds and golden birds, then a beautiful moth with golden highlights.

I was shown a circle which filled with white birds, then a face with white birds in flight in each eye. I saw several people from different periods in time, they were sitting, tied to a chair in a small room with little or no light. I was impressed that they had been mediums in their day.

Here's a lovely image which I received as I sat on my sofa with my eyes closed:

A man walked through a doorway and turned to face me, he had a beaming smile, it was my dad! That was so beautiful.

I had an unusual occurrence in April as a strong influence kept coming into my mind, it seemed that somehow my thoughts were being changed. I had no control over this and I only seemed to notice it each time after it happened, it went on for a couple of hours. It's not been repeated thankfully, I told spirit that it was very confusing for me.

Another unusual experience happened in September, I felt incredibly, strong pulsing in my third eye area, it came and went three times. Each time it felt as if my forehead must be bulging outwards.

So a very interesting year for me, who could give me that feeling in my legs I wonder, and then a couple of sharp reminders from spirit about what I need to be doing, so from here on my time and energy will be focused on this book.

M.E. - My Blessing in Disguise

When The Pupil Is Ready

You may be able to tell what happens in 2015 from the title I've given this chapter, but nothing else would fit. At the end of the year I'm still waiting for actual major changes, but hopefully they're just around the corner.

One night early in the New year, I was in bed thinking about the recent funerals of Paul and Ted that I'd attended. It was a night in which the house was full of creaks and other noises, I also had spells of real cold all over me.

Spirit continued to show me lots of images, many of them white, but not all, birds and keys were common. I was shown a face, white energy poured into its crown and the face became white, then white bird in flight came out of its mouth and flew away just before the face disappeared. On some days I saw lots of white birds, often in pairs. One day I was impressed with October 13th, I think it's the day that my mum had her first heart attack, I can't think of any other connection.

One night in bed I was shown a long scene in which I was flying in something that was a cross between a kite and a hang glider. I had complete control and flew a lot over London, north of the Thames, I always kept below the clouds as I hung underneath the contraption.

My first sitting of the year had been in Portugal on January 1st, during it I was shown a circle of white hands. All had a finger pointing at me, very interesting and a little magical for me.

One night I saw a view of the South Downs, very similar to what can be seen from my sister's house. Suddenly there was a tornado moving across the downs, something impressed me to raise my hands and let my palms face the tornado. The storm disappeared very quickly, wow! wouldn't it be something to do that for real. Another night I saw myself in a street, Eric Sykes came along driving a Routemaster bus. He stopped and began helping some disabled people to get onto the bus, I went to assist him. I soon saw several old friends, now all in spirit, one was Mr Brown who I haven't seen since the 1970's.

On a different night I was shown the small, white image of a man in a suit and hat, he carried a briefcase. Then a white giant came and stood next to him, the man didn't even come up to the giant's knees. The next morning spirit spoke to me about the scene, it was about reaching one's potential, but in the perspective of being able to allow the energy and power of spirit to be used to it's maximum for helping others. Mediums themselves have no power, we are just channels through whom spirit can work. The clearer the channel the stronger the connection with spirit should be, also trust must come into this, for the more that you trust your guides, the more they can trust you and build a stronger connection.

During a circle in late January I was shown an incredibly complicated scene, it was a bit like a production line, and appeared to combine cooking and crafts together. There were some large machines, some were mixing things and a large 'T' went into one. At the last machine there was a crowd of people around it, I thought that I was impressed somehow that this showed my pathway until the next major change, when new people will come into my life. Spirit have shown me so many scenes, but I cannot recall ever seeing one as complex as this.

I was still making regular trips to the UK, on one of my commutes I felt what I can only describe as a spirit presence around my heart. Early in March in the UK I caught the 'wipeout' bug. It had been doing the rounds for a couple of months or more, and it finally got me. I felt so bad that I had to put my flight back a week. It brought back unwanted memories of ME, as in having very low energy.

Back in Portugal I had to take it easy for a couple of weeks until my energy was restored. Towards the end of this time, spirit literally gave me a helping hand, as one day I was pulled up off of the sofa, must be time to do something then. Incidentally soon after returning I was

M.E. - My Blessing in Disguise

woken by the sound of chains rattling on what seemed to be the basement door, three times that night it happened. The next night I was shown a white bird or two on the ceiling, and heard many creaks and noises around the house.

I'm now going to write a sequence of events, it wasn't obvious to me at the time, but having read through my diary I can now see it panning out.

At a circle in early January, Lin had a link for me with a chap named Gordon, he's been to our circle before and brings lovely energy. After the evidence was given he said that he would be 'cracking the whip, and that there was a timeline for me that looks like March'. An interesting message, but it didn't mean anything to me.

During a sitting on February 5th spirit came through and said that they'd spoken through me several times without my knowing. To me this meant that I'd been into deep trance on those occasions. More than one medium has given me a message about this happening at some point.

Onto February 14th, spirit spoke at home to me 'All together now for the big push, and we are doing the pushing'. No explanation was given.

Less than a week after this message on February 19th, spirit told me that 'this team of guides have finished their work with me, a new team will take over to move me through to the next stage of my development'. These guides have been with me for a long time, I think this is the second change like this that I've had.

The next morning, February 20th I was at circle and Lin brought through a message for me. It began with a little philosophy, and then 'The chains are coming off, the wind is changing'. I took this as confirmation of yesterday's message from spirit.

M.E. - My Blessing in Disguise

February 21st, two days after spirit had spoken directly to me about the guides changing, a gruffer spirit voice came through 'The new guides are here, we will speak when necessary'.

Near the end of March I decided to go to circle, I'd kept away because of the bug I'd caught, I wasn't feeling great, but I knew the worst was over. I didn't expect anything from spirit that day, I just wanted to relax in the circle energy. At some point it was obvious to me that a spirit wanted to come through. It was a struggle for a while and during it spirit impressed me with who it was going to be. Eventually one word was spoken, and it was repeated several times before it was understood. It was Celia who deciphered the soft and slightly, husky voice as the word 'Rashid' was spoken. It was a wonderful surprise, I've been waiting since 2002 to hear from him, all the way back to that first séance that I went to. One of our sitters asked Rashid how could they help him, he replied 'It is we who are here to help you', he was gone shortly after as my energy was a bit low.

It would appear that the arrival of Rashid, along with a new team of guides coming in, should mean that spirit are happy that whatever changes were needed within me, have taken place, so as the old saying goes 'When the pupil is ready the master will appear'. This also fitted in with Gordon's timeline, given back in January.
A few weeks later Rashid came through briefly when we sat at Debi's trance circle.

This book has to end somewhere, the arrival of Rashid does seem to be an appropriate place to bring it to a close. My situation has to change at some point, when it does I hope that Rashid will speak regularly and bring his spiritual philosophy through. At the time I originally wrote the ending of this book, I suddenly heard sleigh bells in my right ear, lovely, ho-ho.

I've had so many wonderful experiences courtesy of spirit, that my perspectives on life have had to change. Should any reader has made it through to the end of this book, I hope I've managed to somehow

M.E. - My Blessing in Disguise

convey some of the joy that attuning to spirit and working with spirit can bring. It still feels at present that I've done very little spiritual work, it's as if it's all been preparation for what's to come.

I've said before that I don't regard myself as a natural writer, that view hasn't changed as this has been a painful experience, I've had to wear supports on my wrists and elbow to get me across the finishing line. However, the pains were more than outweighed by the joy of rediscovering so many, long-forgotten, joyful experiences which spirit have brought to me. Describing these experiences has been incredibly difficult, it's all so intangible and yet so real when it's happening. I don't know what I've done to deserve their time, encouragement and love that they've shown me since I've become aware of spirit. I hope that this book has done some justice to it all.

It's taken almost 21 years since the arrival of ME/CFS set the wheels of change in motion in my life. It took a while and some painful changes before I found the Spiritual side. It's been a roller coaster ride, not least the time that I've had to spend in Portugal, a real double edged sword for me.

If this book can bring hope to anyone I'll be well pleased, if it just leads someone to try healing for the first time, or to sit in a circle, it'll have been worth it. I had no idea of where my becoming ill would lead me to, sometimes you have to be so far down before you can find the way up, see the light if you will. I'm so grateful that I found my pathway, probably when I needed it the most, and that spirit were waiting there to help me.

This journey has led me to my spiritual side and to the wonderful knowledge that has come with it. I'm hopeful that the abilities spirit have developed with me, they will wish to use through me in the future, so that they can be used to benefit many others with guidance and healing, if so, then what began on October 1st 1994, when ME rudely crashed into my life, will have truly been 'my blessing in disguise'.

M.E. - My Blessing in Disguise

Thanks

I need to thank Celia for all her help in circle and out, as a mentor and friend, along with her husband Kelvin, Celia has also given me tremendous help in getting this book out there.

Other thanks go to Beverley, Debi and Barbara, my team mates from the Pyramid of Light healing group, Jan for opening my eyes to spirit faces and spirit art, Annie, Lin for the many messages, to all who've shared my circle time, and to all in Spirit who've helped and encouraged me, especially my guides.

Thanks to Anita for the Buqi healing, and for convincing me to start making notes, to Jenny and Paul and all those who gave me healing at the Cornerstone. To Celeste, Michael C, for pushing me into healing, and to those guides who have helped me to help others.

Thanks to all of those who've given me readings, and to those who've given me messages from the platform, including Ann, Lesley, Maureen, Cathy, Betty, to Nic and Steve at the Banyan, the physical mediums David, Scott and Stuart for their seances.

To all family and friends, past and present, to Sheil for our talks, and especially to Sylvia and Paul.

Brian R. Older
Email: bolderdash33@gmail.com

M.E. - My Blessing in Disguise

Printed in Poland
by Amazon Fulfillment
Poland Sp. z o.o., Wrocław